THE BOSS

JURGEN KLOPP AND
THE NEW ANFIELD BOOT ROOM
FROM SHANKS TO KLOPP

BY HARRY HARRIS

EMPIRE
PUBLICATIONS

First published in 2020

EMPIRE PUBLICATIONS
1 Newton Street, Manchester M1 1HW

ISBN: 978-1-909360-74-7

CONTENTS

CONTENTS

ACKNOWLEDGEMENTS

My thanks to Ash & John at Empire Publications. Thanks for exclusive contributions from: John Barnes, Steve McManaman, Craig Johnston, Steve McMahon, Michael Owen

DEDICATION

To All My Liverpool supporting mates of which there are many!

'Our Identity Is Intensity' - Jürgen Klopp

FOREWORD BY ALAN KENNEDY

Now it was tough to select Liverpool's greatest ever top three managers. Although I have selected Bob Paisley as the No. 1, Jürgen Klopp is the nearest to come close to Bob and I think has every chance of being the No 1 should he land, as expected, the club's first ever Premier League title, after leading the club to their first ever World Club Championship in the same year at the Champions League and Super Cup.

I know that, if I said Bob Paisley as the No1, people will accuse me of living in the past, but Bob's record and his place in history not just of Liverpool but the game in general places him at the top.

Also, I have to confess I am ever so grateful to Bob Paisley for signing me form Newcastle and then picking me in the team and winning so many trophies. It's every footballers dream to win trophies, which ever trophies they may be, that's what you set out in your career to achieve.

While I was very happy that Bob gave me my big chance, we also had some disagreements as there were times when he thought I wasn't good enough to play at left back and he put Emlyn Hughes there, or opted for Mark Lawrenson at left back in the '81 World Club Championship. I couldn't argue against that, but it didn't mean that I wasn't disappointed as I believe that you play an out and out left back at left back, and it never quite works when you play someone out of position. That's why Liverpool are fortunate to have Andy Robertson as a settled and undisputed left back. James Milner was tried there, and before him Jamie Carragher around eight years ago, but left back is a specialist position.

Bob Paisley was fair with me, as he is with all the players. He always said that if you didn't let him down and the team was winning, he would continue to give you your chance. It's not that Bob gave me my chance at Liverpool, or the fact that he might have had a crush on my mum or my mum's sister… Our families are both from Hetton-le-Hole, a coal mining community in County Durham. Bob was playing for Bishop Auckland at the time, but I don't think it was because he frequented my mum's fish and chip shop that he signed me when he became Liverpool manager, it might have had something to do with my ability!

When I look back on Bob's career, he was at Anfield before Bill

Alan and mentor Bob Paisley who he believes remains Liverpool's greatest ever manager

Shankly, as player, coach and various other positions, learning all the time from previous managers such as Taylor and then Shankly. But his record is better than anybody's in the game, 19 trophies in nine years, and you can't go against that.

Shankly was more the individual, whereas Bob relied on his team of back room staff in the famous Boot Room. I met Shanks after the Newcastle team I played in were humiliated 3-0 in the 1974 FA Cup Final by Liverpool and he said to me 'you played really well, well done', which is something that has lived with me. Shanks was still around the club when Bob became manager, Shanks was always part of the club; he would wander round as he lived near the training ground and would often pop in, I also met him a few times at Anfield. But I didn't know him close up, the way I got to know Bob.

Kenny Dalglish was coming toward the end of his playing career when he became manager, but I only played the eight games for him. He won the Double in his first season so his record speaks for itself, and this game is all about creating records. When he first stepped up to become manager Kenny told us that every player would be fighting for his place, which is very much the ethos of Bob Paisley's management and something he would also tell the players. But Kenny moved Phil Neal on, he went to Bolton and then Coventry, and I went to Sunderland. Although I thought my departure was a bit premature, in those days there was only one sub, and you wouldn't find many full backs being that one sub. Kenny had Bob to fall back on for advice, and in many ways the Liverpool way rolled on under Kenny just as it had under Bob and Joe Fagan.

Bob was more the quiet type of leader, someone who always said 'let the players do the talking on the pitch' but while the history books say he is the greatest Liverpool manager, I now think that Jürgen Klopp is running him close. It's Jürgen's manner and attitude that impresses me the most, and reminds me so much of Bob Paisley, and the way he connects with the fans and with the club, makes me believe that he can become Liverpool's greatest ever manager.

Sometimes, when I look back at the way managers treated the players, I think "maybe I wouldn't have done that, or wouldn't have done it that way" but I don't get that same sort of feeling with Klopp. Very much like Bob, he lets the players express themselves, and Jürgen understands the modern day player, he also understands the whole club. Jürgen Klopp is the modern day Bob Paisley, and in so many ways mirrors the way the team played 40 years ago, the same sort of effective football, often not necessarily with the best or most expensive players, but the right players, the best players for the right positions, exactly what Bob Paisley would have done.

Someone like John Barnes looks at his own era and would say that there were some better players in the 80s and 90s. He might be right. But as Bob Paisley knew - it's not necessary the best players but the right players, and under Jürgen Klopp this Liverpool team is playing some of the best football for a long, long time. So yes John might have a point that there were better individuals in that time but it's about the right team balance.

After we won the European Cup in Paris, I know that Bob Paisley felt that he had an ageing team and wanted to bring in younger players, and he did just that with Craig Johnson, Ian Rush, Ronnie Whelan and Steve Nicol. Perhaps they were not as outstanding as the individuals in that 1981 European Cup winning team, but they worked. That's why I was so pleased that Jürgen Klopp didn't buy anyone substantial last summer when everyone expected him to do so. He believed in the team, believed in what he was building and he gave confidence to those players, and it has been rewarded.

Pep Guardiola is another modern day manager I admire, and I hate it when people say he spends more, because it isn't how much you spend, it's bringing in the right players for the right positions. Our old chairman

The Boss

John Smith always said "First is First, second is nowhere" and he meant that it in terms of winning the league. Should Jürgen bring the first ever Premier League to Anfield than I would say yes, he would be my greatest ever Liverpool manager.

Alan Kennedy
DECEMBER 2019

INTRODUCTION

"He understands the touchstone for success is straight from Bill Shankly's philosophy: He wants to make the people happy. That means playing the right way – whether it's called rock and roll football, heavy metal football or whatever – with a work ethic that gives his team a realistic chance of winning."

ROBBIE FOWLER

FOR FOUR YEARS NOTHING, THEN LIKE LONDON buses the big prizes came along all at once; the Champions League on June 1, UEFA Super Cup victory over Chelsea in Istanbul in August and the FIFA World Club Championship for the first time in Liverpool's 127-year history just in time for Christmas, and within his sights the club's first title in 30 years, their first ever Premier League title. 2019 was some year for Jürgen Klopp but 2020 could be so much better!

Previously without a trophy at Anfield, Klopp had been much maligned by the likes of Jose Mourinho, a winner at all the clubs he's managed, but the silverware and the biggest titles of all started rolling in to put a far different complexion on the reign of "King Klopp" in the golden year of 2019.

Jürgen Klopp had succeeded where Bob Paisley, Joe Fagan and Rafael Benitez previously failed, to become the first manager in Liverpool's illustrious history to be crowned World Champions. And only the second English team, after Manchester United, to lift the coveted title.

He said after that glorious win over Flamengo in Qatar: "I said beforehand I didn't know what it would feel like, but now I can say it's outstanding. Absolutely sensational. I'm so proud of the boys. Couldn't be better. It feels really great. We are all exhausted pretty much from a really intense game. In moments like this I really struggle to find the right words as it's not my native language for describing my respect for the boys and how they do it. It was an incredible performance in an incredibly difficult game against a good opponent. We did so many good things. So many good football moments. Everybody for different reasons was on the edge pretty much. There were some sensationally good performances. I'm really happy. The atmosphere in the stadium was great, Flamengo have been partying the whole week we've been here but while they can't celebrate that much now, they should be proud of what their team did. But we deserved the win. We were the better side. In some moments we had a really good goalkeeper, and in most other moments we were the dominant team."

Already as high in the affections of the Liverpool fans as some of his illustrious predecessors, some now believed that King Klopp had become every bit as popular as the legendary Bill Shankly, the man who turned Liverpool FC from Second Division backwater into the best team in England. If Shankly, Bob Paisley and Kenny Dalglish are the Gods, then in the words or Eric Clapton, Klopp is knock, knock, knocking on Heaven's Door! Klopp has rekindled the Spirt of Shankly, the glory days of Bob Paisley, and the charisma of Kenny Dalglish and that is some achievement given the way the club started the decade.

Robbie Fowler scored 183 goals in 369 games for his boyhood club to become an undisputed legend at Anfield, named 'God' by the Koppites in the mid 1990s. He has nothing but admiration for the Klopp era as he observed: "It's not just a question of reclaiming its place on the perch Fergie talked about – the Liver bird is soaring. For the generation of fans who have never seen Liverpool win the title, there is a sense that Jürgen is giving the club its pride back. To reach the Champions League final two years running is not down to luck. You don't come back from a three-goal deficit against Barcelona in a semi-final by just hoping the noise of Anfield will frighten them and the cards will fall your way. He knows what he is doing. He understands the touchstone for success is straight from Bill Shankly's philosophy: He wants to make the people happy. That means playing the right way – whether it's called rock and roll football, heavy metal football or whatever – with a work ethic that gives his team a realistic chance of winning. He recognises that success on the pitch has to be earned and is not a God-given right.

"Liverpool have always won stuff, or been in contention for trophies, but when you think of the Klopp era – and how close they came to the title last season – all of a sudden it makes you realise that when I played, we never really came close. This is Liverpool's time."

As this books' exclusive poll among Liverpool's legends shows, Klopp generates the sort of admiration that began with Shankly creating the Boot room legacy of generation of Liverpool teams that dominated the game domestically and in Europe for two decades. Surpassing Shankly would require Klopp to create a legacy of his own, by keeping Liverpool at the pinnacle over a sustained period with even more trophies.

The Legends Poll shows that 'King Klopp' has overtaken King Kenny, another of the Immortals of Anfield, a measure of Klopp's enormous popularity and affinity to the fans. While arch rivals Manchester City craved the Champions League and the golden ticket to become the World's No 1 by winning the World Club title, Reds fans Holy Grail was to end the 30-year wait for the title. Their No 1 priority looked a distinct possibility after Liverpool leapt to a nine point lead over Pep Guardiola's City with a 3-1 Anfield victory in November 2019 with Klopp describing it as "crazy" to be so far ahead so soon into the new season. The lead was further extended as City dropped points to Manchester United and seemed to almost be intimidated by the relentlessness of Liverpool's pursuit of that first Premier League trophy.

Jürgen v Pep had become every bit as enthralling as Wenger v Sir Alex, but in a much less hostile way with the managers at the Etihad and Anfield expressing their huge mutual respect for each other. However much they played down the mind games, though, they were never far from the surface. In November 2018, Guardiola gave a talk at Liverpool University when he said: "I love reading but I don't read. I start to read and then I think Liverpool, Klopp and I can't focus!"

In Klopp's four years in charge, he lifted the Reds from eighth in the Premier League to three straight top-four finishes for the first time in a decade, reaching four cup finals, before being named coach of the year at the Best Fifa Football Awards. In this book, I chart the greatest year in the history of Liverpool through the eyes of some of the club's greatest ever players, celebrity fans as well as ordinary supporters whose lives revolve around The Reds. Klopp described the team's identity as intensity, but he also praised the clubs fans for making Anfield such a cauldron of noise and invincibility.

UEFA's technical experts branded Liverpool the greatest exponents of the modern games speed, intensity and commitment - something Klopp described as "rock and roll" football when he first arrived in England after his phenomenal success with Dortmund. But Klopp wasn't one dimensional and his squad rotation proved his flexibility in a season that he launched the quest to end the 30 years of hurt in pursuit of that elusive title. He explained: "I am not so silly that I say I only want to see a football game where I only see that 'blitz' football. The reason we did that was to implement some important things, like how to press, counter-attack and use situations when we win the ball, which we still do. But, of course, now, especially in the last one-and-half-years, a lot of teams sit back. There are different ways to score. There are different ways to control a game. There are different ways to finish a game."

After writing the official Liverpool FC 'Diary of the Season', which became one of the best selling Liverpool books, an examination of 'King Klopp of the Kop' seemed the natural follow up, charting arguably, one of the clubs' greatest ever seasons. Such has become the reach of Liverpool under Klopp, that Liverpool are closing in on Manchester United and Real Madrid as one of the biggest global brands and that upwardly mobile direction will only be enhanced by winning the World Club Championship. There is no doubt that the Klopp v. Guardiola battle has become the most intense in English football but despite City winning the last two league titles and an unprecedented domestic treble at the Etihad, Klopp has raced ahead in the European and global stakes winning three big trophies in 6 months.

Guardiola says of Klopp: "He has had a huge impact. Liverpool were not a real contender to win the Premier League when he took over, but in three or four years he has done it."

Diego Simeone, one of the most combative managers in the world, executed a wonderful job at Atletico Madrid taking them to two Champions League finals, breaking the stranglehold of Barcelona and Real Madrid and lifting two Europa League titles. Like Klopp he is extremely passionate. The Argentine was asked which manager he admired the most, "A manager that I respect? Jürgen Klopp without a doubt. He had to lose things, as well as winning some beautiful things, but he's always done it with one style. I see him really close to his players."

Former Arsenal legend Ian Wright suggested the Reds will go one better this season as it was time the title was back to Anfield. "What I'm seeing from Liverpool this season, I have to say Man City are magnificent, Liverpool will have to learn from the slip up against Leicester and when City lost to Newcastle," said Wright on Radio 5 Live. "At the end of the day, they lost the league by a point and what I'm making of this, is that what Liverpool learnt from last season is how important it is to not drop points when you have the opportunity to win games at home, that's what it's going to come down to."

Before the season, most people were expecting City to make it three years on the bounce. Wrighty was one of the few in the mainstream media backing the Reds to finally end the wait for a league title. A 4-1 win at Anfield is certainly some way to show they were up for the fight!

The weekend that celebrated Klopp's four years at the club as a time for Robbie Fowler to write in his Mirror column that "the difference now is frightening". He explained: "I think the evolution of this current Reds team says so much about him as a manager. To have the faith, the belief and the understanding of the club to set a four-year plan – as he did – and deliver it shows his mettle.

"I am a big fan of Brendan Rodgers and, under him, I think Liverpool were potentially on the rise again, but Klopp has taken them to a totally different level. What I like about him, is that he *believed* he could."

Fowler recalled an interview with Klopp two years previously when he told him he chose Liverpool as his next destination after Dortmund because they had a balance between the money needed to reach the top and the history and identity of the club and their fans and that he backed himself to make Anfield great again. Fowler argued: "He's not there yet, but he has certainly given Liverpool fans their belief back – and their pride too. I have witnessed that. I took my lad Jacob on the bus tour around the city with the Champions League trophy afterwards. His face after that win was a picture. It was a mixture of marvel and joy in what it meant to be a Liverpool fan at that moment, but also anticipation about what is still to come. That was the first trophy and we all believe there will be more. I went to the party after the final in the team hotel and the joy was on Klopp's face, too - it was the thing I noticed most about him.

"Look, he's a winner, no doubt, but he also wants to give the people something. That joy I saw on his face says he wants to give the fans something to be proud of. He gets what Liverpool is about. He gets what the people of the city are. Most importantly, he gets what it means to people to have that joy in their life. I'm not saying he's not a disciplinarian. That image of him laughing all the time is not true – I've seen him deal with players in the past and he's as tough as they come. But he has heart, too. He does all the tactical stuff, is hugely sophisticated in game plans, science, analysis, but his man-management sets him apart. I've been in and around that club and I can see that Klopp is liked by everyone there. They see his passion, his belief and commitment, and they want to share in it. And the fans see that, too."

Klopp learned basic English watching US sitcom Friends. He listening to radio talk-in shows to help him pick up the language of football and work out different accents. Klopp said: "Before I came here, I listened to talkSPORT. They talk unbelievable bulls★★t, but I picked up English football terms and heard different dialects – Scottish for sure, probably Irish. I carried on listening when I got here. Just half an hour on the way to work and half an hour back improved my language and gave me a range of words."

The admission came in an interview about life and football by celebrity Liverpool fan John Bishop for a new book 'A Game Of Two Halves' in which author Amy Raphael got famous supporters to interview football figures. Proceeds from the sales go to the UN Refugee Agency.

He added: "My English is still not too good, but it's good enough obviously to send out my message."

Klopp conducted a behind the scenes tour of Anfield for baseball star Francisco Lindor as part of a mini-documentary with CNN and Copa90. In the dressing room, Klopp pointed out all the nationalities, differing cultures, and said: 'Oh yes, there is absolutely no problem. Never ever. They would never...' Asked when they get there, he added: 'We come in about an hour and twenty minutes before the game. We are in the hotel before the game. We train at the training ground the day before, go to the hotel and sleep there and then come here.'

Lindor asked about the music that would be played in the dressing room: 'I don't know who is in the mix, but Smally is responsible for the machine, our masseur. He is the only guy who thinks about it... They can hear whatever they want. I listen to music as well but I am 51, if I come in and make the playlist that would be bad!' Smally' is club masseur Paul Small, who a mainstay at Liverpool since joining full-time back in 2002.

Walking into a social area, Klopp added: 'The atmosphere after a game is brilliant. I always take 15 or 20 minutes sitting here after the game. Three or four chefs here cooking food, perfect meat, perfect fish. Everything you'd want after a game. The players eat pasta as well. We all sit around, it's a real social place.'

Klopp then took Lindor and Eli from Copa90 pitchside, confronted by the symbol of Anfield. Klopp referred to the Anfield sign as 'one of the most important things here'. He touched the sign when they lost 5-0 and would not touch it until his team had won some- thing. While on the pitch, they discussed the atmosphere. Klopp said: 'You have to be in early because when teams are outside they sing the anthem [You'll Never Walk Alone]'.

Lindor joked about the comfort of the leather seats in the dug-out: "If we had this, nobody would want to get up!" He laughed when Klopp pointed out that the seats have built-in heating. 'We need all the feeling in our feet.'

They walked over to the Kop, where Klopp talked about the club's heritage and history. He hoped one day to stand on the Kop as a Liverpool supporter as Bill Shankly used to. 'I always wanted to stand one time at Dortmund in the Yellow Wall and so far it has never happened because I was too short of time. But I would do exactly the same here."

I can recall meeting up with the club's CEO Peter Moore at the team hotel ahead of their match with Watford in the season where they finished just a point shy of City and eventually won their 6th European Cup. Peter told me that 'what you see is what you get' with Klopp. He is just the same if he was meeting the Queen or if he was greeting the tea lady at the training ground - not that they have tea ladies anymore! Peter said we would know if he was anywhere in the vacinity of our chat over a coffee, because you could hear his infectious laugh 'miles away'.

Peter commented: "You will know when Jürgen is coming, you will hear his loud laugh before he is 100 yards from us! It's a laugh that is infectious. He has an enormous smile, and a laugh that you respond to whether you are a player or a local kid he wants to reach out to in the community.

"At Liverpool Cathedral on a Monday night he was there for a club fund raising event with young, local children. He spent 45 minutes answering questions from invited guests. Every time he told them a story, and there were lots of stories, he would laugh. Sometimes he knows what's coming, of course, and starts to laugh before he even gets the chance to tell the story, and can hardly get the story.

"He is a charismatic, larger-than-life character, but it's backed up with his incredible motivational skills and his technical know-how. He is perfect for Liverpool, and Liverpool is perfect for him"

It was a great pleasure for me to chronicle the seasons events culminating in such a marvellous success story as Klopp earned his first trophy, however in the Foreword to the Diary of the Season, he made it clear, while still relaxing on a well deserved holiday, that the next season would be even more special.

"The 2018/19 season is one everyone with Liverpool Football Club in their hearts will remember with joy. And not just because of how it ended in Madrid. Yes, of course this was a landmark moment for everyone involved; it's number 6 – it's history. But this journey had so many moments we loved at the time and will be with us for generations. The destination is the most important part of any trip, but the route there can be something amazing also, if you allow it to be. This season meant so much because we experienced these moments together. Players, supporters, management, staff – the whole LFC family. We came together as a community to create and share something special.

"There are many parts that make a great club, but without doubt the most important two are the team and the supporters. At Liverpool we are blessed to have world class in both. And they share so many qualities. Both have passion and courage. Both are filled with belief and desire. Both understand the hard work you need to achieve something worthwhile. Both embrace the values of supporting your own team and helping your mates. Whatever they do, they do it together and for one another. That's how our story came to be this season.

"My players this year did remarkable things. I called them mentality giants after we beat Barcelona, but that's not saying enough. Skill, intelligence, emotion, fitness – they have it all. The most important thing for Liverpool fans when reliving the memories of this season is to remember it's the start – not a conclusion. Madrid wasn't the final chapter for us – I think we're still writing the introduction. When we were travelling around Liverpool with the European Cup on that magical Sunday, the words that I heard sung the loudest were "We're never gonna stop!" That's what this team and club has to live by. We arrived at this point because we were hungry for moments like 1 June.

"Take all the joy from this campaign and do so in the knowledge we want it again. Love the memories and use them to shape our future."

In December, Klopp signed a new contract extension that should he see out his deal, he would be Liverpool's longest-serving manager since Bob Paisley led them from 1974 to 1983. Principal owner John Henry, chairman Tom Werner and FSG president Mike Gordon issued a joint statement in which they said: 'We feel this represents one of the big moments of our stewardship of Liverpool Football Club so far as we believe there is no better manager than Jürgen. The decision also keeps with the club's overall strategy of building from a position of strength. It means Jürgen will oversee the ongoing transition from Melwood to the new Kirkby training base as the club continues to pursue a vision of being elite in all facets of the industry. It also provides us with continuity with the existing football operations management structure, overseen by sporting director Michael Edwards, whose input into the project cannot be overestimated. He has been – and will continue to be – as indispensably important as anyone else to the direction of Liverpool Football Club. In Jürgen and Michael we are blessed with world-class leadership."

Bill Shankly's iconic image graced the front cover of the match day programme to celebrate his 60 years to the day he took over as manager and began the Anfield Dynasty and the conveyor belt of managers known as the Boot Room. The timing couldn't have been better as Klopp was reinstating those values and clearly intended to fulfil them with his contract extension.

Wearing his beloved red club tracksuit and holding a leather ball in his left hand, he was pointing with the forefinger on his right hand with one of his famous sayings. 'Liverpool was made for me and I was made for Liverpool,' it said in capital letters behind his image.

As the Mail on Sunday reported: "It was 60 years to the day since the father of modern Liverpool took charge of his first game for the club and it feels as though his spirit is still abroad at this stadium where he enjoyed so many triumphs. Great managers have come and gone since Shankly but none have felt like his reincarnation quite so much as Jürgen Klopp. For Klopp, just as it was for Shankly, fraternity is everything in football. For Klopp, just as it was for Shankly, it is the intensity of the brotherhood between players and the unity between club and fans that drives a team onwards and gives it an edge over its competitors. Shankly was a socialist with a manifesto. As his team prepared to go, temporarily, 11 points clear at the top of the table, Klopp set out his own."

Bruce Grobbelaar described Klopp as "Shankly reincarnated", in an enormous compliment. He said: "Jürgen Klopp is Shankly reincarnated in a German body. He gets this club."

Jürgen Klopp, voted the greatest coach in the world following the 2019 European Cup triumph in Madrid

1: THE BEST COACH IN THE WORLD

JÜRGEN KLOPP MIGHT NOT YET BE UNIVERSALLY regarded as the greatest manager in Liverpool's history but in 2019 in a ceremony in Milan he was voted the world's greatest coach by FIFA and he was naturally proud of his achievement.

"Wow, it's quite heavy! What can I say?" Klopp said accepting the award, "I have to say thank you to a lot of people obviously. I have to start at the beginning with my family sitting at home and probably watching. It's great – nobody would have expected that I stand here 20 years ago, 10 years ago, five years ago, four years ago probably! And how close it can be; Mauricio, we won that game [the Champions League final] – that's why I'm here and not you. That's how football is, but we all know what an incredible job you did, what an incredible job Pep did, what so many coaches out there did.

"Coming back to saying thank you, I have to say thank you to my outstanding club, Liverpool FC – who doesn't love it has no heart! That's not true, you can love other clubs as well."

Klopp become the first Premier League manager to sign up to the Common Goal movement, donating 1% of his salary to the charity. He made the announcement after being named FIFA coach of the year. The initiative, which funds organisations around the world that use football to tackle social issues, was launched by Manchester United and Spain midfielder Juan Mata in 2017. Speaking on stage at the Milan ceremony, Klopp said: "A few people obviously know it - if not, Google it. It's a great thing." Quoted on the Common Goal website, he added: "While it is flattering to receive an individual award today, in football and in life, nothing is possible without teamwork. That is why I would like to celebrate this occasion by sharing that I am joining Common Goal and pledging 1% of my earnings to help change the world through football. Since Common Goal started two years ago, the movement has grown steadily proving it is a simple, effective and safe mechanism for players and managers to give back through football. As a team, even with a minimum pledge of just 1%, together the football industry is capable of transforming the world. Now is the time for those interested to take a step forward." Common Goal chief executive and co-founder Jürgen Griesbeck said: "We are thrilled to welcome Jürgen Klopp onto the team. At a time when our world is facing social divides, increasing global inequality and political polarisation, his contribution exceeds the financial and will inspire football fans and non-football fans across the planet."

Other coaches signed up to the scheme included Manchester United's Casey Stoney and Denmark's Kasper Hjulmand. Premier League's Bruno Salter, Leon Balogun (Brighton), Charlie Daniels (Bournemouth), Kasper Schmeichel (Leicester) and Isaac Christie-Davie (Liverpool).

In a column for The Players' Tribune Klopp related how "honoured" he felt. "But I really don't like to stand on a stage with a trophy all by myself. Everything I have accomplished in this game is only possible because of everyone around me. Not just my players, but my family and my sons and everyone who has been with me since the beginning, when I was a very, very average person."

The German revealed what he said to his players before they reached the Champions League final after overcoming losing 3-0 to Barcelona in their first leg was "the worst result imaginable." Preparing for the second leg, Klopp said: "My team talk was very straightforward. Mostly, I talked about tactics. But I also told them the truth. I said: 'We have to play without two of the best strikers in the world. The world outside is saying it is not possible. And let's be honest, it's probably impossible. But because it's you? Because it's you, we have a chance.' I really believed that. It wasn't about their technical ability as footballers. It was about who they were as human beings, and everything they had overcome in life. The only thing that I added was: 'If we fail, then let's fail in the most beautiful way.' Of course, it is easy for me to say those words. I am just the guy yelling from the touchline. It is much harder for the players to actually do it. But because of those boys, and because of the 54,000 people at Anfield, we did the impossible."

The outcome is etched in the memory but Klopp had to rely on replays to see Alexander-Arnold's cheeky corner that saw Divock Origi nick the winner as he had turned to his assistant to discuss a sub when the right-back sprung the surprise set-piece and had only the noise of the crowd to tell him Liverpool had completed the stunning comeback. Klopp said: "Unfortunately, the most incredible moment in the history of the Champions League... I didn't actually see it. Maybe this is a good metaphor for the life of a football manager, I don't know. But I completely missed Trent Alexander-Arnold's moment of pure genius."

Klopp channels his inner Rocky Balboa when giving speeches as "football is the only thing more inspiring than cinema". It dates back to his days working in a warehouse where they stored movie reels - shortly after becoming a young father - gave him the grounding and inspiration for the work he is doing now. "When I was 20, I experienced the moment that completely changed my life. I was still a kid myself, but I had also just become a father. It was not perfect timing, let's be honest. I was playing amateur football and going to university during the day. To pay for school, I was working in a warehouse where they stored movies for the cinema. And for the young people out there, we are not talking about DVDs. This was the late '80s, when everything was still on film. The trucks would come at 6am to pick up the new movies, and we would load and unload those huge metal canisters. They were quite heavy, honestly. You would be praying that they weren't showing something with four reels, like Ben-Hur or something. That was going to be a bad day for you."

The early exposure to film stayed with Klopp on his journey through management. He used Sylvester Stallone's Italian Stallion as inspiration during his time with Borussia Dortmund. He admired the passion and work ethic taught by the iconic film series. But most of his young Dortmund squad were too young to have seen the movies when he showed clips of Rocky IV before a crunch game against Bayern Munich. That didn't stop him going full Mickey Goldmill before Liverpool's legendary Champions League comeback against Barcelona last season.

Klopp's planning is meticulous, even appointing a dedicated 'throw-in' coach in the season leading up to his first trophy success with the Champions League. Dane Thomas Gronnemark started working on a part-time basis during the club's pre-season training camp to minimise the number of errors from set-plays. He primarily 'coached' full-backs, Robertson, Gomez, Alexander-Arnold, Clyne and Moreno, while Milner, Mane, Wijnaldum were part of the sessions. Gronnemark, who previously worked with Midtjylland and Bundesliga sides Schalke and Hertha Berlin was approached directly by Klopp to bring the methods of his 'Long Throw Academy' to Anfield. He worked with Denmark's Athletics and Bobsled teams. A dedicated trainer for throw-ins was a first in English football. Klopp estimated Liverpool take or defend around 50 throw-ins per match, and felt his players squandered possession too often from these set plays.

Rather than encouraging a long-throw, Gronnemark advised on the most effective way of using the restart to launch attacks, and how to avoid putting team mates under pressure when in their own half. His travelled to Liverpool for a couple of sessions a month. Gronnemark completed the world record for the longest ever throw-in – over 56 yards. "When I heard about Thomas, it was clear to me I wanted to meet him. When I met him, it was 100% clear I wanted to employ him. You cannot have enough specialists around you. He has already made a difference. I think it's not only important to me, it's important to everybody. To be honest, I'd never heard about a throw-in coach. How it is as a football manager, you know a lot about different things – I played the game, I've been managing since around about 18 years or so – but that doesn't mean I'm a goalkeeper specialist and I'm obviously not a throw-in specialist. I know about different movements, what we always did, but it was not 100 per cent clear – maybe it's my fault – how I can improve the guy with the ball, not only the movements of all the other guys. When I heard about Thomas, it was clear to me I wanted to meet him; when I met him, it was 100 per cent clear I wanted to employ him. Now he is here and we work on that from time to time. We use his information as well during the weeks when he is not here. We use it of course for the Academy as well. It's good. You cannot have enough specialists around you. I must always be the guy who makes the decisions on when we use all these specialists but you cannot have enough. We have the fitness, medical department, we have the nutrition, and now we have somebody for throw-ins. He's a good guy, to be honest. He has already [made a difference]. The boys like it; when you have somebody who knows what he is talking about, it always helps when you want to improve something."

"I know it is totally the weirdest job in the world," Gronnemark told BBC Sport. Former Stoke midfielder Rory Delap is the best known long throw-in expert in the Premier League era. Gronnemark said his brief at Anfield was "not to turn Liverpool into the second Stoke". The Dane, who had been working with teams since 2004, said Klopp contacted him as he was "curious". "If I was a defender I would not want to be on the end of one of Gomez's throw-ins," said Gronnemark. "In general against Liverpool I would not want to put the ball out for a throw-in. I am not saying Liverpool will do a lot of long throw-ins, but you never know when they may do it."

Klopp encouraged goalkeeping coach John Achterberg to take out rugby pads to toughen up Alisson, a technique used on Mignolet and Karius. The sessions involved crosses into the area while someone blocks and buffets the keeper with the pads. 'It is what the goalkeepers always do,' said Klopp. 'It is not really rugby; it is goalkeeper training. All the boys did it. Alisson is doing it as well. It makes sense to do it. We have these situations in training constantly when we do set pieces – the box is full with 22 players. Maybe that is a bit much, but 15 certainly. It is busy, we do it often so that the goalkeeper gets used to that. It is all about timing (when to come for crosses). We'll see how that is. We brought him here because of the things that he is already good at. That is what we want him do. It is not that the goal- keeper has to change completely now for this league, we have to help him too in situations. That is how it is always is. There is not just one player responsible for something. We have to have the right formation around set pieces; set pieces can be quite different here. So far, it has been absolutely ok. But it is not solely about Alisson (improving the defensive record). It is down to the whole team."

Klopp also brought in nutritionist Mona Nemmer. His latest recruit at the start of the new season which turned out to be the best start imaginable, in came sports psychologist Lee Richardson, who had spells with Watford and Blackburn as a player and managed Chesterfield. He spends three days a week at the club's training ground on an ad hoc basis. The 50-year-old was also filling the role of sport psychology consultant for the Lancashire County Cricket Club, as well as his own performance management company, AIM-FOR. Pro surfer Sebastian Steudtner gave a series of talks over the summer.

Richardson's arrival coincided with the exit of former sports psychiatrist Steve Peters, who was brought in by Brendan Rodgers. Richardson has had an instant influence as Klopp told The Athletic: "He was a player, then a manager and then he studied sports psychology. He's working for us which is great. He works very specifically with the boys and I have no idea what they are talking about. I am not interested. It's just a nice add on. It's just for us the next step. It's difficult to find the right people with how I see it in that part of the business. Now we feel pretty good with him on board and that's cool." He arrived on the recommendation of Philipp Jacobsen, who joined Liverpool in 2018 as medical rehabilitation and performance manager.

Klopp recalled his switch from striker to right-back as a player in Germany, and explained how versatility is key for Liverpool. He was asked to take duties as manager midway through the 2000/01 season after Eckhard Krautzun's dismissal at Mainz, steering them clear of relegation after retiring as a player. Prior to that, he made 340 appearances for Mainz, with 95 coming under Wolfgang Frank, who he credits as his biggest influence as a manager, who switched Klopp from the role of first-choice centre-forward to starting right-back. He was "always a striker" because he "had a good header and was really quick," but "technical-wise I was not too good. From a nowadays point of view, I would say [moving to right-back] makes complete sense: I would have done the same to me. I would have made myself, maybe a centre-half, but I would have put me in the back. Because really quick, good attitude... but not brilliant with the ball."

On the game that changed his career, Klopp allowed him to go from his own "biggest enemy" to having been "just happy to have a game." He added: "We were a lower-league team, but I scored 10 to 12 goals a year. That was OK. But then at one point a new manager came in, he was the best manager I ever had: Wolfgang Frank. He changed the system. It was a friendly game in the pre-season, we had a game against a team from one league lower, they were first in that league, we were last in the [one above]. That's a difficult game to play as friendly, and he said 'OK, we change the system'. He made the line-up and in that line-up I was at right-back. Half-time in that game was 6-0 to us, we played incredibly, we defended like lions, it was really brilliant. Then we changed completely and the second half team played 0-0, so we won 6-0 and from that moment on, the team from the first half played for the next 50 games and I was right-back. That's how it started, and from that moment on I was the right-back. [I was] 100 percent [fine with changing]. For me there's was no problem.

"I was my biggest enemy, because I hated my football, I really didn't like it. When I tried to stop a ball, it bounced. I had these inner talks. I was really not a supporter of myself, but only wanted to play. If he told me 'you look like a decent goalkeeper'...give me the gloves, I do it. So I was just happy to have a game, and the pressure went off my shoulders as well. Because in a team [like Mainz] and you don't score a lot of goals as the main striker, each chance you miss it's not like there'll be another one. I was not involved anymore in that, and I still scored two, three, four goals on average, it was OK."

Asked about the number of versatile players throughout the Bundesliga, he disagreed that it was German-specific, highlighting a host of examples in his Liverpool squad, that it "helps a lot" to have a variety of options for every role, spread out over a smaller core of players. "We have them as well, James Milner can play around 13 positions probably, he probably would be the first choice if all the goalies were out. Fabinho can play at least two, Trent can play a lot, so we have that. We don't have that many specialists. People think sometimes it's a weakness if you're that versatile, because you think 'OK, I don't have a fixed position, he puts me in there, there, there, then I'm out'. It is [a strength]. It helps in building a squad, especially. That helps a lot. Because you don't have a specialist in these positions, you have three, four, five players that can play really different positions, that helps you a lot."

Back in 2018 Wijnaldum said: "It is a quality, but also a weakness. If players can only be in one position, managers do not even think about moving them.' Wijnaldum is one of Liverpool's most versatile players, helping him to make the third-most appearances under Klopp since his appointment in 2015. Only Milner and Firmino featured more over the past four years.

★

In 2001 Jürgen took over German Second Division club Mainz following an unremarkable ten-year playing career at the club. The then 34 year-old won 6 out of 7 games to steer Mainz to safety and within three years he had got them promoted to the German top flight. Despite having the smallest budget in the league, Mainz finished in respectable mid-table for several seasons before they were relegated in 2006 and after failing to gain promotion the following year Klopp resigned at the end of the 2007/08 season.

A call soon came from giants Bayern Munich and Borussia Dortmund and Jürgen chose the latter. During his time at the Westfalenstadion Klopp made his name with a tactic called *gegenpresse*, where players attack the ball when they give it away rather than falling back into defensive positions. This all-action style made Dortmund exciting to watch and eventually brought trophies to the fanatical supporters from the Ruhr, Germany's industrial heartland; the Bundesliga title was eventually wrestled away from Bayern in 2011 and 2012, along with several domestic cups and a Champions League final appearance which they lost to Bayern at Wembley in 2013. However by 2015 Klopp was getting diminishing returns with Borussia and there were fall-outs with match officials amid frustration that the club sold many of its best players to rivals. Bayern, most notably Polish striker Robert Lewandowski. Klopp left the club at the end of the season and ended up at Liverpool a few months later.

During his time in Germany Klopp's football was characterised by all out attacking play or 'Heavy Metal football' as the man himself described it, while he was regarded as a supreme man-manager who was able to create an unbreakable bond between himself and his players. Yet it isn't all squirrels and picnics; it was later revealed that players are reluctant to confront him because of his imposing stature. Asked in an edition of *France Football* if he has been afraid of anyone, Klopp replied: "No, never. Fear is never a good thing, even when you have to tell a player that you are not renewing his contract. I think I have a natural authority. I have a voice that carries, and I am 6ft 3.6ins. Apart from Virgil van Dijk and perhaps Joel Matip, who are nice men, no-one is bigger than me."

Klopp's determination is to entertain at all costs, as he told the respected French publication; "What is my style of play? Well, you know what? I have been a coach for 18 years and I haven't even thought about this question, despite being asked this a lot. I don't really get what it means. I love the game, it's as simple as that. It intrigues me 95 per cent of the time. When I watch a match, I always see things I like, if not, it would be a waste of time. Entertainment is the most important part of football. There are too many serious problems in the world to make football boring too. I want to see happiness with my players, passion in their eyes and a desire to fight. I want to see them bursting [with energy maybe he means], to surprise me, to look what's on their right, to try and make a pass to their left, that sort of thing."

Former Porto coach Vitor Matos was described as Liverpool's "signing of the season" by assistant manager Pep Ljinders. Matos is Liverpool's "connector" since being brought in as an elite development coach by Klopp over the summer. Matos said: "Working with Jürgen is like having a masterclass! I am very pleased and happy for the opportunity to work with the best. Really, Jürgen is not only about understanding football, a player or a youth player, he is more than that, it is how he understands life and its values. For me, this fascinating way of seeing things is unbelievable, it's really unbelievable.

"Normally we say that the character of the team is the character of the coach and we can see Jürgen's impact on everything in the club. The way he is as a person makes an influence on the training sessions, in the pre-match meetings, on the environment at Melwood. There is a famous doctor in Portugal who says, 'They who only know about medicine, don't know anything about medicine' and I say that a coach who only knows about football doesn't know anything about football. Jürgen is the perfect example of that. The way he fills all the game ideas, all the tactical principles, all the team organisation with passion and with love is amazing because that is what gives you the way of playing. It's been really amazing to work with him."

Matos explained his role. "My biggest goal is to create development. You can create development in different ways but the most important thing is that you understand football as a collective game. It's something that is built on the interactions between the players and these interactions that you have are related to your way of playing, to your identity, so you can see: 'OK, this is Liverpool 's way of playing.' Development or individual development is also connected with this: these game ideas and this way of playing will force the individual development of the players. My role is to say: 'OK, we have these Academy players. How can we help them learn the game ideas of the first team, and how can we use those game ideas to continue their individual development?' My first idea when I arrived was that I needed to know every one of the U18 and U23 players and discuss, 'What's the big idea for him?' I needed to know which person I need to speak to and work with to achieve this. It's about knowing the club, knowing what the expectation is for a youth player to come and train here [at Melwood]."

Former Liverpool Chief Executive Ian Ayre commented in an interview in the *Sunday People*: "I was back last weekend and the club are going in the right direction, and, for me, Jürgen Klopp is the anchor. Every now and again in life you meet someone or see something in an organisation where someone is just a complete fit. It's like when you meet the girl of your dreams and with Jürgen, he is simply everything a Liverpool manager should be. He ticks every box. He just fits. I grew up in the era of Bill Shankly and he had everyone hanging off every word. People loved him and won't find any Liverpool fans who don't feel that way about Jürgen either. I love his manner, but he's the same with everybody. He just gets the club, the culture. Brendan and Rafa had that too, but in different ways. They may have been great coaches or tacticians but this is different because Jürgen brings everything, that true connection with the city, the fans, the owners."

Of course Klopp has got in hot water on occasions for getting carried away in the heat of the moment. "No, I don't regret it, in a way — but it should not have happened. I did it. I broke a rule, I pay for it. That's how it is. I'm not sure football is all about a manager running on the pitch. It didn't happen to 500,000 others. I know that I am rather on the jump and on the run when something happens. When I did it at Mainz, it was for a very important goal and after that it didn't happen any more. At Dortmund, I ran down the side-line when we became champions. The only difference is that when I did it at Mainz, I don't think I broke a rule. I was on the pitch and then the referee told me to get off and I went around the side. I passed the ball and I fell over."

Klopp once damaged a hamstring while celebrating, "That was with a jump at Stuttgart. I jumped in front of the opposite dugout but nobody – nobody – thought it was disrespectful. It's a cultural thing. It's not for you to change and me to explain how the rules are. I did it. I broke a rule, I pay for it. I don't think I have had any problems with dugouts apart from a few words but that is normal. A match ban, for me, would have been too much. Paying money – and not because I earn so much money – a fine is there to make you aware and make sure you don't do it again. I will not do it again, as so much as I can avoid it. Now I know it, I will not to do it. There were 14 years between the first one and the last one. It cannot happen any more – for the next 14 years."

Klopp jokingly confessed that he actually has no idea why he does what he does; he only knows how to react to situations. He has earned a reputation as one of the most charismatic, emotional managers around, with a natural affinity for motivation and man-management. As such, his team talks have become the stuff of legend, with many reports over the years detailing the inspirational things he supposedly told his players to motivate various great Liverpool performances. Speaking to The Athletic, however, Klopp confessed that rather than planning his speeches and player interactions carefully, he tends to just gets caught up in the moment and lets his emotions take control. "Sorry, I would write a book about the things I do if I knew why I did them," he confessed. "But I could never write a book because I have no clue about how these things work. I just react in situations. My job, my life is 24/7 thinking about what happens here. The meetings are based on our past if you want — what happened after the last game, what happened yesterday, things like this. What can we use? I always react. I don't usually remember what I say. If the boys didn't say things in the press afterwards then I wouldn't even know I'd said it.

"I remember Divock Origi after the Dortmund game (back in 2016). He said: 'The boss told us at half-time that if we turned the game around it would be a story we'd all be able to tell our grandchildren about so it would be really worth giving it a try.' But if it was that easy I'd tell them things like that constantly! We always want stories to tell the grandkids!

When we start a team meeting the only thing I really know what I am going to say is the first sentence."

The off-the-cuff a strategy has clearly worked for Klopp. The two-time Bundesliga winner has transformed Liverpool into European champions and one of the continent's most in-form sides over the last couple of years. Klopp insisted that his job is all about taking a reactive approach to what is going on around him. "All that happens through the week, it stays in my mind, I don't write anything down," he added. "I just think about what's worth telling the boys. S**t session, very good session, whatever, little things. I know how it sounds and it should not sound like this — like I know always to say the right words. But I do trust myself 100% to find the right words."

Brendan Rodgers left shortly after promoting Pepijn "Pep" Lijnders, but Klopp's kept the Dutchman on as his first team coach. Klopp was disappointed when Lijnders left in January 2018 for a managerial role at NEC in the Netherlands. But he soon offered Lijnders the chance to return as his assistant.

"He was convinced we could conquer a lot together," says Lijnders, who accepted Klopp's offer and left NEC after half a season. "Jürgen can touch someone straight to the heart. He knows exactly what he wants and when we were on the phone it felt just right." Lijnders said in a *Guardian* interview: "Jürgen is the leader and face of the team, the one who defines the character and who stimulates everyone. Pete [Peter Krawietz] is responsible for the analysis and prepares everything in regards to videos which are shown to the players. I'm responsible for the training process. Together we decide what kind of aspects we want to develop for the team and then I create the exercises. It's quite simple; it's just about the continuing stimulation of our mentality to conquer the ball as quick and as high up the pitch as possible. That element comes back in every exercise. We as staff always try to find ways so the players can be more spontaneous and more creative."

Training drills help shape Liverpool's identity. "The players first have to understand the importance of counter-pressing to our team. They have to feel it, not with the head, but with the heart. They start the exercise with the idea to keep the ball, but in the event of losing it they have to be directly on top of things. When a team lose the ball in training, you will hear me, Jürgen or Pete screaming: 'Go! Get it back! Don't stop!' It's so loud they'll even hear that in Manchester, haha. They have to understand why it's so important. That power and emotion is our game. Because our identity is intensity. That comes back in every drill. And that's what I like about coaching: that you can stimulate certain common behaviour and create a lot by specific team training. That's what I live for."

Lijnders says the manager and captain reflects the identity of the club. "The heart of the team is the heart of the coach. So the character of the coach will become the character of the team in the long term. That's it. Because there is no stronger weapon than your own example. If I'm a disciplined coach, then I don't need to discipline the players. Our captains Hendo and Milly, together with Virgil, are so disciplined, which means the rest of the group doesn't need to be disciplined. There is a saying from [Theodore] Roosevelt which says: 'People don't care how much you know, until they know how much you care.' Jürgen does really care about the squad and his staff. Players will understand and absorb more of our philosophy when they feel how much we care about them."

Lijnders spotted another Klopp strength: "He is able to give a completely different perception to a situation inside a few minutes." Such as the Barcelona game last season. "We lost 3-0, but afterwards Jürgen said in the dressing room: 'The only team in the world who can overturn this defeat against Barcelona is us.' It gave the squad a boost, also because of the way we had played that night. When the players walked towards the coach there was already a different feeling."

Occasionally they meet at their homes but most of the time they are at Melwood, where a glass cage adjacent to the Melwood building was specially built for Klopp and Lijnders to house a paddle tennis court. "It's a combination of tennis and squash and because of the glass walls the ball can bounce, which keeps it in play," Lijnders says. "The court is actually meant for two v two, so it's not only a battle against each other, but also yourself. It's fantastic. Perhaps we play two to three times a week, sometimes more often. A perfect way to switch off. You can't play without 100% concentration. For us it's great to just think about nothing during those games. And sometimes it is in these moments that we find a brilliant solution for something."

Former England manager Fabio Capello praised Klopp for creating "something magic" at Anfield, comparing hiss style to Pep Guardiola's. He observed: "Klopp has made something magic for me. The atmosphere of Anfield is fantastic, the team is like the fans. The connection is fantastic between the team, Klopp and fans, it's a unique thing. Guardiola is different. I think he plays the team like a theatre. The fans a theatre. The show is really good but it's a theatre."

Carlo Ancelotti said of Klopp, now a rival manager on Merseyside but then at Napoli, "He is a friend, a complicated opponent to face with great experience. He is a great manager." When Klopp was informed of how complimentary the Italian had been been, he reacted: "I like him a lot; an incredible player, a great manager and a fantastic guy. In Germany, we call him a smart fox. All these very positive things about me are nice but it is tactics. Carlo's been in the business for so long. He wants to bring the nice fella out of me! We're ready for a real battle. I don't care too much for what people say about us or how they see our situation. This is a fantastic manager, a fantastic team and an emotional crowd so that will be a real challenge They are a good team in a good moment. Even the last game was not bad against Juventus. They are in good shape, second in the league, impressive results. We played against Sarri and his new team on Saturday and now we play against his old team, so it will be interesting. It's not exactly the same anymore because they changed style and lost Jorginho, but they're very quick up front, have good footballers, a good counter-press, a good counter... it will be interesting."

Klopp was returning to Napoli, the scene of one of his biggest regrets in football as he vowed to change after viewing his "pathetic" behaviour in Napoli in 2013. "Pathetic," was Klopp's assessment of his behaviour which resulted in a two- game European touchline ban. He watched most of the game on a TV in the stadium after being sent off inside half an hour for an angry outburst at the fourth official. The footage of him ranting went viral. Klopp was furious that defender Neven Subotic wasn't allowed back onto the pitch sooner after an injury, allowing Higuain to open the scoring. Napoli won 2-1. "I apologised immediately after the game to my team, the fourth official and the referee as well," Klopp said. "I have to accept the consequences for my actions. I was like a clown out there. That was stupid. My emotions turned a well-run game into a hectic affair. I did not show my prettiest face out there. I told myself I did not want to see such pictures of me again and I thought I could do it. It was absolutely my mistake."

Now he said: "I understand why I was not happy but the reaction was too much and they gave me a ban. I had to watch two games from the stands, one against Arsenal at home. But my behaviour was not too good, especially in the German Bundesliga before that, but nothing has happened any more. Maybe it was my last time when I was a bit too excited. I know it'll not happen again. During the game here, I tried to go into the stand and it was not nice. I was sitting there and getting all the comments from people, so for the second half I had to do something and I watched the game with the groundsman in a little room with a Diego Maradona shirt on the wall. A few things are the same for me since then and a few things have changed in a better way."

Klopp and Guardiola were inducted into the League Managers Association's Hall of Fame, presented with silver salver to commemorate their inductions by LMA president Gareth Southgate and fellow Hall of Famer Sir Alex Ferguson at a gala evening in Manchester. They followed in the footsteps of legends including Brian Clough, Sir Bobby Robson and Arsene Wenger by being added to the LMA's esteemed list of coaches.

'This is really special,' Klopp said. 'To be a part of this incredible group of managers is big, really big. Tonight my family and coaches are here. I wanted them all to be here because it is very important in our family history. When I first heard about it [the honour] I couldn't believe it. I've now been in England for a bit longer than four years and I've enjoyed each second, to be honest. I saw all the names with the pictures when I came in, it's really impressive. I don't often feel pride but, in this moment, I'm very proud because this is something really, really special."

Guardiola said: 'I do not have any words to express my gratitude. To be part of this family. It is an incredible honour to be a part of it, for the rest of my life and for generations, to be in this Hall of Fame in English football. What a privilege. When you come down the corridor and see all the big names, big managers, big personalities being here that would've helped to make football better, football that we have right now. I think all the managers here that have been inducted into the Hall of Fame is because we were in incredible clubs with incredible players. As long as we can help them and try to think on the same side and the same page, that's the only reason we can do what we do as managers. Without the quality of the players we have, the managers cannot have success."

LMA chairman Howard Wilkinson said Klopp and Guardiola had shown 'incredible drive, innovation and dedication' in their roles. 'Since arriving in England, they have built two of the best teams in Premier League history and have done so with humility and honour,' Wilkinson said. Both managers style of play was praised by Sir Alex Ferguson, who said: "They are teams with courage. They play to win all the time, they play to attack all the time." LMA Chief Executive Richard Bevan added: "Tonight, the LMA honoured two of the greatest managers of this generation. Pep has achieved remarkable success with three of the world's biggest clubs. His incredible haul of major domestic and continental titles across Europe demonstrate how his coaching and leadership has combined tactical inspiration with an insatiable will to win, to enable the highest level of performance from his players and staff. Not only has Jürgen redefined man-management in the modern era, he has established a footballing identity which each of his teams has personified. Through hard-work and exceptional coaching, he has delivered performance levels and consistency rarely seen in European football. The LMA congratulates both managers on their achievements and looks forward to seeing them continue their pursuit of excellence with their respective clubs."

Klopp tries to live 'a normal life' outside of football management, and when asked, in a BBC podcast, what part of the job he likes the least he said: 'It's a very intense job, I have done it for 19 years but if I didn't do this job I would do another intense job. The only difference is it's in public. That's the only part I don't like. It pays my bills but being constantly under observation is not too nice. I have a completely normal life. I go home, walk the dog, from time to time I go to the pub, but not very often because people would say "Ah, he's drinking. Ah, he's smoking!"The public part is not something I enjoy. I accept it but I don't enjoy it. The first sip of a pint and you are live on social media. I have no problem telling people to respect my borders."

Of course he had to keep a lid on his players' egos after winning the Champions League, but he didn't find that too difficult, "the conscious decision we made with the boys was, as Liverpool players, it was not about winning one thing. It is about winning and there is no limit. The moment we did it was important - but it did not give us a feeling it was done. We like to think we would meet up in 20 to 30 years, look back and mix up the years. Was it 2019 or 2020? So far, so good. We try to squeeze everything we can get from our time together. There is no pressure, it is just opportunity."

Klopp considers himself a man of the players, but he has clear defining lines of friendship and respect. "All my former players have my number and we stay in contact. I support them still, apart from the moment we play each other. If we win 5-1 I would prefer my former player scores the one. It is like a family and friends forever. When I was a very young manager [at Mainz] and I knew my players did not earn very much, I had to tell some of my best friends they would not get another contract and I did not know which way it would go for them. Now it is a different level and I do not put the players on the streets, they will find another club. I do not push them in a dark room and leave them there. The future is still bright for them, and sometimes it is not the right place in our team any more. It is being completely honest in these moments, it is not that I enjoy it. Everything has its time and it's the same with a contract as well. I have never kept a player because I like him so much."

Klopp has been surprised by the emergence of some gifted young players, notably Alexander-Arnold. "I have known Trent Alexander-Arnold since he was 17 years old. He was a big talent but we were not sure he could do it physically. Now he is a machine - so he is a big surprise."

Boris Becker is his great idol, He explained: "He is the same age group as me and he is my hero. When he was 17 in 1985 and won his first Wimbledon, it was one of the biggest days in my life too. My wife and his former wife organised a meeting because he was always on my non-existent bucket list. In that moment, I could not speak, which is difficult to believe. I always knew we could be really good friends - and for that evening, we behaved as such."

Klopp joined the Reds in 2015 after the sacking of Brendan Rodgers, and settled quickly into life on Merseyside. "It was pretty quick that it felt like home to be honest. That's really strange because it was a different country and I didn't know any people, but it worked out pretty well for some reason. It's good – better than I expected obviously."

2: THE REAL JÜRGEN KLOPP

JÜRGEN KLOPP MADE HISTORY FOR LIVERPOOL as they became champions of the world for the first time, and became the only English team to win the Champions League, Super Cup and World Club Championship in the same year. After being crowned the world champions goalkeeper Alisson, who rarely gives interviews, provided an insight into the dressing room philosophy, Klopp's messages and why they are not intimidated by the club's glorious history.

The Brazilian number one said: "I think we, as a team, are making the things special. The boss keeps us together and we try to make the difference not just on the pitch but off the pitch with the supporters. Every time we say, 'We are Liverpool, this means more' maybe it makes no sense for those who are not Liverpool supporters but we really try to make this special for everybody. Not just for us players, but the supporters also who are all around the world following us. We need to give the best on the pitch. They have already the history but we are making history again. Football is like this. Winning for Liverpool is even more special. We try to do our best, we are thinking about always the next game we have in front of us. We have many games to play, we are just halfway through the season so we have a long way to go and we need to keep playing who we are playing."

Before that glorious night in Qatar, Klopp had posted his 100th league win with an impressive record breaking 5-2 Merseyside derby victory to become the fastest Liverpool manager to achieve the landmark, taking just 159 games to do so, surpassing Rafael Benitez, who took 189 games. Klopp is the second-fastest manager to 100 wins ever, falling behind only Jose Mourinho (142) in the rankings. Even the great Sir Alex is unable to match Klopp's numbers, needing 162 games to bring up his century while Arsenal legend Arsene Wenger took 20 games more than Klopp. It can only be a matter of time and there will be a statue of the German erected outside Anfield.

Those who know what makes the modern day Klopp tick are those closest to him, the players and his back room staff. Sadio Mane hailed Klopp as the best manager in the world. As Liverpool sat top of the table,

Mane was Liverpool's top scorer so far in the league with seven goals, when he detailed Klopp's influence. "There are a lot of good managers in Europe but what I can say is that our manager always has the right words and the right things to manage his team, especially knowing how to deal with his team. I would always trust his influence on the team. He is a winner and I would say he is the best in the world." The Senegalese striker described his relationship with Klopp whom he described as a 'great' man. Klopp trusts Mane implicitly and is comfortable deploying the no.10 anywhere across the frontline. There was a time when the strike force relied heavily on Mo Salah, but Mane has developed into the team's most important attacker under Klopp's guidance. "His secret, I think, is to be the team's dad. Between us, everything clicked straight away. We all love him like a father and we fear him like one too. He takes up a lot of space in my life, and not just in football. He's great as a person. I trust him blindly, like most of the dressing room, I think."

James Milner compared Klopp to the formidable former Manchester United manager Sir Alex Ferguson. Sir Alex had promised to "knock Liverpool off their ★★★★ing perch", but now Klopp was threatening to get the Liver bird back on it! Klopp famously said he needed to win the Premier League or the Champions League "or the next job might be in Switzerland". He landed the Champions League just about in time!

Milner launched his book Ask A Footballer, and told talkSPORT his manager uses press conferences the way managers such as Sir Alex Ferguson did to set the tone for a game. He said: "He's the same as some older managers, like Sir Alex as he thinks the battle starts there. He gives 100 per cent every single day and has been fantastic for the club since he's been here."

Klopp makes his players smile, but he is also strict. Milner said: "The manager is pretty much 'what you see is what you get'. He doesn't have a front for the cameras where he's different behind closed doors. He has that jokey side with us but he can also stick the boot in. He demands the best, the highest standards. He has changed a bit since he came in and realised he can relax a bit more. But the characters in the squad and the players he's got aren't going to take the foot off the gas. You see from him bouncing around on the sidelines how much it means to him."

Klopp is in equal parts friendly, intense and hands-on. During the off-season and international breaks, Klopp expects regular text message updates from his players, even to the extent of informing him how they feel coming off the pitch, others on set fitness programmes must send daily completion messages.

Milner sends a short "Session done" and his manager usually replies with a thumbs-up emoji, and more recently Klopp with cowboy hats. Milner isn't quite sure what the cowboy hat is supposed to mean! Milner once received a picture message - Klopp sitting in a hot tub, beaming. "He looked like he was enjoying himself," Milner told the i newspaper. "He's not been happy a few times when people haven't messaged him. I don't know if people thought it was a joke the first time he asked and nobody texted him. He said, "Boys make sure you message me otherwise there's going to be fines bandied about." It's important, that information.

"That's what he's like: he loves his job, he's 100 per cent in it, he's so focused and demands the highest levels, but he enjoys himself while he does it and can have a joke. Can he do anything to help the player? Can they come back for treatment? He'll be thinking about his next team. He wants to have that information."

Milner can't help but love the way Klopp really wore CR7 boxer shorts did when making his final team talk before Liverpool faced Ronaldo's Real Madrid in the 2018 Champions league Final. "He thinks deeply about what he's going to say before a game – and the CR7 thing broke the ice. This was just before we went to the ground for the final and we had our usual 15-minute meeting. He just lifted his top and had Cristiano's boxer shorts on. Everyone started laughing – as you would before a Champions League final against one of the best players in the world and you're manager's wearing his boxer shorts. He just relaxed everyone. That's why he's such a good manager."

It wasn't so funny, though, when Klopp left Milner out of the next Final despite starting virtually every Champions League game. Milner found himself on the bench in the final, but no word of explanation from the boss. "He didn't say anything. He only explained his thinking to me after the game. He said he wanted me on the field at the end. If it got nervy he wanted me playing – especially if it went to extra time or penalties. I was obviously disappointed but you win things as a squad. After a day you think: 'What can I do to help us win this trophy?' Anyway I came on after an hour and we won. When you get over the line it's amazing and you remember all the games you've played – like beating Barcelona 4-0 at Anfield. Winning it was incredible."

Jordan Henderson believed there was 'no better manager' to help him go to the next level. Having signed a new five-year deal, he was excited about the prospect to bring more silverware to Anfield than the solitary League Cup he managed in seven years. "I feel in good shape, and I also think I can improve and be better in areas. Under Jürgen Klopp there's no better manager to do that really," he told the Daily Mirror. "As a manager, tactically he is amazing. What he has done at this football club since he came in is phenomenal really, the transformation. That's no disrespect to Brendan and anyone before. But I look at the transformation from when he first came in to where it is now and it has certainly gone up in terms of everything. He has brought the whole club together – the fans, the players, the staff. He has made younger players and older players even better. He is such a massive influence."

One of the beneficiaries of Klopp's reign has been Andy Robertson. When the Scot signed a new contract he was effusive, "He is different class with everyone, and was with me from the moment I came here. He helps improving you as a player and told me what he expected when my chance came, and when it did, I knew I had to take it. Now I feel an established member of the squad, and it's a privilege playing at such a massive club. If there is something that has struck me it has been the need for greater mentality and physicality that you need doing it the Liverpool way, and I can see how much fitter I've become and aiming to improve virtually every single game, but most important has been the mentality and attitude that you develop here, an essential part of the make up of the team."

Trent Alexander-Arnold pointed to Klopp's motivational skills and high standards are the reasons for such consistent levels of results. Given his debut by Klopp in January 2017, he passed the 100-game milestone in the 2-1 win at Aston Villa. Alexander-Arnold told the Liverpool Echo, "He is someone who motivates everyone that is around. He is someone you want to play for, someone you feel as though you need to perform for. Especially with the way that the squad is now, you need to perform week in, week out to keep your place. He keeps that mentality within the squad and we never settle for what we have or the success we have had so far. There is a determination in this squad to get better and improve and achieve more."

Klopp referred to striker Roberto Firmino as the 'engine' of the team. "We get along so well. He's an excellent coach, an amazing person, so passionate on the pitch", the Brazilian said in an interview with Eight by Eight magazine. "When he says that [I'm the engine of the team], to me, it's a sign that I'm giving back what he wants. It motivates me to keep going, to do the things he asks. It was Klopp's idea to fix me as a

No.9. But I accepted this role and adapted to it. Now I want to continue in this position until the end of my career."

Klopp marked the four-year anniversary of his appointment in the Anfield in October. Dejan Lovren is one of only a handful of Reds who has remained at the club. The Croatia international identified off-the-field instructions which help fostered a greater team spirit, "We started to believe when he [Klopp] said: 'From doubters to believers'," said Lovren. "He changed things in the club, from small details like saying good morning to everyone, to cleaning your table. I think some part of these details are missing in some clubs. We are, I think, raised at my age that when you see an older person you will say, 'Good morning'. It is about respect. When you have this outside of the pitch you will feel it also on the pitch. It is simple things. It is about the food as well. He brought in people who are the best in these positions [head of nutrition, Mona Nemmer, from Bayern Munich in 2016], and he knows what he is doing."

Naby Keita echoed the dressing room feeling that their manager enjoys a light-hearted relationship with his players but that there are no favourites. Keita believes Klopp's power of communication makes him such an excellent manager. "I don't think he has any particular favourites or he has picked anyone out for a special mention, he communicates very freely and openly with all the players," Keita told Sky Sports. "He likes to laugh and joke around, he has a very light relationship with all the players."

Mane knew instantly that Liverpool was the right club for him when he met Klopp, as he recalled that first meeting when he was signing from Salzberg with Dortmund also chasing him. Klopp was talking, a lot, while Mane was quiet, as he is a quiet type. He thought it was going to be tricky working for such an extrovert. But as he got to know his manager more, he says: "Klopp is a really nice guy. Everybody loves him and that is more important to be honest (than all the talking!). He is a bit of a funny guy but at the same time he is a serious guy. Usually when I am talking to him off the pitch it is about personal things. Things about lifestyle and life, and that is important to me. I think I have somebody I can confide in"

When asked if Mane specifically was Klopp's favourite, the striker replied: "If I can get to the level of Mo maybe I will be his favourite one day."

The Egyptian described his close relationship with Klopp. "From my first day with the Reds, he has treated me like a friend. We talked together and there was something very strong between us right away. That has continued from the beginning."

Fabinho is better known by two nicknames in the dressing room.

Klopp referred to the Brazilian as 'Dyson' last month to underline his importance following his impressive display in a victory over Spurs. Fabinho is more commonly referred to by a South American term meaning 'the skinny one' after Virgil van Dijk's suggestion. Asked about the 'Dyson' tag, Fabinho said: 'A few people call me this! Between us players I'm more known as Flaco but they're cool nicknames. Before the coach used it [Dyson], another player used it - I think Milner might have said it. It's a cool nickname but the other one that the majority of the players use, Flaco, that was started by Virgil and everybody started calling me it.'

Virgil Van Dijk gave an insight into Klopp's motivational qualities in an interview with BBC 5 Live Sport's Football Daily, "Obviously believing in yourself, never give up, always work hard, stay full of confidence. He gives you the confidence that you definitely need, he tells you straight if you don't do it well to be fair as well. Personally, I'm a big fan of that – to have someone who is pretty straight, who shouts at you when you need it. Sometimes I need a bit of shouting to me as well. He's a fantastic coach."

Wijnaldum gave an insight into Klopp's man-management. "I've certainly grown as a player during my time here. The expectations are so high at such a big club and that drives you on to become better. I can't speak for every player but I have a good relationship with him. He has helped me a lot. He can be hard, because he's always on your case and saying what he thinks. But he's honest and I like that. It's always in the right way, always for the right reasons. It's not to make you feel bad or anything like that. He's really hard but, on the other side, he keeps your confidence high. He says that mistakes are just part of football. I remember against Leicester I made a mistake and it led to a goal. He wasn't angry about the mistake, he was more angry about my reaction afterwards. He thought I was too busy thinking about it rather than just putting it behind me. Before I signed for Liverpool I was playing for Newcastle as a No 10. Basically, I was always attacking, I didn't have to do much defensive work, I didn't play as the No.6 or the No.8. Learning to play different roles has made me a more all-round midfielder. It makes it easier for you to play more often and it makes it easier for the manager if he has players who can be used in different positions. I think I've shown I have the defensive discipline to play deep as the No.6 and start the build ups with my passing. I can also play higher up the pitch and make a difference in the opposition area. Being able to do both has helped me to play so many games." The Dutchman said he almost joined Spurs, but his talk with Klopp swung it Liverpool's way. "I had a really good conversation with Pochettino, but we didn't come to an agreement," Wijnaldum told the PFA. "Not just me – Newcastle also didn't come to an agreement with Tottenham. When I spoke with Jürgen, he made me feel really good. He gave me a lot of confidence because he said he liked my way of playing football. Three days after our meeting they had reached a deal and I didn't think twice. This is one of the biggest clubs in the world. I wanted to make the transfer and I'm happy that I did. Everyone talks about winning something and we have to make sure we take that next step. We have the confidence that we can do it. You want to be able to look back and feel you were part of Liverpool's great history – win something here and they will always I want to be remembered as a Liverpool player who was part of something special."

Harry Wilson, on loan at Bournemouth, gets text messages of encouragement from Klopp. Wilson played regularly under Klopp during pre-season but – having spent last season on loan at Derby County – was allowed to join the Cherries for a second successive season-long loan. Klopp was in touch regularly with the 22-year-old. Speaking while on international duty with Wales, Wilson spoke about Klopp's message to congratulate at him after he scored against Manchester City. "I get the odd message off the manager. He says he has been watching and after I scored against Manchester City he congratulated me on the goal. It gives you a boost to see that, and it is great he is keeping an eye on me." When Wilson was making a name for himself at Derby, his standout moment, particularly for Liverpool fans, came in Derby's shock victory against United at Old Trafford in the Carabao Cup. "He [Klopp] dropped me a text to tell me he'd watched it and he was delighted with the performance - and the goal! A couple of weeks ago there was another message saying, 'Good result, good goal - keep going'. When you get those texts, it is a massive boost. You know you aren't forgotten."

Former Liverpool centre half Sami Hyypia promised Klopp's players a lifetime of adulation if they land the title. More than a decade after leaving the club, Hyypia, 46, was still revered as part of the miracle of Istanbul in 2005. But landing Liverpool's first League title in 30 years would bring immortality. "Everyone remembers you when you win trophies – even 15 or 20 years on, When I'm back in Liverpool, everyone mentions that night in Istanbul in 2005 – something like that stays with the fans. No one forgets those achievements. That's why this city will go crazy if they manage to win the title this year. When we won in Istanbul, the club hadn't won the European Cup for 21 years, so there was great emotion. It was a huge release. And it will be the same next May if we win the title – because it's been so long. There will be wild celebrations and also a place in history for the players. It will be special." The Finn said he won't miss the party next time, after heading home following Klopp's triumph in Madrid against Spurs. "Last May, I was in Madrid and people were trying to get me to fly back to Liverpool to celebrate, but I couldn't because I had to be in Finland the next day. I saw the pictures and the footage of the celebrations and I was sad that I couldn't have been there because it was tremendous," said Hyypia, speaking on behalf of Carlsberg, official beer of Liverpool FC. "But I promise I won't miss the party if we become champions next year."

While Liverpool stretched their lead over Manchester City in the first third of the season, Hyypia knew there was a long road ahead, but he also knew Klopp and his players won't allow their focus to waver. "It's a great thing that no one left last summer – they kept all their big players. And, when I see them play, it looks like everyone wants to be there to play for this club and be in this team. I watch them and it seems they are having fun playing at such an extraordinarily high level – but they are also demanding of each other. That's why they won't ease up. I saw the episode with Mo Salah and Sadio Mane, but, far from thinking that was damaging to the dressing room spirit, I thought that showed how strong it is. It just shows that everyone wants to win together and what a great group Klopp has built with that dynamic. It's always good to have that kind of openness where players can call each other out. That's part of the culture of winning. All successful teams have that desire, which means they demand more from each other. I remember some sparks flying between players when I was at Anfield – and that's only good for the team."

With City likely to fight until the end, Hyypia believed if Liverpool triumphed it will make victory even more remarkable. "If someone creates a great team like City, you can't stop that. We lost one game and City won the title, so you have to hold up your hands as we did all we could to win it. They even gave us credit for pushing them to the very end. That's why, if we win, it'll be even better as City are just so good. To win in an era where your rival is so good merely heightens the achievement."

If Klopp does deliver the title, he would "never have to do anything again in Liverpool", said former Reds keeper Chris Kirkland, who told Sport Witness, "I've always been a Liverpool fan and my first game was when I was seven years old standing in the Kop. As a Liverpool fan, it's brilliant. It's exciting times. I think Jürgen deserves a lot of credit. Three or four years ago there was a bit of negativity around the club, but he's brought the whole club back together. I go down to Melwood quite a bit and am lucky enough to watch the training. No matter who's down there, whether it's the person taking the bins out, someone cooking the food or washing the kit, he treats everyone exactly the same way. He's got so much time for everybody and has brought that feel-good factor back. The fans know that – they adore him and they won the Champions League last year. If he can get us the league title for the first time in 30 years, he'll never have to do anything again in Liverpool because he'll be a hero. There's a long way to go. The win against Man City was a huge game and nine points is a big gap but it's Man City you're talking about – they pulled it back last year. But I'm hoping this is the year. It's been bubbling for a couple of years, we won the Champions League last year for the first time since 2005. It's been bubbling since he [Klopp] came to the club and he's transformed it completely. They have some world-class players. If we can keep the big players fit... I think in the next two months they play Saturday-Tuesday-Sunday-Wednesday every week after the international break until Christmas, so that's going to be a challenging period for them to keep everyone fit. But if they do that, I'm definitely backing them to win it."

Alisson revealed what Klopp said to him behind-closed-doors in the wake of his big mistake in his early days in English football. In an interview with Italian newspaper La Gazzetta dello Sport, he discussed how his relationship with the Liverpool boss has unfolded. "When the clubs got together [to discuss the transfer], Klopp gave me a call on Face Time and explained his project and what we would do together. I have admired him since the days of Dortmund. I like being trained by him, because he does not talk a lot but he always knows what to say and how to do it. He is an intelligent man of character. [After Leicester] he came into the dressing room and started joking. He dealt with it in the best way possible, since I already knew I'd embarrassed myself. Then he told me not to lose faith and to carry on playing that way."

Mario Gotze hailed Klopp as his "footballing father" and believed the Liverpool manager's human qualities set him apart from Guardiola. Gotze is one of a handful of players to have operated under two of this generation's most celebrated coaching talents. "Pep Guardiola was technically one of the best coaches, [playing under him was a] tremendous enrichment," Gotze told DAZN as part of the 'Being Mario Gotze' documentary. But I had the feeling that he thinks only on the pitch and leaves out the people and the outside. The empathy was not that big. It was not easy for me, just because I came from Kloppo, who was like a footballing father. Pep was the complete difference. A world-class coach needs empathy, every athlete is also human and you should combine both [tactics and empathy]." Before returning to Signal Iduna Park, Gotze was tempted by a Klopp reunion. I decided to leave Bayern and Jürgen Klopp was interested in getting me to Liverpool. And I was also interested in working with him again. It [the desire to work with Klopp again] still exists. He is a world-class coach and that's why it's always an option. I decided to join Borussia Dortmund, but it was not a decision against Liverpool or Jürgen Klopp."

3: GETTING BACK ON THAT PERCH

WHEN LIVERPOOL CHIEF EXECUTIVE PETER Moore announced that he considered that The Reds were "back on our perch", Jürgen Klopp wondered what he was talking about! The phrase was famously used by former Manchester United manager Sir Alex Ferguson about the Anfield club's dominance when he arrived at Old Trafford in November 1986, later declaring that his first job was to "knock Liverpool right off their f——— perch". It took Fergie 25 years and 13 Premier League titles to do so but by the time of his retirement in 2013 United had set a new English top-flight record of 20 titles, compared to Liverpool's 18. The score was 16-7 when Sir Alex took over and Fergie's turn of phrase has clearly irritated Liverpool supporters down the years.

Moore, a lifelong Liverpool fan, was appointed by Fenway Sports Group - the American company which bought Liverpool for £300m in 2010 - in February 2017. He believed Liverpool had regained their old status when they were crowned European champions for the sixth time.

"We are back on our perch, as we famously say," Moore told former Liverpool striker Michael Robinson, now one of Spain's leading sports broadcasters, during an interview at the World Football Summit in Madrid.

Jürgen Klopp's response was typical. He claimed he not to know what a 'perch' is. "I'll try to Google it but I am not sure I will find out what it means exactly," he said.

But he was sure whatever it meant, it would not add any pressure, to his already pressurised job. "No, absolutely no extra pressure. Not at all. What I heard is how it often is in life, without the context. We are all adults and we say things and sometimes people have to deal with things that I say and in this case people seem to think I have to deal with things Peter said. I'm not angry about him or whatever. I like Peter. So now if people come to me constantly and ask, 'are you still on the perch or not?' I still won't understand what the word perch means."

Sir Alex had ended United's 26-year wait for the title before establishing his side as the dominant force in the country, overtaking Liverpool's record of 18 titles, and putting United back on their perch as he promised. "He is one of the biggest, if not the biggest, in world football," Klopp said "You can say that with all the things he achieved. Where he started, where he came from and what he did with the club. All that stuff. It's just incredible. As a young manager - a couple of years ago I was a young manager - it's not allowed to compare yourself or think about what he is doing and then compare to what you're doing. It was a completely different world. It's a different job. I always admired him. From a distance it's easy. I'm not sure how it would have been if I was here 20 years at Liverpool and you always have this battle all the time. Then maybe it's different because he was a very competitive guy saying some things before he played against Liverpool. I'm pretty sure when he was in charge he didn't want us to be successful. Maybe he doesn't want that now but the opinion is probably not that strong anymore because he said already a couple of times, I heard, that he likes what we are doing here." Klopp met him for the first time in Nyon as part of a conference for Champions League coaches while he was Dortmund boss. "I asked if someone was here and they said, 'Yes Sir Alex Ferguson is in the breakfast room'. I came in and he was like, 'Oh Jürgen, come here'," he said. "I came in and for the first half an hour I had no clue what we were talking about because of the Scottish thing. I tried to be really, really friendly and step by step I got it. It's still the same with Kenny Dalglish. He is a really nice person. I respect him a lot. Obviously he thinks I'm not completely blind as a manager so that's good."

At his first press conference he promised he would turn doubters to believers. "So, he's bringing passion to the... English?" Was Arsène Wenger's take on the appointment. The high intensity, high pressing rock & roll *gegenpressing* football synonymous with Klopp at Dortmund comes with hard work on the training ground that would transform Liverpool.

Klopp, Fenway Sports Group president Mike Gordon and sporting director Michael Edwards dictate the playing policy which led to decisions to sign Mo Salah despite his failure at Chelsea, and breaking world records for van Dijk and Alisson, and at the other end of the scale capturing a relegated cut-price Scotland left-back, Andy Robertson. Gordon operates from from Massachusetts, whose philosophy is one of "speaking your mind at Liverpool isn't 'allowed' — it's mandatory". Gordon, a Boston asset-manager drawn into FSG, took over the daily running of Liverpool in summer 2012. He appointed Ian Graham, a Cambridge physics graduate whose football research firm was produced data for Spurs that inspired several Daniel Levy transfers. Graham is a

Liverpool fan so his arrival at Anfield seemed to fulfil his destiny. Edwards played for Peterborough's reserves, who blossomed as an analyst at Harry Redknapp's Portsmouth. He worked on player stats, having worked for Prozone, and graduated to head of performance analysis at Tottenham. Edwards' team compiled a 60-page dossier on Klopp.

Key signings were made via meticulous research, combining Graham's data with the scouting reports. Signings are the recommendation of the Klopp-Edwards-Gordon brains trust. Klopp is a huge attraction for new recruits; Van Dijk, Alisson and Salah had options at Atletico Madrid and Paris Saint-Germain. Klopp said: "I came from a very small club [Mainz] where I played for 11 years then was manager. Everyone treated me like a friend. Then I went to Dortmund and after the pre-season we were friends. The players were young, even younger than my sons, so I was for them a pretty old friend — but that's how it was. I realised pretty early the relationship in England between nearly all members of staff and players to the manager is completely different to what I was used to. The first thing they said was 'how do you want to have that, that, that?' And I said 'well how did you do it before?' They said 'that's not important, what do you want'? It's like they hand you a blank bit of paper and you write down all your rules. But it's commonsense: if I want to be in the stadium at 1.15 before a 3pm game I have no clue how far the stadium is, I have no clue when the bus starts! So it took a while before people knew who I am and how I am."

Ultra modern techniques might be used behind the scenes, but not social media for the manager. Klopp once said: "I think my smartest decision in life was not to use social media. I don't read it if people criticise me on social media. They can write whatever they want and it never would faze me because I don't know it. I don't read it" but social media was good for him. In Tenerife, March 2017, on a cup break a video was posted of Klopp laughing when Lovren fell on his backside in training and was hit on the head by a ball as he lay prostate. When Salah was named the Football Writers' Player of the Year last season, he was unable to attend, so sent a speech to be read out on the night. It went viral. "I read and hear about him being a wonderful role model for Egypt – North Africa – for the wider Arabic world and for Muslims. This of course is true – but he is a role model FULL STOP. Regardless of race or religion – country or region of birth. The only "labels" we should put on Mo is what a good person he is and what a fantastic footballer he is – and by the way – the first part of that is more important in life than the second."

"Jürgen is one of the more holistic human beings you will ever meet," said Moore. "He is able to keep the ship going straight, motivate not just the players but his staff, the coaching staff, the sports science staff - he keeps everyone on an even keel. His personality is infectious. His charisma is without question. Even when you have lost he makes you think there is a brighter sunshine ahead."

Moore was as much referring to Liverpool's financial situation, with owners Fenway Sports Group transforming the club from the verge of bankruptcy to one of the top five richest in the world in nine years. In Moore's eyes, Manchester United were no longer on the perch, and it was now Manchester City that posed the biggest challenge to Liverpool. Yet, it might well have been different had Klopp ended up at Old Trafford.

Klopp's wife had urged him not to take over Manchester United while he was still at Borussia Dortmund, eventually joining the Reds instead. Phil Thompson revealed the part wife Ulla Sandrock played. He told Denmark's TV2: "I interviewed Klopp for Sky, and I asked if he and Liverpool were created for each other. He looked at me and asked 'Why?' Then Klopp told me he could have taken over Manchester United, but his wife said it wasn't right. When Liverpool arrived, his wife said it was right. There is something strange there. It is as if he's created for Liverpool."

Since Moore's arrival, The Reds have reached two Champions League finals under Klopp and started work on a state-of-the-art training ground at Kirkby. "What the Fenway Sports Group have done at Liverpool over the past nine years is nothing short of miraculous," added Moore. "They have gone through ups and downs but have stayed the course and never taken a penny out of the club."

The new Main Stand opened in 2016 lifting capacity above 54,000, while the club signed Virgil van Dijk for £75m and Alisson for £67m in 2018. Liverpool spend £16m on a digital strategy aimed at increasing engagement with a supporter base they estimate at 771 million followers. "Football is a virtuous cycle," Moore observed. "You drive revenues so you can afford to buy a goalkeeper or a centre-half that will win you games. When you win games, sponsors want to be part of your story, so they write you a cheque. You take that money and buy better players. They win you more games." Klopp and owners Fenway Sports Group awoke a 'sleeping giant' managing director Billy Hogan proclaimed. The club was transformed off the field in the six years since Hogan joined as chief commercial officer with FSG overseeing the redevelopment of Anfield and the impending move to a new training ground, while Klopp led a resurgence on the pitch. "There's a huge desire to return the club to where we believe it belongs at the top of world football,' Hogan told the Liverpool Echo. "Sitting here today, the club is in a tremendously positive place. The football is terrific, the team is playing great and we're all excited about the future." Hogan paid tribute to the impact Klopp on and off the field. 'Jürgen is a big personality and he's also tremendously supportive. The "Klopp factor" is more than just about his interaction with football, it's across the whole club. He's a tremendous fit and we're so happy that he's here. We're starting to see the culmination of the strategy we've been following. Getting to this place, seeing the way this team is playing and the amount of talent in the squad — seeing what the guys have done at Melwood and the academy — is fantastic. If you go back to when FSG first started looking at Liverpool as an opportunity, people were referring to the club as a sleeping giant. I think that's something that's been proven to be true."

Klopp knew Liverpool were an attractive club for the biggest players in the world, however there's no chance of signing some of the top superstars such as Kylian Mbappe, out of reach of even the richest Premier League clubs. Reports in Spain suggested the 20-year-old could be a possible replacement for Salah, with Real Madrid eyeing the Egyptian winger. Via the internet fans made it known they would love the club to lure the young French winger to their club. Klopp, who tried to sign Mbappe before he joined PSG in 2017, admits Liverpool simply cannot afford him. Bought for 180m euros, Real Madrid are willing to pay 280m euros! He earns 30m euros a year after tax! Klopp said: "I don't see any club at the moment who can buy Kylian Mbappe from PSG. And we are involved in the clubs that cannot do it, it is as easy as that. OK, from a sporting point of view, there are not a lot of reasons to not sign him, what a player he is. It is about the money of course. No chance. Absolutely no chance. Sorry for killing that story."

When asked why there aren't any French players in his team, Klopp told French TV channel Canal+: "There's no reason for it, there's no reason for it. Kylian plays for PSG. Griezmann has joined Barcelona. Obviously you know how good your team is. We would like a French player but some of them are too expensive for us."

Klopp's prime concern was to stop a talent drain such as Luis Suarez and Raheem Sterling leaving Anfield. "We want to be a club in the future for sure whose players don't want to leave," he said in 2016. "That's very important. But it will only be possible with success and the atmosphere we create in and around the club." Although forced to sell Philippe Coutinho to Barcelona in January 2018 for £142m, Liverpool remained a 'go to' destination for the best players, but not if moneybags clubs like PSG and City want to compete, then it's not so easy or straightforward. "I don't think we can compare with Man City, I have no idea which players want to go to Man City, but good players obviously have in the last couple of years, there is no doubt about that," Klopp said. "We have reasons, good reasons why players want to join us, that is clear. City had a very successful spell though, in the last 10 years they have been champions a couple of times. So it is different tastes and that leads to different decisions. I don't think we struggle with convincing players. You can feel it, this year, last year, you can see in the eyes of a player, I am not sure if honour is the right word, but it is good that we speak to them. The club is in a really good position, but unfortunately it does not lead to a situation where you win all the football games. It has to be done on the pitch. Image-wise, it maybe [always] was, but now I think it is easier to live the life of a Liverpool supporter and that means automatically being in a situation to sign the players you want to sign."

Klopp successfully created healthy competition for places, as he told the Liverpool Echo: "How do we improve? You only have to look at your passport, as long as you are not dead, you can improve, that is how it is. That's how it is for all of us, so I don't have to convince them. And they know if they don't then there is another player who can the same position, in a different way, maybe, but for sure not sure and that is the pressure the boys have to deal with. It is not massive [pressure] because we don't use that fact because we really see ourselves as a unit and whoever is in the best shape has to play. So it not about your name, it is 'you're in the best shape to play' because the [difference in] quality is that [small]. The boys are really close to each other and there is not a massive difference between them, so that is good. It keeps them on their toes, playing for Liverpool keeps them on their toes.

"We don't have fringe players here, we only have first team players and a few young guns. We now play a lot Tuesday, Wednesday and Saturday, so we will have to see about [changes]. We don't just play a lot of football we travel a lot, but you know that. Every team has to do that, we don't go for excuses. Other teams have difficult situations, as well, it is like that. You want to play Champions League, desperately and then it starts, you don't say 'oh my God, look at all these games' that makes no sense. It is good.'

Klopp knew his players deep desire was to keep on winning, hungry for more trophies. "It is just the simple thought about what a career should be keeps them on their toes and the idea of a collection of silverware, not only one. So there is a lot to come and it is not difficult [to keep players focused]. From a character point of view, we fit really well. The team and the staff and I, we have done really well because we are pretty similar. We don't think too much about the long term targets, the next game is our final and we play a lot of finals in our season."

Teenagers Harvey Elliott and Sepp van den Berg were the only summer transfer window acquisitions, emphasising that Klopp felt his squad was strong enough, although if he did have an addition in mind, it might have been a question of their availability, and price, when he said: "The players we thought about to make this team better were really expensive and we could not spend the money. That is how it is."

Looking at Mbappe, he added: "To see a player better than him, or with potential to be better or play exactly the same as him, is really difficult. That is what it was. That was the situation. But was not that we were not real, but we did not want to make five or six changes. Not at all. This team is at a wonderful age, there is still space for improvement, completely fine. We want to do something and we could have done a lot, but could not do the right thing and we only wanted to do the right thing. That is the reason we kept this squad, because it is really good and if you wanted to improve it you have to do it with the right players, not just some players to fix whatever. That is not possible."

Manchester United manager Ole Gunnar Solskjaer grew up a Liverpool supporter and the current Liverpool side influenced his approach as manager when he began his career in Norway. Solskjaer took Molde to Marbella for their pre-season training camp, where Liverpool relocated for warm-weather training. Solskjaer met Klopp and posed for a photograph taken by the Molde press officer Per Lille. Solskjaer briefly spoke about studying Klopp when he was coach of Dortmund and admitted he wanted to 'copy' his counter-attacks. "It was nice to meet him," Solskjaer said, "I studied him when he was in Dortmund, and that kind of football is something we want to copy - especially the way he counter-attacks and plays offensive, with the speed and intensity they have in their game. That's something we aspire to do ourselves. It will, of course, take some time, but his type of football is inspiring."

As if to underline the ongoing boom at the club, Liverpool unveiled ambitious plans to redevelop the Anfield Road End to take their stadium capacity beyond 61,000. The club entered into a public consultation with the hope of being able to submit a planning application for the development in the first half of 2020. Should Liverpool not meet opposition to their proposal, the structure behind the goal to the left of tunnel would be boosted by an extra 7,000 seats, taking the Anfield Road capacity to 16,000 – the Kop, with 12,500 seats, would become the smallest stand in the stadium. Of the 7,000 seats, 5,000 go to general admission, a further 2,000 for corporate hospitality; the size of the structure, meanwhile, would see part of Anfield Road, which is a two-way thoroughfare for vehicles, permanently closed to traffic.

The project would cost £60m, an indication of the club's current financial health is that they would be able to fund it self-sufficiently. When they built the new Main Stand in 2015-16, owners Fenway Sports Group provided a £110m loan. Liverpool – who would be open to the prospect of selling naming rights for the Anfield Road End – were also currently building a new £50m training ground in Kirkby, which will be ready for business in July 2020, but chief financial officer Andy Hughes says the time is right for this project. 'Our ambition is to increase the capacity of Anfield stadium and allow more fans to enjoy some of the best football in the world," said Hughes. "We have always been looking at a long-term development plan for Anfield and we have been looking specifically at Anfield Road as the next step. We have deliberately phased these investments, as they are big projects in their own right. They require funding. So of the big steps we chose to do the Main Stand first, the training ground second and Anfield Road third. We are currently still in the development process for the training ground. That is looking to complete this summer so the timing to move on to design, planning and initiation of the Anfield Road development is right now.'

4: THE JOY OF SIX

THE ROCKY THEME TUNE PERFECTLY SUMMED up the epic struggle to topple champions Manchester City and their even more expensive squad under another world class manager in Pep Guardiola. But just like his hero Sly Stallone, Jürgen Klopp came agonising close to landing the big title but in the he had to settle for a points defeat - albeit just one point.

However unlike Rocky, quickly made up for the fans' disappointment when his players got up from the canvas and delivered a knock out blow in the final of the Champions League beating Spurs. It was ironic that City's owners coveted the European crown, while the Liverpool faithful wanted the end of the long wait for the title and both ended up with the other team's most heartfelt desire.

Liverpool might have won an impressive eighteen titles in their illustrious history, but the last one was an awfully long time ago, and not even a record busting start to the season seemed to be able to topple a team many regarded the best in Europe, if not the world. In the final media conference prior to the big kick off, Klopp was asked what the key would be to closing a 25-point gap on City from their previous title winning season. "We are still Rocky Balboa, not Ivan Drago," he retorted in reference to the fourth film of the iconic boxing epic.

"Thank you, Jürgen," was Pep Guardiola's response. "For nine years I've lived with it, no problem. Every season except the first one when I arrived at Barcelona, when I had people who didn't know I was a manager, since then we have always been the favourites. But thank you, Jürgen. You are so kind."

He set out and used Liverpool's phenomenal season to inspire his own players; he told them throughout the season, if they slip up just the once, Liverpool would be behind them ready to pounce. In Rocky IV the all-American hero travelled to Siberia where he trains in primitive surroundings before confronting Drago, the seemingly unbeatable opponent, it was the perfect analogy as Liverpool were in City's faces for the entire season.

Klopp identified the weaknesses immediately after losing to Real Madrid in the Champions League Final, not merely in the one game, but over the course of the season, and went about minimising those weaknesses, with a massive spend to provide more punch, as he planned to go the distance, but City had even greater spending power if they needed it.

He laughed about the Rocky analogy — he has seen all the films 'many, many times' and the fourth one is his favourite. 'I don't want to be the underdog,' said Klopp. 'I want to win and Rocky won. It's the only difference. So now we have the best tools of all? It's not true. Manchester City had a fantastic team last year and they have now brought in Riyad Mahrez. It doesn't make them weaker. Our potential is good, what we do with it we will see, and that's only the quality we have. I only want from us that we fight, not that we are the underdog. I am not interested in be- ing the underdog. Yes, it has happened a few times but not because I wanted to be, but because it was a fact. I don't see us an underdog, I see us as a team that challenges... the ones who have to do more, who have to run more, who have to jump more. That's all.'

Liverpool finished fourth the previous season, but it was the huge 25 point gap that concerned Klopp. Liverpool's emphatic Champions League quarter-final victory over Pep's side, plus a league win over City, suggested they were much closer than the 25 point deficit indicated and that they could mount their biggest challenge once they had recruited key additions. 'You all ask me about the gap to City and what we have to do, it has nothing to do with City. City took three points from us, we took three points from them but we lost them in other games. Win all of them and it is good but it is pretty difficult to do because not only the other Big Six, you see how Wolverhampton acts, how Fulham acts and how Everton acts – they are all ambitious. I don't think too much about what we have to do; I thought about it pre-season but now we have to be in this championship mood. It is like you jump in the water and dive and then let's go for it until you don't have enough air any more or oxygen and you have to go up again. That is the plan, that we really go for it.'

Alisson was a key acquisition, the Brazilian was, until Chelsea signed Kepa Arrizabalaga for £72m, the world's most expensive goalkeeper at £67m move from Roma. Klopp had no worries about the 25-year-old making an instant impact. "Just be a goalkeeper. Be yourself, in this case, because he is very calm and laid back - and that helps," said Klopp ahead of the opening game. "It's about making the right decisions in the right moments. It's all good. He's settled really quick, as if he's been here longer than two weeks. That's all fine."

Liverpool were the summer's biggest spenders. Klopp justified it: "My own expectations are always pretty high, we'll have to make the most of it (the pressure after spending a lot). It's always my expectation to reach the highest level but it doesn't work all the time. I think for us it was pretty normal there would be one point where we spend more money. The last few years I've had to sit here and defend our transfer behaviour, we sold more than we brought in. It all makes sense, we had to create a squad which is strong enough and wide enough to cope with the Premier League. People ask me is it the best squad I've ever had? I don't think about that. It's about what we make of it, how often we deliver, how often we bring ourselves in a mood to fight against all these Premier League teams who want to have our points."

Klopp knew Emre Can would be leaving, so he brought in Brazilian Fabinho for £44m plus Naby Keita. "We knew early enough that it was pretty likely he would leave and we were able to plan."

Liverpool were searching for their first trophy under Klopp after losing in a League Cup, Europa League and Champions League final. Klopp was in his fourth season, having taken charge in October 2015 after leaving Borussia Dortmund, and believed Anfield the perfect stage for him to deliver success. Klopp spent £176.8m in the summer window in the quest for major honours. But Klopp prefers being the underdog: "I don't want the 'best team' in England. If a team is better than yours, then you have to work out how to be at their level, and then how to beat them. I have never wanted to have the best team. I have never wanted to be the best player or the best manager. What interests me is to beat the best. The best team today in England is Manchester City. That means that other teams are not the best. The goal then is to beat City as often as possible."

Klopp said Liverpool were "in a league that brings together six of the world's biggest clubs, who are all fighting for four Champions League places," which made his task "very difficult." He added: "Apart from Manchester City, who were way ahead early on, it was a huge relief for all the others to qualify. Liverpool's history is made up of battles. And when you battle, you never expect it to be easy. Why would it be now? Yes, we're aiming for the stars, but we respect the game. I feel the size of the club and above all the honour given to me to lead the team. Last year, I turned 50 and I invited quite a lot of people to celebrate. I hadn't seen some of them for 20 years. The words that I heard most were: 'Who would have thought it? That you would, one day, be manager of

Liverpool?' It's true that when you're born in the Black Forest and you have played in Germany's seventh division, it seems improbable. I didn't even dream of being a professional or having a career in football... so for me, I'm at the club that suits me to achieve every goal."

Klopp never took his eyes off the big picture and an unlikely move in the transfer market. Shaqiri endured relegation at Stoke, scored a wonderful goal for Switzerland at the World Cup, found himself reprimanded by Fifa for a goal celebration that politicised his Albanian-Kosovan heritage, and was bought by Klopp, who said of the signing: "I think the English phrase is a 'no-brainer'."

Shaqiri paid tribute to Klopp. "When he arrived here, the club was totally different. You can see the people have a lot of respect for him and his work. The progress of this club, this team is getting higher every year. He is going about it the right way. Nothing is impossible. We can be everything we want to be. We beat City in the league and the Champions League last season, so I think we can win everything in the world. It has to be our ambition, against whoever we play, to dominate the game. I came here to try to win titles. This club needs to have the ambition to win titles, to be one of the best clubs in the world"

Klopp questioned why Liverpool were perceived as City's only challengers, and why only in England can you seemingly "win the title in the transfer market". He said: "I couldn't be less interested in what other people say of us. What people say is sometimes nice, sometimes not so nice, but it is always not important. What is important is that we know what we want to be, and we want to be a challenger. How can we be something different? We didn't win anything in the last few years, that's the truth. And the other teams, I can't see that they've got weaker. So why should we [be the only challengers] because we made a few signings? It's only an English thing, where you can win the league in the transfer window. It's not possible. It's not interesting. We did our business, other teams did theirs last year, two years ago, whatever. We did it this year because we felt it was the right moment to do so, that's all! We enjoy our role, and all the rest is not important to us."

Then Manchester United manager Jose Mourinho had led the Old Trafford to the runners-up a huge 19 points behind City but was touchy when asked if he should still be considered a great if he did not win a title at United, "Do you ask that question to the manager that finished third in the Premier League or fourth? Because he never wins anything internationally, for example." A clear reference to Klopp and Spurs boss

Mauricio Pochettino. It was a barb that would back fire on the 'Special One' as he was sacked following a 3-1 defeat at Anfield that December bringing a fractious reign at Old Trafford to a close.

By contrast Klopp was in good humour discussing a charity game, joking that he wanted to sort out 'the plumbing issue, electricity and the pool' when he comes face to face with his landlord Brendan Rodgers at Parkhead on the touchline for the Match For Cancer. Having taken over from Rodgers in October 2015, Klopp moved into the Formby mansion his predecessor had bought from Steven Gerrard.

In a video message on Celtic's Twitter page, he joked that he was looking forward to seeing Rodgers for the first time since the house was let to him. 'It will be fun for sure. Especially because I meet my landlord, I think for the first time since he left Liverpool and I came here. We have a lot of things to talk about. The plumbing issue, electricity, the pool and stuff like that. So Brendan, hope you are in good shape and we can sort a few things that day.' He was excited to visit Glasgow and Parkhead for the first time: 'It's my first time in your wonderful, famous stadium and probably my first time in Glasgow in general, so a big day for me and hopefully a very nice day for all of you. As a manger it's always difficult to prepare a game, in this specific case it's even more difficult because nobody can blame me for recruitment, or scouting. He then joked: 'I have nothing to do with the team, maybe nothing to do with the lineup, because James Milner is in my team and he's a very demanding person. He will tell me probably "he plays there, he plays there".'

Klopp demanded desire in enormous quantities to get forward and score late goals despite being physically tired. 'In these moments the fuel is really low and maybe the players need a bit of help from an angry manager - 'run or I will kill you' - and they did that with a fantastic counter attack.'

Klopp responded after Gary Neville suggested Liverpool should ignore the Champions League to focus on the league which he believes they had a realistic chance of winning. Klopp asked for Neville to come and explain to him how that would work and questioned whether he should play the youth team.

"How would that work? We don't play Champions League or what?" Klopp asked at his press conference. "Gary should come over and tell me exactly how that works. How do you prepare for a game when you don't focus on it? I don't understand, do we play our kids or what? I don't know what he means with that, to be honest. We have to play football. A lot of people watch our games when we play Champions League and that's our job that we do the best we can do in all these games. That's what we try. I don't know exactly what it means but to focus on one competition can only be if maybe you are already out of the competition nearly. If it's late in the season that you see you have a chance to do that or do this and all that stuff. Last year, for example, we had no chance to focus on one competition because we had to qualify for the Champions League and I don't think that even Gary Neville would have said, 'Quarter-finals of the Champions League, let City win'. I don't want to be too critical as I don't know exactly how he said it, but it's a bit silly, sitting in an office talking about football, it's different to doing the job.'

In an interview with The Times, Gary Neville thought Liverpool could win the league if they were able to rest their star men week-on-week, something they particularly need due to their high pressing game "The Champions League - if I was Liverpool, I would kick it into touch," Neville suggested. "I know that's very hard to do but if they could go into February, March, April without it, I think they could have a real chance [of winning the league] if they had free weeks."

Klopp's philosophy was to ensure his players felt enthused by what happened to them the previous season in losing the Final against Madrid, and the determination to get back to the Final to put that right, rather than become subdued by the Final defeat. "No damage. No. Absolutely not. It is a different club to the club I joined. We got a lot of respect because of the way we played last season. Everyone who saw the Final saw that we could have won it against a side in a completely different moment. They see the games we played. They saw City. They saw Rome. They saw Porto. Going to the Final needed 10 or 12 outstanding performances. They saw so many games which we played in a really good way. There was a lot of respect. It is important for the club and the players. The players we spoke to in the summer were different talks to those I had the previous year or before. We are in the place we want to be without being satisfied with anything. We are a challenger again for pretty much everything, especially in each game. I don't think there is any game in the world where you would say beforehand, 'No chance Liverpool', which is good. That doesn't mean we will win. But that means it is clear that we have a chance if we play our best."

He added: "The best way is when you are experienced you use your new knowledge and start again like a virgin. It is a nice experience, it is a nice memory, but at the end we have to start new, using the experience but not relying on it. We are in a really good moment, but we are not a little bit satisfied. There is nothing in us that thinks that's it. It's good but we want it better for the club."

Klopp did not want to be second best to City, comparing Liverpool's battle for supremacy with tennis rivalry between Germans Becker and Michael Stich. Stich won only one major to Becker's six as City's recent trophy haul outstrips Liverpool. "We cannot wait until City are not there any more. We want to fight them. We want to have battles with them, 100 per cent. We still have to be a bit more passionate. I grew up in a time when Boris Becker and Michael Stich were the best tennis players in Germany and maybe for a few years in the world. Michael Stich was an outstanding tennis player, maybe better than Boris Becker, but he was not Boris Becker."

Klopp marked three years at Anfield with an excellent interview with Joes' Melissa Reddy, where Klopp echoed Bill Shankly's famous "if you are second you are nothing", saying he knows being a runner-up won't do: "If somebody wants to judge me because of the last three years then I know what people are saying, and it's the truth. I lost the last six finals [three with Liverpool), it's not something that's really enjoyable, but you can see it from two points. Yes we lost, but at the same time we reached them, that's not cool but in most sports second place is OK. If you go to the Olympic Games and you come home with a silver medal, it's still something but in football it's nothing. It's nothing for me as well, so I don't get up in the morning and say 'I'll reach another final' or whatever. It's not like this, I want to win and I know that's the responsibility."

On his arrival, Klopp was "pretty sure" he would win a title within four years. "I really wanted a change after 14 years managing in Germany, where I knew everything, I knew each team. If you would have asked me about a side in the fifth division, I could have told you the names of at least four of their players. Then I came to England and everything is new. Yes, I watched English football before, but I was busy in Germany with my league and with Champions League and stuff. Then, you come here, we play a team - let's say Hull - and you don't know one player. For the preparations you have pretty much three days so you watch their games completely differently because I had completely no idea of what they do. In Germany, meanwhile, I knew inside-out how every team played. The start at Liverpool was really busy because we had to learn a lot of things while also playing in the Europa League, but it was exactly what I wanted - a new challenge for myself. I wanted to get rid of some routines which were normal after spending such a long time in Germany as a manager and have kind of a new start. I really feel it's a big privilege to have the chance to do so, because it's like an energiser it gives you a real boost, which helps.

"I'm a much better manager now than I was three years ago. I tried to prepare myself a little bit language-wise. I downloaded an app, which I have still and it helped me a lot. I felt that I needed to improve my English a bit, because like a lot of people of my generation in Germany, we learnt it in school, but then we don't use it too much. I tried, at least, to think of a few things that I could say in the meetings with the players and had a look what the English word was for that. That was all my preparations pretty much, because I couldn't do a lot. We left a country and our lives there behind, if you want, so we had to organise a few things. It was quite busy these four days, quite busy, and it was not a lot about football."

Klopp's first opportunity to share his outlook was with Liverpool's in-house TV channel; wanting supporters to change from "doubters to believers." He reiterated that during his first press conference, asking for patience to develop the team. "It was obvious something was wrong at Liverpool, so it was clear that we need a new relationship and that's actually the basis for everything - the people. The first day the manager comes in, all are happy I think most of the time. From that moment on, it only can get worse, step-by-step because you cannot reach all the expectation, it's not possible. I don't know exactly what the people thought about what I could do when I came in, probably they thought 'do something similar like what you did at Dortmund.' Even at Dortmund we needed a start. What I was asking for was just to give us time to start new, because if you don't do that and if we have to start the next game and have in our backpack the last 400 games, that doesn't work. It was cool that they brought a new face in and, of course, if you were used to difficulties in the past then you doubt everything, even the positive things.

"I'm pretty sure a lot of people thought as well, 'okay, a new guy in, but will be the same as always? They have a good few games and in the end, they will win nothing.' And actually it happened like that. I have said it a few times: I have no idea when we will win something, but I'm sure this club will win something. I don't know when so let's have the best times of our lives until then. Let's enjoy the world, let's enjoy the football, let's enjoy the journey and it's what we did so far - it was a good time. Nobody wants to look back in 10 or 20 years and say 'so the best time we had without winning anything was when Klopp was here. It was so funny and all that stuff'. That's not really something you want to achieve, we still have time to do something special and we know that to underline the development and progress, we have to do it. Times change, and to be honest, it is much more difficult than it was in the past. If you think about it, we are maybe in the best moment for ages, but a few other clubs are the same and they made the same steps so that makes it really hard.

"It looks like we are really on a good way and the only thing I can guarantee is that we constantly develop. Our little problem is many other clubs develop as well so it's never that you improve 20% and the others get 20% weaker. They try to do the same, to reach the next level, and that's the challenge we all face. It is interesting, but tough as well. As I said in my first press conference here, if anybody thinks that I can perform wonders, then it could become really difficult in the future, because I can't. I'm a pretty hard-working person, I'm pretty well paid, so I should work hard actually. That's what I do, I try to find solutions for different problems or situations and that's how I understand the job. The only thing I can do is to put all I have - my knowledge, passion, heart, experience, everything - I throw it into this club, 100 per cent. I don't keep anything back and it should work actually at one point. You have to bring yourself in the best situation that you are able to and use it - that's what we do. When we win something, this city will explode - I'm sure - in a very positive way."

Back then the new manager couldn't have possibly imagined that he would set a new Liverpool record of the most points after the opening 15 games in the entire history of the club, and yet still be two points behind champions City until their defeat at Stamford Bridge on Saturday, December 8, a few hours after Liverpool won on the south coast, 4-0 at Bournemouth.

Klopp said: 'We are the ones who have to do more. We have to fight more. That must be our attitude. We have to be like Rocky.'

The highlight of the season proved to be that stunning comeback against Barcelona in the semi-final, overturning a three-goal defeat from the first leg. It was a truly unforgettable night at Anfield that somehow emerged out of sheer adversity; the huge deficit, no away goal, and the quality of the opposition. And without key players Divock Origi and Gini Wijnaldum proved to be the unlikely heroes making up for the loss of Salah and Firmino. Origi played the central role, flanked by Mané and Shaqiri, who had been involved during the first half of the season, but hadn't started a game since January. Trent Alexander-Arnold was back after his omission from the first leg. Having already won La Liga before their weekend date with Celta Vigo, Ernesto Valverde rested his entire starting team. But they were all back, unchanged from the first leg.

Salah wore a black T-shirt with giant lettering and a simple message: 'NEVER GIVE UP'. Liverpool got the perfect start when Sadio Mané anticipated a loose defensive header by Jordi Alba, slipped a pass to Henderson, whose shot was saved but fell to Origi who tapped in the early goal. Fabinho was booked for a tackle on Suarez, having set the tone with a crunching challenge on Messi. Robertson also went down, after a kick backwards from Suarez. He played on until half-time but Klopp withdrew him at the break and Wijnaldum was on. Six minutes in Alexander-Arnold won the ball back from Alba after losing possession and steered a low pass square across the area, Wijnaldum's side-foot finish crept under ter Stegen's arm and in at the Kop end, and 122 seconds later it was 3-0 – Wijnaldum again. Origi overhit a cross from the right but it was picked up by Shaqiri, who exchanged passes with Milner, before swinging in a cross for Wijnaldum to rise above the rooted defence to head it past a stranded ter Stegen.

The most gripping of ties was decided by some incredible quick thinking from Alexander-Arnold. He won a corner, then caught the defence fast asleep and looking like it was organised on Hackney Marshes! He placed the ball in the corner, started to walk off as Shaqiri trotted over to take the kick, then quickly turned and fired in a low corner towards Origi, whose first time shot flew past a startled ter Stegen. Off he ran to celebrate with teammates and substitutes in front of a delirious Kop.

The whole Liverpool contingent formed a line to sing You'll Never Walk Alone in front of the Kop. Klopp's side had led at half-time in 26 games in 2018/19 and won every one. Liverpool had now hosted 19 European semi-finals, winning 15, drawing three and losing only one. It was Barcelona's heaviest defeat against an English side.

Wijnaldum commented: "Unbelievable. After the game in Spain we were confident we could score four and win 4-0. People outside doubted us and thought we couldn't do it. But once again we showed everything is possible in football. I was really angry that the manager put me on the bench. I just tried to help my team, I'm happy I could do that with two goals. [The manager] told us [after the first leg that] the tie was totally winnable. He said we should have every belief we could still win."

Despite a stirring run in Europe, the domestic season ended in disappointment. Liverpool ended their Premier League campaign with a 2-0 home win over Wolves with a brace from Mane, but it was Manchester City who retained the title on the final day of the season, pushed every inch of the way by Liverpool. City had to win each of their final 14 league games of the campaign to succeed by a single point and their triumph at Brighton, after being a goal down, capped a remarkable title race.

Sadio Mané shared the Golden Boot with Mo Salah and Pierre-Emerick Aubameyang but ultimately there was huge disappointment at Anfield, yet at the same time remarkable pride at the extraordinary effort. Klopp's team lost only one game, were unbeaten at home, amassed 97 points which would have won every other Premier League except the last two.

Everywhere in the stadium phones were on, some had radio commentary as they kept praying for more miracles with news from the South Coast. Cheers went up as rumours – at first incorrect – of a Brighton goal. But then there was actually one. Glenn Murray had opened the scoring for the Seagulls. Agüero quickly levelled and City went ahead through Laporte and with both contenders leading at half-time Mahrez made it 3-1, then 4-1 from Gundogan.

A 21st clean sheet of the league campaign gave Alisson the Golden Glove, and Mané nodded home yet another assist from Alexander-Arnold to match Salah on 22 goals, and for the full-back to break the record for defensive assists with 12. Alex Oxlade-Chamberlain came on to another rousing reception.

Players and their families gave a lap of honour. The title had been so, so close; close enough for a replica trophy to be stationed at Anfield in case City faltered. But a club-record 97 points was one short.

Salah and van Dijk became the first outfield Liverpool players since Martin Skrtel in 2010/11 to feature in every Premier League game, Alisson was also ever-present in the league. The Reds went unbeaten at home for a second successive league season for the first time since 1979/80.

Liverpool captain Jordan Henderson said afterwards, "No regrets. We have been outstanding all season and left everything out on the pitch. We have lost one game. People might talk about the draws but we tried everything to win those games. We gave everything over the whole season. City are a fantastic side and you take your hat off to them. Next season we give everything to win it."

Ahead of Liverpool's only fixture ever played in June, Klopp gave the players five days off. Following the final league game, the squad took part in light recovery sessions at Melwood, then relaxed with short holidays before warm-weather training in Marbella. The manager took his squad there before the previous season's final against Real and prior to the tie against Bayern. Klopp described it as "two proper weeks as a pre-season".

The three-week gap persuaded Klopp that, in addition to the usual short-sided games in training, something more was required to keep his side in tune. He arranged a practice match behind closed doors against Benfica B, the Portuguese side's reserve team that plays in their home league's second tier. The two teams' coaches collaborated to set up Benfica's team as closely as possible in terms of personnel and tactics to that of surprise finalists Tottenham. Spurs had made remarkable progress, scraping through their initial group before relying on last minute goals, one given, one not, against Manchester City and Ajax respectively, to make it to a first Champions League final.

Klopp knew defeat to Real Madrid in the previous season's final in Kiev was a powerful motivational factor. "[The defeat in the final] had a big influence on us," he said. "I remember that situation when we stood in the queue at Kiev in our tracksuits on the way home. Heads down, very frustrated, everyone very disappointed. You weren't allowed to be angry. There were a lot of different emotions. But the plan was: we'll come again. We'll be there again. Now we are.

"Each team who lost a final will think about putting it right. We have the chance to do that. That was the kick-start for the development of this team. This team doesn't compare to the team last year. These boys want to be there. It's not like [we think] 'Oh, it's coming up' and we get scared. We are a completely different team to last year."

The long gap between games wasn't ideal, but that the players' commitment had been exemplary. "The best moment for the final would've been five minutes after we beat Barcelona," Klopp said. "[But] the mood in the team is brilliant. The work rate and attitude. The best piece of character of this team is the constant readiness for development."

Thousands more fans than could possibly be accommodated in the stadium poured into Madrid, and on match day a wave of red gathered in the fanzone at Plaza Salvador Dalí. Fans proudly wore "Never Give Up" T-shirts.

Tottenham's Harry Kane started, 53 days after an injury in the quarter-final against Manchester City, with semi-final hero Lucas Moura dropping to the bench. Milner missed out, but Roberto Firmino – absent since limping out of the first leg against Barcelona – led the line.

After just 22 seconds the defining moment arrived. Van Dijk won a header on halfway, Wiljnaldum touched on to Henderson who released Mané with a first-time ball over the top. As Mané weighed his options on the corner of the box, Moussa Sissoko tracked back and raised his right arm as Mané tried to clip the ball into the centre. It struck Sissoko's chest and outstretched arm. Referee Damir Skomina pointed straight to the penalty spot. VAR confirmed the award. Salah thumped it down the middle as Lloris dived to his left. Salah's opener was the second-fastest goal in a Champions League final (1 min 48 secs), only behind Paolo Maldini (50 secs) for AC Milan versus Liverpool in 2005.

Around the hour mark, Firmino was replaced by Origi and Wijnaldum by Milner, and with four minutes of normal time remaining, the Reds found a vital second goal. Robertson curled in a dangerous pass looking for Salah, which was put behind by Rose off his shoulder. Milner's corner was flicked out by Son to van Dijk, whose shot was blocked by Dier. The ball looped up and Dier tried to head out but another challenge from van Dijk meant it dropped to Matip, who played it short to Origi. With one touch to set, the Belgian swept his finish into the far corner. Origi scored with all three of his shots in the Champions League this season.

"Allez, allez, allez" rang out around the stadium, followed by "You'll Never Walk Alone" before a chorus of whistles urged the end of the match. With just 35.4% possession, Liverpool became the first side to win the Champions League final with less of the ball than the opposition since Jose Mourinho's Inter Milan beat Bayern Munich in 2010. In truth, Spurs had been kept at arm's length for the majority of the game with star man Harry Kane clearly not 100% fit.

At the final whistle Jürgen Klopp rejoiced, as well he might when he said: "I'm so happy for our boys, I'm so happy for all these [fans] and I'm so happy for my family [who] suffer every year when we go to a final in the last game of the season and we lose. So they deserve it more than anyone as they are so supportive. Did you ever see a team like this, fighting with absolutely no fuel in the tank anymore? And then a goalkeeper who makes difficult things look easy. It'll be the best night of my life."

Klopp hugged every player. Steven Gerrard exchanged handshakes with friends in the crowd. Henderson found his father Brian, the pair embracing. "It's just very emotional," said Brian. "The tears come. You start shaking. You grab your wife, you grab your daughter-in-law, you grab anybody that's around you... just so, so happy."

Liverpool legend Ian Rush brought out the trophy, newly engraved and now with a pair of red ribbons. The players accepted their medals from UEFA president Aleksander C eferin, with Liverpool owner John W Henry looking on from the podium. Henderson raised the trophy, then the players went over to join the fans as Queen's "We Are the Champions" rang out, the fans singing along.

A group led by Fabinho and Firmino grabbed Klopp and the whole team raised him above their shoulders, giving the manager the bumps to the delight of the supporters. The manager then conducted his own set of cheers.

In the dressing room, the players danced, sang and posed with the trophy, taking selfies with their medals. In the centre of town thousands of jubilant fans celebrated the victory. Back home in Liverpool, fans poured out of the pubs to celebrate in the streets. Reds fans around the world joined the celebrations.

More than 100,000 Liverpool fans made the trip to Madrid, more than five times as many lined the streets of the city for the homecoming trophy parade the following day as a convoy of vehicles – the main team bus at its centre – made its way along Queen's Drive, along Rocky Lane and through West Derby, along Leeds Street and down to the waterfront to finish at The Strand.

Klopp had his legs dangling off the back corner of the main team bus, sipping a beer, smiling and waving to the assembled fans. Some players wore tops with a gold number "6" and "Champions of Europe" on the back.

Klopp gave his final thoughts from the top of the bus, reflecting on how important his and his team's achievement was for the Red half of the city.

"It's so overwhelming what the people are doing," he said. "When you have a direct eye contact and you see how much it means to them that's touching, to be honest. It's brilliant. You see in their eyes how much it means. It's unbelievable. Crazy."

5: SCOUSERS RULE THE WORLD!

FOLLOWING THE TRIUMPH IN MADRID, THE REDS took part in the FIFA Club World Cup as representatives of Europe. The Club World Cup represented a unique opportunity for the Reds to become the first English club to win the international treble of the Champions League, Super Cup and CWC. The champions of each continent and hosts Qatar meet over 10 days in a knockout competition to decide who is crowned the world's top club side, with Liverpool going in at the semi-final stage. Liverpool's two games were played at the 48,000-seater Khalifa International Stadium, a 2022 World Cup venue. They were meant to be at the Education City Stadium in Doha but the new ground was not signed off in time, so the games were moved at late notice.

Liverpool had the chance to be crowned champions of the world for the first time. Despite winning six European Cups, they never won a world final. They lost the 1981 Intercontinental Cup to Flamengo and again in 1984 to Independiente - and refused to take part in 1977 or 1978. They played in one Fifa Club World Cup - losing 1-0 in the final to Sao Paolo in Japan in 2005 after beating Costa Rican club Saprissa 3-0 in the semi-finals. Real Madrid were Club World Cup champions last season and were able to wear those glorious golden patches on their kit because of it.

The Club World Cup trophy went to Europe in each of the past six years, with Real Madrid winning the past three finals. The holders do not automatically qualify, so Real cannot defend their title. The only European team to fail to win in the past 12 years was Chelsea in 2012. Manchester United won the tournament in 2008.

Klopp named his squad for the 2019 tournament, which did not Matip and Fabinho who were injured: Alisson, van Dijk, Wijnaldum, Lovren, Milner, Keita, Firmino, Mane, Salah, Gomez, Adrian, Henderson, Oxlade-Chamberlain, Lallana, Lonergan, Shaqiri, Brewster, Robertson, Origi, Jones, Alexander-Arnold, Elliott, Williams.

There was domestic controversy following Liverpool's unexpected progression to the quarter-finals of the League Cup. The Reds had won their last tie over Arsenal at Anfield despite fielding a weakened team and had been drawn away Aston Villa but the quarter-finals clashed with the FIFA tournament. In the event the club managed to persuade the powers that be that they be allowed to field their under-23 team in the tie. It was quite some contrast to the time when Manchester United were blamed for devaluing the FA Cup in 2000 after being forced to play in an earlier version of the tournament at the FA's behest! United barred themselves from the tournament and the FA still didn't win the race to host the 2006 World Cup.

Only two of the players that started the last Carabao Cup game were not travelling, so the side at Aston Villa would be even younger that the side that beat Arsenal on penalties. "I think it's a really nice opportunity for younger players," said Klopp. "No-one gives us a chance, but I'd love to be part of that game. There's no pressure from me. They get to play in a great stadium. There was not one date which would have worked. We will not suffer, it is not possible. The solution is not perfect, but we tried to make it as perfect as possible." Brewster, Elliott, Jones and Williams could have played in the cup tie at home, and then flew out immediately afterwards to sit on the bench for their Club World Cup semi-final. Klopp said 'not for one second' did he consider splitting the squad and leaving some senior players behind for the League Cup side, which will be managed by Under-23 boss Neil Critchley. "We had to do it like this. I think it's a really nice opportunity for the younger players to face that (Villa). I know everybody thinks 'no chance' but football is a wonderful game. There was absolutely no chance to do it differently, in the moment when it was clear when it would be played and all the other dates were absolutely not possible for us to play it later. At the end we will not suffer because of it. That's not possible. If somebody thought I should have done it differently, I cannot change that.'

Liverpool supported calls by human rights groups for investigations into the deaths of migrant workers in Qatar, in a report in The Guardian. Peter Moore sought assurances from the Qatar "supreme committee" about the progress of investigations into the deaths of two men who had been working on the construction of football stadiums. Liverpool's position was explained in a letter from Moore to Nicholas McGeehan and James Lynch, directors of the Fair/Square human rights organisation, who asked him in November to make a public statement of concern about workers' rights and deaths in Qatar. McGeehan and Lynch highlighted the death of a Networker who died in his lodgings during his period of employment as a scaffolder at the Education City stadium, which was originally the venue for Liverpool's matches. Moore said in his reply that Liverpool had "sought background detail assurances" from the supreme committee. Liverpool's games had since moved to the Khalifa International stadium, and Moore said they had also discussed with the supreme committee the ongoing investigation headed by Sir Robert Akenhead into the death in January 2017 of a British construction worker who fell from rigging at that stadium.

"Like any responsible organisation, we support your assertion that any and all unexplained deaths should be investigated thoroughly and that bereaved families should receive the justice they deserve," Moore wrote in his reply to McGeehan and Lynch. "Furthermore we also believe that employees should be treated with fairness and respect, which is why we adhere to our own anti-slavery policy and why we are committed to paying the real living wage, among various measures of this kind. These are the standards that we set for ourselves and by which we would hope to be judged given they fall within our own remits and responsibilities. Nevertheless, we remain a sporting organisation and it is important that we are not drawn into global issues on the basis of where our involvement in various competitions dictates that our fixtures take place. So while we respect and understand the reasons why you have sought a public pronouncement from us, we hope you will respect and understand why we feel such a course of action would not be appropriate. Having already stated that while we do not visit any country with the objective of bringing about change, but any resultant positive changes would be welcomed, I would like to take the opportunity to reiterate that particular message." McGeehan told the Guardian that he welcomed Liverpool's intervention: "In their detailed expression of support for investigations into worker deaths and compensation for families, Liverpool have demonstrated more clarity of thought than Fifa and all of their sponsors put together."

After beating Watford at Anfield to cement their lead at the top of the Premier League, Klopp expressed dissatisfaction with FIFA's organisation of the Club World Cup. It had been confirmed that, with building work on Education City Stadium not yet complete, the majority of the tournament's fixtures would be played at the nearby Khalifa Stadium. Klopp said: "If we wouldn't go to Qatar we would play midweek Aston Villa and then West Ham, right? The only difference is we fly for seven hours and then it is warmer. I think it is raining there. It doesn't help the one pitch we are all playing on – sensationally good organising, all the games on the one pitch. We will see how the one pitch will be. We don't have more games. We have one game more when we play West Ham, not sure when that is yet. Until then, we try to sort it as well as possible for us. With the Gini injury today, Dejan four days ago, our squad is not getting bigger. That's of course not cool. But that would be the same problem if we went to Villa and played the Carabao Cup quarter-final."

Liverpool faced Monterrey in the semi-final after the Mexico side beat Al-Sadd 3-2. Left-back Leonel Vangioni gave Monterrey the lead with an unbelievable 35-yard rocket before Rogelio Funes Mori doubled their advantage in first-half stoppage time. Baghdad Bounedjah pulled one back for Al-Sadd before Carlos Rodriguez restored Monterrey's two-goal lead. Abdelkarim Hassan scored a late consolation but Monterrey hung on. Monterrey qualified as winners of the Concacaf Champions League, for sides from North America, Central America and the Caribbean, for the fourth time. They've been Mexican champions on four occasions. They played free-flowing, attacking football and looked threatening going forward, albeit against a shaky Al-Sadd defence. The twin-brother of ex-Everton defender Ramiro Funes Mori, Rogelio, looked good and took his goal well.

Brazil's Flamengo faced Saudi Arabia's Al Hilal in the other semi-final. Klopp hadn't done much background research on Flamengo. The Rio de Janeiro club qualified after a late double from Gabriel Barbosa, known as Gabigol, saw them beat River Plate 2-1 in the final of the Copa Libertadores. That was their first continental trophy since 1981, though they won six league titles in the last four decades. He made little impact at Inter Milan, but he gained five caps for Brazil, scored twice in a dramatic final five minutes when Flamengo came from a goal down to beat River Plate. He then got sent off for sarcastically applauding a refereeing decision! He tempted fate by touching the trophy on the way out on to the pitch, a move generally considered to be bad luck, so he was not lacking in self belief!

Flamengo were the reigning champions of Brazil with former Chelsea left-back Felipe Luis and ex-Juventus midfielder Diego captaining the side. Klopp told ESPN Brazil "I know they've won the Copa Libertadores and I know a couple of players, obviously. But, I have about the same knowledge as we usually have before we play a team in the Champions League for the first time. So that's three, four days before we play them. We have a [semi final] in between, and it must be enough to prepare for the game. So in this moment, it would be a shame if I'd know much more about any Brazilian team than I know about Bournemouth. I [had] to prepare for Bournemouth on the weekend, that [was] my priority. And then, as I said, we'll be prepared. That should be enough. We respect them a lot, but we're not sure we'll play them, because both have to win the semi-final. And at this moment, I don't know who we'll play there, so let's see."

Brazil legend Zico once led Flamengo through the greatest period in their history. They had won the 1981 Copa Libertadores and standing between them and the crown of world champions were Bob Paisley's Liverpool after the Kenny Dalglish inspired team picked up a third European title in five seasons beating Real Madrid in Paris that year. "The biggest difference was maybe Liverpool didn't have information about our players but we already knew about all of them," says Zico, "Nowadays you already have a scout... at the time, fortunately we had one assistant coach and he had all the video and details of the Liverpool players and team." What stood out to Flamengo was that Liverpool's back four left space in behind. "We were already training to play quicker passes so we can put the ball in the back," Zico recalled. By half-time Flamengo were three up and twice their No 10 had played a quick ball behind Liverpool's backline for Nunes to score. Zico was man of the match in the 3-0 win and 38 years on, the two sides were on course to meet again.

This time it would be vastly different. 'Jürgen Klopp gave another life to Liverpool — it's totally different, the Liverpool before and after,' Zico said. 'If the final is Liverpool and Flamengo it will be what football fans expect — high pressure, high transitions, always trying to score and go for goal. It will be a fantastic game.'

13 December 1981, Tokyo - Att: 62,000
LIVERPOOL 0-3 FLAMENGO (BRA)
(Nunes 12, 41, Adilio 34)

Mark Lawrenson recalled how the players refused at first to go over to Japan for the 1981 World Club Championship game because of a pay dispute. "There was nothing in our contracts to say we had to play this game." Fortunately it was sorted out, but it wasn't the best mind set for the team. Worse still, they were poorly prepared as Lawrenson admits: "We didn't fully appreciate the demands of what was expected. We played Arsenal on a Tuesday night in the League Cup then got a coach to Heathrow. There was an issue with not being able to fly over

Russian airspace at the time, so we had to go west to go east with a stop in Anchorage. As for the flight, you could say it was 'relaxed'. Ted Croker, from the FA, was part of the group that travelled. When we met him at the airport, everyone greeted him as 'Mr Croker' — after nine hours out to Anchorage and a 'few' drinks, it was 'all right, Ted!' [We were] jet-lagged so badly no one could sleep as they stayed by Tokyo Tower so a few ended up on a nearby driving range at 4am. We thought it was an exhibition but Flamengo — who had been in Japan for 10 days — had other ideas. It was a sandy pitch but you could see the incredible touch of the Brazilians. Zico did things that made you go 'Wow!' We were well beaten." The flight back was in keeping with the entire trip, flying into Birmingham due to heavy snow closing Heathrow. It took another six hours to drive back on a heavily congested M6. "Looking back, it's a bit of a regret. I won plenty of things with Liverpool but the Club World Cup would have been a nice addition."

December 9, 1984. Tokyo - - Att: 62,000
LIVERPOOL 0-1 INDEPENDIENTE (ARG)
(Percudani 6)

Lawrenson was injured on the flight out to Tokyo, a tightening of the hamstring after sitting down for 18 hours. They flew economy both ways and Anchorage was again the stopover destination. His fitness test was running up the slope of an underground car park at the hotel. Gary Gillespie took his place, and he recalls "The trophy wasn't high on our list of priorities. We were having a difficult time in the League and the focus was on winning that again — we were going for four titles in a row — but we really should have beaten Independiente. I got sucked out of position early on and they scored with a ball over the top. We were the better side but you have to give them credit. They took it so seriously and had some top players — such as Jorge Burruchaga who went on to win the World Cup with Argentina 18 months later.

"The one thing the trip was memorable for was meeting Rod Stewart on the way back home. I've still got the photographs. Kenny Dalglish knew Rod and he invited all the Scottish lads in our squad for a drink with him — it wasn't just the aeroplane getting refuelled! There were six Scots in total but I seem to remember a few of our team-mates made themselves honorary Scotsmen so they did not miss out."

December 18, 2005. Yokohama - Att: 66,821
LIVERPOOL 0-1 SAO PAOLO (BRA)
(Mineiro 27)

Peter Crouch had been at the club for only four months so he was delighted to be involved, but he admits it wasn't an easy competition to prepare for as he explained: "We had been on a brilliant run at home and kept 10 consecutive clean sheets. I had also just scored my first goals for Liverpool, so I was full of confidence."

Unfortunately Crouch and some of the players found it impossible to acclimatise in Japan. Crouch roomed with Steve Finnan and recalls: "For the first few nights, we were awake at 3am playing the computer game Super Mario Kart." Jetlag didn't prevent Crouch scoring twice in the semi-final against the Costa Rican side Deportivo Saprissa. But the final was one of the most frustrating for Crouch. He says: "We hit the post, hit the crossbar and had two goals disallowed for offside. We should have won, as we battered them in the second half, but it wasn't to be. To make matters worse, I only came on for the last five minutes. Afterwards, we went out for a drink in a karaoke bar. There was me, Pepe Reina, Jamie Carragher, Steven Gerrard, Xabi Alonso, Didi Hamann, all singing Liverpool songs with the crowd. There were no camera phones, no problems — just everyone having a good time. Come closing time, the fun really started. There was only one taxi available and, to put it bluntly, I wasn't missing it as we were in the middle of nowhere. With no more room, Didi tried to get on the roof and that is when the police were called!

"He and Carra ended up getting chased around the streets by the police and I believe they gave Didi, who wasn't the quickest, the opportunity to spend the night with them! He turned up at our hotel the next morning, still in his tracksuit, and just joined us for breakfast without saying a word. It was a memorable trip but it is one where I have some regret. I can understand why Mark and Gary both feel it was an opportunity lost, as I feel the same. It would have been great to get that medal. Hopefully the current squad will put it right."

Jamie Carragher described losing the last Club World Cup final as one of the biggest regrets of his career. Despite enormous talents such as Kenny Dalglish, Mark Lawrenson and Graeme Souness it was so bad in Tokyo the club did not even bother entering in 1977 and 1978.

Manchester United remained the only English team to have won the title following a 1-0 win over Ecuadorian side LDU Quito in 2008.

They also won the old version of the World Club Championship beating Brazilian club Palmerias in 1999.

After a seven-hour flight, the squad had arrived at their luxurious hotel on a dark, rainy, Doha evening, under police escort, as thousands of fans prepared to descend on this small city on the coast of the Persian Gulf. A vocal crowd were singing in the rain as they checked-in for the week. "The amount of people who have contacted us has been mind-blowing," Amina Al-Ali, of the Doha-based fan group Qatar Reds said he'd been contacted by many fans wanting to witness the teams bid for world champions, they were expecting 7,000 fans. Qatar Reds said the most common questions from fans related to transport, hotels, fan zones - and the weather. In pleasant temperatures and thunderstorms, the one pitch was absorbing it all. If Liverpool reached the final, the pitch would have endured four games over three days; the forecast was for more rain. One official who had lived there for five years said he'd never seen such a sustained period of rain.

It will also be raining microphones and recorders as the players will experience another first for a Premier League club - they will conduct every post-match interview before they return to the dressing room. Every player must now walk through the Mixed Zone before they return to their dressing rooms, but they do not have to stop for waiting journalists. Previously, one or two players do a few, short, interviews immediately after the game - in a 'Flash Zone' - before they have a team debrief, shower, get changed and speak to a much larger group of reporters in a 'Mixed Zone'. FIFA changed its rules following a new approach in the Women's World Cup 2019 and U17 World Cup in Brazil. "The aim of this new process is… to give players more time for their post-match recovery," explained FIFA. Klopp's players would either embrace the new routine or find it an irritation immediately after an intense game.

Klopp insisted he was the "wrong person" to address concerns over Qatar's human rights record when questioned about them during his pre-match media briefing. Concerns were periodically voiced about the country hosting this event and the 2022 World Cup because of its stance on homosexuality and immigrant workers' rights. "Organisers have to think about these things, not the athletes," Klopp said. "When sportsmen have to decide to be part of a competition, it's not right." According to a report by the International Trades Union Confederation in 2013, more than 1,200 workers from Nepal and India had died on construction projects in Qatar linked to the World Cup, including non-football infrastructure schemes, in the previous three years. The ITUC said at the time that if deaths continued at that rate then they could reach 4,000 - although it dropped its complaints against Qatar following improvements in workers' rights.

Qatar disputed those figures, saying the deaths cannot be linked directly to the World Cup. In February Amnesty International insisted that although progress has been made, Qatar "must step up efforts to honour labour rights promises" before the 2022 World Cup begins.

"I have an opinion on football but this is a real serious thing to talk about I think and the answers should come from people who know more about it," Klopp said. "I have to be influential in football but not in politics. Anything I say wouldn't help, it would just create another headline, positive or negative. I like that you ask the question but I think I am the wrong person. My personal opinion, I have one of course, is of course I think we should all be treated equally, that is clear. But we don't have the time to judge things when we are here, we only have time for training."

Paul Amman, founder of Liverpool LGBT+ fans group Kop Out, was invited by the organisers of the 2020 World Cup to visit the country the previous month with his husband. Amman, who was not in Qatar for the Monterrey match, although other members of Kop Out were, told BBC Sport: "Qatar has moved significantly in recent years, especially in migrant workers' rights and in capacity and capability to host major events. I do not feel this has moved enough yet, but there is still progress being made and to be made. Football and its fans have a power to help change things for the better in Qatar for migrant workers, for LGBT+ people, and for our experience and safety at tournaments. The experience has led my husband to confirm that it was right that we took the chance and visited."

Amnesty International continued to push for improved human rights in the country, "ever since Qatar was named World Cup hosts for 2022, we've been pressing the authorities to drastically improve working conditions for the country's two million migrant workers," said Kate Allen, director of Amnesty International UK.

The game against Monterrey was live on BBC Two and iPlayer, but first Klopp was interested in how his kids would do in the League Cup as he said it was the "only solution" Liverpool could find and described it as a "very exciting opportunity for us".

"In the last few years we got kicked out of the cup competitions with our first team, but this year we have given the youngsters the opportunity, they showed up against Arsenal and that is what we expect," Klopp said. "We knew first we would be invited to the Club World Cup before we knew how far we would get in the Carabao Cup. We do not fly 3,000 miles not to show up. Our life is certainly dealing with difficult situations. We will be prepared and we will try to win the football game. We do not see ourselves as the favourites, we are challengers. We are here to represent Liverpool and Europe."

He said Liverpool "respect Monterrey a lot". He added: "Monterrey are in a pretty good way at the moment. They have a way to play and they change system when they are in front. I was impressed by the things I saw and we are full of respect. I visited Mexico in the summer for the first time, it was brilliant, I can recommend that! We know Monterrey's situation, the coach coming back, not losing a game. They have a very specific way of playing, tactically good players. It's interesting. I don't want to talk too much about tactics as you can imagine. There are a lot of Mexican players in Europe, they are quick and technically good. They are influenced by South Americans, very emotional.

"We don't see much Arabic football in Europe, but you could see Al Sadd with Xavi they were ready. The only team I haven't seen is Flamengo so far. We have an Arabic player in our team in Mohamed Salah. We are representing our own club, we don't have the burden of showing South America how we play football. We need to show we are ready. That's all we are concerned about. Compliments, thank you, but they don't really help us. We are more concerned about the game. We are always optimistic, ready to work hard, we will find a line-up to work hard and respect the opponent."

Klopp stating that the Club World Cup is, in fact, the "most important" for the Reds at the moment. Asked whether there was a lack of respect for the Club World Cup in England, Klopp responded: "I'm not sure, I don't know about respect in England. We are here now, we are completely focused on that. If you asked me beforehand if you think there should be a Club World Cup in the middle of our season I would say no, that's my honest opinion. We speak about that constantly. The importance is easy, we are here so it's the most important competition in the world for us at this moment.

"We have been made very welcome, well organised, we were asked to come here. We are here to represent Liverpool first and foremost. We qualified and were invited. When you come to other countries you have to respect their countries. I have to respect the rules of England having moved there. The weather isn't as good as I expected here, though, to be honest.

The format was due to change in 2021, with 24 teams from six confederations starting in June. The European Club Association called for European clubs to boycott that competition and Klopp has significant reservations. "Can it be an even bigger tournament in future? I think the FIFA plan is a team world cup in the summer, but it's in a summer where the African Cup [of Nations] is as well and there are other competitions as well. That doesn't work out, they have to sit together on a table and have to make sure that we have great competitions but not in the same time. Obviously a lot of people are interested, I like being here, we want to show up here, we have a lot of fans in this part of the world, they usually have to come to us or follow us at night time if they want to watch our games, so that's nice to become closer from time to time, but from the organisation point of view, everybody needs to think about it. FIFA cannot plan a tournament in the summer and UEFA says 'ok we play one' as well in the same moment and the South American confederation says 'sorry but our tournament is more important'. You cannot just add on tournaments, it doesn't work."

Klopp's concerns of a rain sodden, over sued pitch were drying out. "We spoke yesterday with our groundsman who is here. My concern was from England. But when we arrived on Sunday it was half-raining, but our groundsman said it was built on sand and took the water off. Pitch hopefully no concern. The training ground yesterday was brilliant, absolutely brilliant."

Klopp was told he is a good manager by a journalist. Milner, sitting next to him, at the media conference, was laughing! Klopp replied: "Thank you! There was a question there? Speed football you call it? Full throttle I used to call it when I was younger. We train like that!"

Milner on Klopp and the positive difference he makes: "He can be the other side of the coin, aggressive in the other way as well! You need that energy. It's massive for us."

Klopp commented: "I don't see myself as a cheerleader, my job is to help the boys as much as I can especially in intense periods it is tough. We still have a few things in our tank."

The only mishap in the build up was Klopp forgetting his security pass and was shown the door when he tried to gain entry to the breakfast room. It was a long haul back to his room, but he conceded it was his fault, that the security belonged to the host nation, and not his club, and he couldn't complain not having the appropriate pass around his neck! "The security staff here are not with us they are from Qatar. I came out of the elevator, wanted to turn right and was stopped. I showed him my badge and he just looked at me and said "pass". We have to wear this kind of pass that proves we're a member of LFC. I said "Ok sorry", it's a big hotel but I went all the way back to my room to get the pass. It was my fault, not his fault. We think we are the centre of attention but we are not so it's a reminder that there are a lot of places in the world where other things are important and now we play football, so that's it.'

There was some shock team news announced shortly before kick off, with Henderson filling in at centre back with Van Dijk out due to illness. Klopp named two keepers on the bench! "The solution we have was not planned like this," Klopp told the BBC before the semi-final about his issues in defence. "We knew it would be a centre-midfield player if the others were not available. In this case it is Virgil. We have trained it already so we thought it could be difficult. That must be enough. If a player is ill then there is no chance to risk him because he is not even out of the room. He is really struggling but obviously he is on the way to getting better, but obviously tonight, no chance." Klopp made other rotational changed, explaining: "We said we needed fresh legs again. It's a football-playing side so everybody needs to be responsible for defending because we have defensive-minded players out."

Steve McManaman knew the general public were divided back home on the value of this tournament, despite it being so highly regarded just about everywhere else in the world, as he explained: "I think in this country they're not really bothered about it. When I played in Madrid and we played the teams from Argentina and the teams from Brazil, it was a huge, huge thing to win. They really wanted to win it. The Argentinian team we faced in the final were Boca Juniors and they took thousands and thousands of fans to Tokyo back then, so it means a different type of success in different countries. I think in England it's probably quite frowned upon because it comes during a busy Christmas period and of course you've got the League Cup fixtures, but I personally think it's important to win it. If Liverpool can be crowned as the best team in the world, then why not be crowned the best team in the world?"

Late substitute Roberto Firmino side footed the winner in injury time to reach the final against Flamengo with the winner going into the start of three minutes of extra time. Salah at first showed skill with a sharp turn and change of pace, but when surrounded by the touch line, touched it back to his full-back showing great resilience and determination to keep the play alive. Klopp's team never know when to give up and specialised in late, late winners. Kloppage time!

Keita opened the scoring in the first half from a brilliant Salah pass, but Rogelio Funes Mori equalised a couple of minutes later. Klopp observed: "Naby is a player who can score goals. It is not the highest number of games he's played for us, but he's scored a lot of goals already, important goals as well. Absolutely brilliant how he did that and there is so much more to come. Maybe if you know Naby a bit longer you would say, 'OK, that looked really good but there is still some space'. That's absolutely brilliant news for us."

Allison was man of the match with a string of superb saves, while the Monterrey keeper was also in top form as the game swung end to end as the Mexican side put up a brave and skilful display. Despite only 31% possession, Monterrey had eight shots on target compared to Liverpool's six. Monterrey had 16 shots in total and there was a moment of relief when Gomez, the only recognised centre-back in the squad, was only shown a yellow card for stopping a dangerous counter-attack. Klopp was forced to bring on regulars Mane, Firmino and Alexander-Arnold and but was rewarded.

The stadium announcer asked fans "who's come to see Mohamed Salah" adding "let's get this party started" as the game kicked off. Every time Salah touched the ball there was a roar of excitement as fans came with flags and banners with his name across them. At half-time, the DJ played songs from David Guetta and the Red Hot Chilli Peppers and a Mexican wave broke out in the second half. It was an occasion like no other but Liverpool came through unscathed - eventually.

Klopp, who was booked after a fracas with his rival coach on the touchline, enthused: "All you need is Allison Becker, Allison Becker. He was there in the decisive moments. A really hard game and then you can bring on the boys. Wonderful goal, great game, super atmosphere. We have no clue about Virgil, we thought he would be fine. We will see. We have brought in a few kids and see what we can do line-up wise. We want to play the final and see what we can do."

Klopp had only one genuine centre back and Jordan Henderson played at the back for the first time and confessed that "it was a bit different", with enormous understatement. He explained what happened to van Dijk, "It was an easy decision actually because he couldn't train.

Yes, he was yesterday on the [training] pitch for a couple of minutes until the media left [the session] and then, unfortunately, he had to leave as well. Not because of the media, just because he didn't feel well. So yesterday no training was possible, this morning no training possible, so it was an easy decision – he couldn't play. It was difficult for Hendo to deal with, but he did really well. We will see, I don't know how quick he can recover. We will see."

The boss confessed that he was "afraid of extra time, to be honest!" He explained: "I was more than happy when Bobby scored that goal. We had to do a few changes as we had no other options. We left players out so we could have the opportunity if the game wasn't decided. That Bobby scored was just wonderful. I'm really happy with the performance as I knew before the game it would be really tough. So many strange things happened. It was the most offensive midfield I have ever put out in a competitive game. Henderson centre-back for the first time. We didn't have much height at centre-back. Why should we think European football stands over all? But you can't judge a team from one game. Monterrey had good players. We had a really new line-up and were dominant in a lot of moments. We were not here to show Europe was stronger. We were just here to win the game."

In their semi-final, Flamengo had come from behind to comfortably beat Al Hilal 24 hours earlier, a task completed with virtually a fully-fit squad. They posed a more difficult prospect, but Klopp promised his team would improve, describing the final as a "Tough game, a really tough game. But we watched the game (against Al Hilal), I saw a lot and we will watch more games," said Klopp. "One game is important but it is not all about that. It was an open game for a long period. We will see who deals better with the circumstances, who has more right decisions. We will be a different opponent, of course. We have now to 'collect our bones'. I don't know who exactly will be ready for the next game, so we will see. I saw the bench of Monterrey, there were like 10, 15 players on it, I don't know. Probably Flamengo's season is over, they are here with the full squad pretty much as well. We have just to recover as quick as possible and to make ourselves ready."

Flamengo coach Jorge Jesus was familiar with Liverpool as he was in charge of Benfica when the two met in the 2009-10 Europa League quarter-finals, winning 2-1 in Lisbon before being beaten 4-1 at Anfield. Klopp commented: "With Jorge Jesus as a manager, of course there's a European influence and that's it, but the players themselves already have quality. If there would not be a European coach, it would already be difficult. With Jorge Jesus, (he is) very experienced, very successful in Portugal and now in Brazil as well. We have a lot of respect for that but at the end we will try our best and we will see how it will work out."

Klopp had a run in with the Monterrey coach Antonio Mohamed after the Argentine demanded the referee send off Gomez. Klopp was furious as his opposite number waved an imaginary card in the air. The touchline antics went viral, with Liverpool fans loving their managers' passion and commitment to the cause.

★

Flamengo would be 'treated as heroes' if they lifted the trophy, while Liverpool returned to face Leicester on Boxing Day! South American clubs placed greater significance in winning global club tournaments compared to widespread indifference in England. Indeed Manchester United's record as two-time world champions is virtually unknown in English football while everyone knows Liverpool have lifted the European Cup 6 times.

"The situation is different for them and us," Klopp admitted, "they got sent with the clear order to win it and come back as heroes. We got told, stay at home and play the Carabao Cup. That is a massive difference and we cannot change that. My teams want to win the competition, even if we know it is very difficult. The view on it in Europe is different to that in South America. We want to change that view, we feel it has changed a little bit. Of course, Liverpool fans want us to win but lots of the other fans in Europe don't care about the competition. You saw how much Monterrey fought in their two games here and it will be the same with Flamengo.'

Klopp opted not to try to motivate by telling his player they would become legends if they brought the trophy back to Merseyside. "That is not something I will use in a meeting, that you can become a legend if you win a competition. That keeps your mind away from necessary things. If people see them as legends after, then great, but you cannot approach it like that. If Flamengo win it, they will probably have a proper party. We play Leicester City. We cannot make this competition bigger for Europe but for us it is the most important for the moment, it is the one game we play tomorrow so let's try everything.'

In Jürgen Klopp's homeland the competition was not viewed

seriously but his attitude changed as he looked forward to picking up yet another trophy, even if he did not know what it looked like! "Winning it would be great and I don't even know exactly know how the trophy looks but I didn't know that about the Super Cup either. Before that, I didn't know how people spoke about it... Before the game people said: 'do you really need it?' Then you play it and you win it and it feels incredible. It was really a big one. So let's see what we can tomorrow. As a kid in Germany, I was not aware of it, no. You want to be the domestic champion, win a domestic cup and then want to win a European trophy and that's what we want. That's where football ends usually for the team. But really, you do not win something so people will say, 'oh, you won it'. You win it to celebrate it, and I know Liverpool fans will celebrate like crazy, and other people will say, 'who cares?' But I could not care less. I do not worry what it means to other people. Win because you are there. Let's give it a proper try."

Liverpool's fixture pile up remained on the manager's mind with the heavy Christmas schedule followed by the FA Cup in January. "The problem that we have is the Premier League have decided we have a winter break and the FA decided the re-game [replay] if you have to play, if you draw in the fourth round, you play the re-game in that week. It's incredible. It's just in the winter break. Right? That's when they set the game. OK, how is that possible? Nobody speaks about these things. I really don't understand that. Look at that. They are the games, we can't do more games. The problem we have now is nobody speaks enough. We don't speak enough to each other so the Premier League, the Football League, the FA, UEFA, FIFA, everyone is planning their own things and nobody follows that so there is no common schedule for everybody."

Sensing the potential for a fixture backlog several months ago, Klopp spoke with his players about their attitude toward the World Club tournament. He said: "We spoke about it a few months ago and asked how did they want to play it. It wasn't that they could decide but how do you see it? They said: 'we go!' Since then it's never changed. For them it never changed. I never had to convince my team to come and play the competition. They were completely on fire from the first moment when they heard about it. The boys are 100 per cent clear, they didn't need Ali telling them or Bobby telling them, or Fabinho telling them about the importance for them, they are footballers, they are sportsmen and they want to win everything they can. We are playing against a side from a country and continent where this competition means everything to everyone and, in England, we have to explain why we come here. That's how Europe looks at the world, that we are the centre of attention. Since we are here we respect it more and more second by second because you get a feeling for it and you watch the games and it is all or nothing with everyone fighting for everything. We are here and we want to win the competition of course but we have to respect there is another team and they want to win it as well. That's what we do."

Gabriel Barbosa, Flamengo's best player, hinted he would love to play with Roberto Firmino but Klopp refused to discuss any interest in the striker who was sure to use the contest as a shop window to display his talents before the Liverpool manager. "We show our respect for opponents with attitude. We show it on the pitch," said Klopp, "We are not here as European champions. We are here as Liverpool FC wanting to win this game. Flamengo has a strong team and we are not too bad as well. It's about who has better solutions for better moments, not who has better players. I love my squad. I have the best team I wish for. I don't think about other players from other teams.

"I know what we have to expect. Flamengo will be intense, organised, Jorge Jesus has changed their fortunes and most of their things. They have different ways of playing and they have real quality in the centre of the park, they are cheeky on the wings and they can shoot from distance - just like a successful team should be. This is the first time that I have faced a Brazilian team but this is also the first time Flamengo have played a team like Liverpool."

Goalkeeper Allison knew more than most what to expect. As a 14 year old he was inspired by Internacional beating Barcelona in this tournament. "Ali told me he went completely mad," said Klopp. Klopp challenged his team to take a giant leap by comparing the achievement of lifting the Club World Cup to US astronaut Neil Armstrong landing on the moon for the first time. "I don't know how you approach something that has never been done before, like landing on the moon. We'll just try to play a really, really good game and win against a good side. It's football and it is how it sounds. The team, World Cup winner, you don't often get the chance to do so and for most of them, with the countries they play for, they never have a chance to win a World Cup so this is for me also the only chance. But who cares about me, don't worry about me but it feels like a really big opportunity. I don't feel pressure but I feel a real opportunity and I want to do it."

Such are the heights of Klopp and his players ambitions that maybe the moon isn't aiming high enough! It was put to him: You have the opportunity to do something Liverpool have never done."

"Yes, train in the sun!"

On the night it was Brazilian Bobby Firmino who struck in extra time to land Liverpool's first ever Fifa Club World Cup triumph in the club's 127-year history beating the brilliant Brazilian champions. Firmino scored a dramatic injury-time winner against Monterrey to produce a super composed finish in the 99th minute as the Reds became the second English side to win the tournament, after Manchester United in 2008.

In a dramatic end to normal time, Liverpool had seen an injury-time penalty decision overturned after Mane was tackled from behind from Rafinha, with referee Abdulrahman Al Jassim reversing his own initial verdict after checking the pitchside monitor following a consultation with the video assistant referee. Firmino had squandered an opportunity to put Liverpool ahead inside the opening minute firing over from close range. Keita and Alexander-Arnold also wasted early gilt edged chances as the Premier League leaders made a blistering start. Firmino also agonisingly hit the post and Salah shot first time narrowly wide shortly after half-time, but Flamengo posed a real threat, Barbosa's bicycle-kick saved by Brazilian Alisson.

Liverpool suffered an injury blow as Oxlade-Chamberlain fell awkwardly on his ankle. As a stretcher was brought on, Klopp lifted his baseball cap and muttered: "oh f***ing hell." With the prospect of extra time looming Henderson's powerful, curled strike from the edge of the box was superbly tipped over by Flamengo goalkeeper Diego Alves, who earlier seemed to be incapacitated by cramp. Mo Salah was also denied by Alves as the Premier League side were able to see out the second period despite the young substitute Lincoln blazing over from close range with their best chance of the game right at the end.

Klopp needed his strongest side to navigate this difficult contest, and after failing to capitalise on an excellent start, Liverpool came under pressure as tricky winger Bruno Henrique threatened down the right. Yet the 99th-minute winner vindicated Klopp's decision to pursue a first Club World Cup triumph over progress in the Carabao Cup, while delivering an entertaining final to a massive global audience.

Klopp was delighted for Firmino but he stressed his confidence that one of his deadly strike force always tend to hurt the opposition. "The best thing about our three boys up there and all the others, if one is not scoring then the other one is scoring or the other two are scoring. Divock Origi, for example, and nobody is talking about him, scored incredibly important goals. Xherdan Shaqiri has scored incredibly important goals last year or set them up. Mo Salah scores for us an incredible number of goals, all of them very important, but not always. Then Sadio is stepping up and scores incredibly important goals. Now here, we needed obviously Bobby's goal and here they are. I couldn't be more happy for him that he could score that goal because before the game we spoke about a lot about what this competition means to Brazil, to South American people and especially Brazilian people. And we have two Brazilians and he's one of them. It means the world to him and it helped us a lot. On top of that, it was a sensational goal, completely calm. You see the last goal helped obviously to bring these things back and I'm really, really delighted for him."

Former Brazil, and of course QPR, keeper Julio Cesar brought out the Club World Cup trophy looking like most Brazilians, glum faced. Jamie Webster belted out Allez Allez Allez as the players and coaching staff shook hands and received their medals before Henderson lifted that coveted piece of silverware joined by Oxlade-Chamberlain on crutches. But Liverpool now had a new theme tune; in the words of Freddie Mercury and Queen "We Are The Champions…We are the Champions…of the World!"

Klopp saluted a "wonderful night" after creating history in Doha, the first time Liverpool won the title having lost on their previous three attempts, to become the first English team to win the European Cup, UEFA Super Cup and Club World Cup in the same year. Klopp said: "It was a wonderful night for us, for the club, for everybody who is with us. It's a tough period for us, but the boys, game after game after game, they really show the desire to make the next step, show the desire to win the next game, show the desire to win the next challenge. Tonight, we couldn't do more than win this game and winning (the title) for the first time for this wonderful club. Flamengo is a really, really good team and tonight we were the better team. That's why we won. The boys dug in again and massively put in a performance. They keep getting tested constantly - our life is like this. At the moment we pass test after test after test. We have to make sure we pass further tests as well."

Klopp had succeeded where Bob Paisley, Joe Fagan and Rafael Benitez had previously failed. "I said beforehand I didn't know what it would feel like, but now I can say it's outstanding. Absolutely sensational.

I'm so proud of the boys. Couldn't be better. It feels really great. We are all exhausted pretty much from a really intense game. It was not our best game we have ever played but it was enough to win. We were the better side. In some moments we had a really good goalkeeper, and in most other moments we were the dominant team. Late goals, we don't want to need them but they were necessary and important. The boys have improved a lot over these months and when you start believing you believe through the full 90 minutes and in this case 120 minutes."

Klopp led the players over to the corner of the Khalifa International Stadium reserved for the allocation of 1,500 travelling supporters. But when Klopp tried to go behind the goal and on to the running track closer to the fans, over zealous FIFA representatives blocked their way. Footage surfaced of the players celebrating in the dressing rom. Robertson shared a snap of the team huddled around the trophy. Alisson, Alexander-Arnold and Adrian shared selfies with the trophy. 'Championes, Championes, Ole Ole Ole' was heard ringing out in the changing rooms. Injured Fabinho congratulated his team-mates from his home.

The following morning, in the West Bay area of the Qatari capital, the manager and players were photographed on the beach, throwing Santa hats in the air as the temperature edged into the 20s before preparing to return home, to complete a 7,000-mile round trip, with their place at the top of the Premier League strengthened as Leicester's defeat by Manchester City maintained their 10 point lead, although they now also had a match in hand. Since Liverpool had beaten Watford, Leicester had dropped five points, making the game at the King Power Stadium on Boxing Day a must-win for Brendan Rodgers' side. Klopp's side become the first English team to win the international treble in the same year of European Cup, UEFA Super Cup and FIFA Club World Cup, but it's the 30-year wait for their first Premier League title the fans craved more than anything in the New Year.

After over seven years without silverware, Liverpool had added three to their vast collection in just over half a season. Not long ago Klopp said he was king of the semi-finals having lost seven finals in a row. No longer. Three final victories in a row turned that on its head.

6: SUPER CUP WINNERS

AFTER MANCHESTER CITY WON THE Community Shield on penalties, after edging Liverpool Wembley to take the first piece of silverware of the new season so it was imperative that Jürgen Klopp delivered the Super Cup to regain the feel good factor of winning the 6th European Cup. But Liverpool looked good enough to challenge champions City for sure, and the Shield went to Pep Guardiola only after Georginio Wijnaldum's penalty saved by Claudio Bravo, before Gabriel Jesus scored the winning kick.

Their first confrontation of the new season between the two outstanding sides in the country did not disappoint. Raheem Sterling scored his first goal against his old club when he turned home David Silva's flick-on from close range. In the second half Sterling struck the post, van Dijk's shot hit the underside of the bar and Salah hit a post, but they finally levelled when Joel Matip headed home Van Dijk's cross. At that stage Liverpool looked the most likely, with Salah having at least three chances – coming closest when his header was incredibly cleared off the line by a Kyle Walker bicycle kick.

The showpiece opener of the season went straight to penalties, with City scoring all of theirs. It had been an entertaining start to the season, but both clubs had far bigger fish to fry.

A change to the way City played saw Bravo take short goal-kicks in his box to Nicolas Otamendi, taking advantage of the new laws allowing passing teams like City and Liverpool to take advantage. Liverpool were determined to make sure the domestic season, at least, doesn't end the way it began last year, with City winning the Community Shield, and ending up with a domestic treble.

Before the game, Jürgen Klopp was surprised the Community Shield is not taken more seriously and questioned the point of it all. It was the first of seven competitions Liverpool would take part in this season, with their Premier League opener against Norwich followed by the UEFA Super Cup against Chelsea in Istanbul. Despite his reservations, Klopp named the strongest team he could - including nine who started the Champions League final in June. Mane had yet to returns to training after his Africa Cup of Nations final defeat, while Firmino and Salah played less than 90 minutes in pre-season friendlies after summer internationals.

City and Liverpool had produced one of the great title races last season, with Guardiola's side beating Klopp's 98 points to 97, and judging by this game, it would be a battle between the two again. Before the game there were the usual mind games, Klopp's barbs about spending that Guardiola did not appreciate. Guardiola got so animated at giving instructions during a break in play that he came onto the pitch and was shown a yellow card, another of football's new laws. Guardiola described it as an "incredible final from both sides". He added: "At this level the difference is nothing. One penalty, one point." But he thought Manchester United, Arsenal, Tottenham, Chelsea would mount a challenge.

Afterwards Klopp commented, "Wow, it was a really good performance, a powerful one in the second half. Both teams had a similar pre-season. I spoke to Kevin de Bruyne after the game and we both said we don't really know where we are yet. The least we deserved was the equaliser, one save decided it and I cannot be disappointed today. The performance was much more important than a win. We know we are still here, we can still play proper football."

Yet a few days later Liverpool cemented their standing in European circles as they landed their first piece of silverware of the season, but more importantly began the process of cementing their 6th European Cup success with victory over Chelsea in the UEFA Super at the Besiktas Park in Istanbul. The Super Cup has enormous kudos in European circles, but has never been too highly regarded in England. In recent years it had become the domain of Spanish clubs with the previous five winners all hailing from La Liga. For the first time in 14 years, the prestigious Super Cup was heading to England as it was the first time it has been contested between two Premier League sides. Seven Super Cup finals had been between domestic rivals - five involving Spanish teams, including four since 2014, and two all-Italian ones.

For the first time in history, a woman refereed a major European men's game, France's Stephanie Frappart was in charge. In April, she became the first woman to take charge of a French domestic men's Ligue 1 match when she was the referee for the game between Amiens and Strasbourg. She has been included in the pool of referees for the 2019/20 Ligue 1 season. Frappart was the referee for the Women's World Cup final between the Netherlands and the USA.

In the opening round of Premier League games Liverpool and

Chelsea had been involved in high-scoring games. The Reds kicked off their domestic campaign with a 4-1 thumping of Norwich in the season opener on Friday, while Chelsea lost 4-0 to Manchester United on Sunday. While that suggested that The Blues new boss Frank Lampard could expect nothing but the runners up medals, historically, games in Europe between these two sides were always close. It was the 11th time Liverpool and Chelsea met in a UEFA competition, five ending in a draw. Liverpool had two wins to Chelsea's three, with only one game having been won a by a margin of more than one goal.

Liverpool were aiming for an incredible seven trophies, six or even five trophies would still be unprecedented in England. The best previous haul was Manchester United's haul of four in 2008-09; Premier League, League Cup, Community Shield and Club World Cup. Klopp was thrilled to be involved in his fourth major European final in three years, the first time he managed a team in a Super Cup, having lost finals of both the Champions League and Europa League. He said: "The Super Cup itself is not a cup that I've really loved to watch in the past. The Super Cup is the final proof; if you are not in that game, it means you didn't win the final. That's completely different this year, so we're looking forward to it. It's a big one."

Frank Lampard had endured a debut in the dugout to forget as his young side collapsed 4-0 at Manchester United, although the scoreline was harsh on the Blues as they dominated in the first half with 55% possession and hit the woodwork twice but paid the price for a relatively inexperienced forward line that included Tammy Abraham and Mason Mount, who were making their first Premier League starts for Chelsea but with Chelsea still under a transfer embargo, Lampard was keen to put his faith in the club's young players.

Liverpool landed their second big European prize within three months, albeit on penalties. A second penalty shoot out hard on the heels of the Community Shield. But this time, what a story it turned out to be for Klopp's stand in keeper, Adrian, who weeks after training with a semi-pro team, saved a penalty to win the European Super Cup. Champions League holders Liverpool and Europa League winners Chelsea finished extra time at 2-2, and in the shoot out Adrian made the crucial save with his legs to deny Tammy Abraham and give his team a 5-4 win on penalties, in his first start for Liverpool after regular goalkeeper Alisson suffered a calf injury last Friday in the Premier League opener.

Klopp couldn't help himself in a typically unusual celebration. "What a story," Klopp said. "Adrian! Like Rocky! He kept his nerves together. He's loud in the dressing room already. I don't think he's won a lot in his life so it's good for him to win it. He made some unbelievable saves, both keepers did, so I'm really happy for him."

Chelsea took the lead in the 36th minute when Christian Pulisic exposed poor positioning by right back Joe Gomez to pass for Olivier Giroud to shoot low past Adrian. Liverpool stormed back after the break, Fabinho's 48th-minute pass opening up the Chelsea defence and leaving Sadio Mane with an easy finish off Mohamed Salah's flick. In extra time, Mane put Liverpool ahead from a Roberto Firmino cross, but Chelsea quickly responded with a penalty from Jorginho. Stephanie Frappart, the first female referee to oversee a major men's European final denied Liverpool a penalty after just six minutes when Mane's overhead kick hit Andreas Christensen's arm, which seemed to be out of a strictly "natural" position. There was no full review by the video assistant referee system. Twice Chelsea put the ball into the net through Pulisic and substitute Mason Mount, but Frappart and her assistants ruled both efforts out for clear offside.

Klopp added: "It was a very difficult game for both teams, it was all about winning it and we did that in the end. Nobody in the stadium wanted extra-time, it was a killer. I'm not sure about the penalty but who cares now. We started well then dropped off... we could talk about football but it's too late now. We had to fight and the boys did tonight."

Skipper Jordan Henderson praised Adrian, "I'm delighted for Adrian who's just come into the club and he's the hero. We're delighted to win because we want to win as many trophies as we can, so we'll enjoy it tonight but then focus on recovering for a big game on Saturday."

Adrian said: "Welcome to Liverpool! It's been a crazy week. I'm really happy for the team, I'm happy to play for Liverpool and happy for the fans. It was a long game but in the end a great finish for us."

Klopp won his first piece of silverware as Liverpool boss in June when they beat Tottenham in the Champions League final. "I just think Klopp is trying to get this Liverpool team in the mentality of trying to win everything," Craig Burley said on ESPN FC, "Like [Steve Nicol's] halcyon days when he was there, just wiping teams away. The winning habit is a good habit whether it's on penalties or four or 5-0. I think that's the thing with Klopp. He wants his time at Liverpool, however long that is, to be the biggest success it can be. If he can add a Premier League title to this, and more importantly the Champions League, then that's what he's all about."

Steve Nicol felt Klopp's celebration was a message to football fans who have doubted his trophy-winning credentials. "Do you think he's thinking about 'I hope all these people that said I can never win a final are queuing up to congratulate me?' I think so, yeah [Klopp is trying to build a winning DNA], absolutely. Once it's in there, I'll tell you what, it's a formidable thing to carry around with you. But I'll tell you what though, losing, it does the same thing the other way round."

The Philosophy Of Jürgen Klopp

"I like it a lot that we have such a positive moment and the people really have a lot of good, good moments during the season. Hopefully it may continue like this."

In a special feature with club sponsor Western Union, 'The world according to Jürgen Klopp', the Liverpool manager detailed his approach to management. Typical, and modestly, he gave so much credit for the team he assembled around him, and that he has complete confidence in those who form part of the support network at Melwood, a crucial factor for him to lead strongly and successfully.

"I try everything to be as successful as possible. I live 100 per cent for the boys, with the boys, what we do for the club. I think that's leadership in the first case. As a leader you cannot be the last who comes in and the first who goes out; you don't always have to be the first coming in or the last going out, but you have to be an example. We have enough confidence and that's very important for a leader. If I would expect from myself that I know everything and I'm the best in everything, I couldn't have confidence. But I don't expect that. I know I'm good in a couple of things, really good in a few things, and that's enough. My confidence is big enough that I can really let people grow next to me, it's no problem. I need experts around me. It's really very important that you are empathetic, that you try to understand the people around you, and that you give real support to the people around you. Then everybody can act. That's what leadership is: have strong people around you with a better knowledge in different departments than yourself, don't act like you know everything, be ready to admit, 'I have no clue in the moment, give me a couple of minutes and then I will have a clue probably. That's how I understand it but it's no real 'philosophy', it's just my way of life."

Klopp has become aware of the scale of the club. "This club is so unbelievably big, it's incredible," he said. "It feels really good and gives us a lot of power and, for me, absolutely no pressure. I sometimes try to imagine how it is in all the living rooms all over the world; millions and millions of people when we are playing are completely concentrated on what we are doing. During the week they follow us wherever we go, they read everything about us, and it's very positive – it's the best thing you can do in your spare time actually... if you love football, obviously."

Klopp highlighted the five key elements of leadership:

1. ALLOW PEOPLE TO HAVE FREEDOM

In the beginning, when a new player is coming in, I don't give them any information. It's like, 'let them play'. You learn more about your players each day and how to treat them, how to deal with them.

2. ALWAYS HAVE A RESPONSE

Players always need something to respond to – I needed it as a player as well. There are two reasons I am so energetic on the sideline. One is my character – although I am a lot calmer than I was – and the other is that I am kind of the reserve tank for the boys. If I feel the energy level goes a bit down, then I am still there and can kick their butt, whatever they need. It is better to be angry with me than feel 'it's too intense today'.

3. RELATIONSHIPS WITH OTHERS ARE EVERYTHING

All we do in life is about relationships. Otherwise, if you only want to be responsible for the things you do and not anyone else, then live in a forest alone or on a mountain alone. As a football team, we have to work really closely together. Each of our players knows the name of each person who works at Melwood. It's not for me to create an atmosphere in a room – each person in our team is responsible for that. It's worked out well. We all win for each other; we do it for (kitchen staff) Carol (Farrell) and Caroline (Guest), because we know how important it is for them. That makes it more valuable, more worthy. If you have a bigger group to do it for, it feels better for yourself.

4. LEAD BY EXAMPLE

As a leader you cannot be the last who comes in and the first who goes out. You don't always have to be the first and last, but you do have to be an example. I try everything to be as successful as possible. I live 100% for the boys, with the boys, doing what we can for the club. It's not really a philosophy, it's just my way of life.

5. DON'T BE AFRAID TO USE OTHERS

Confidence is very important for a leader. I know I am really good at a few things, and that's enough. But my confidence is big enough that I can really let people grow next to me, that's no problem. I need experts around me. It's also really important that you have empathy, that you try and understand the people around you and give them real support. That's what leadership is – you have strong people around you with better knowledge than you; you don't act like you know everything; and you're ready to admit that you have no clue in a particular moment.

★

A fascinating analysis of leadership by Karen Ferris, entitled "The Klopp Effect Lessons in Leadership" focuses on ten key areas. Karen describes herself as "acclaimed internationally as an author and speaker, with industry acknowledgement of my reputation as a Thought Leader, I provide both strategic and practical advice and insights to my audiences."

Analysing the 10 key Klopp traits, Karen added: "These are 10 leadership traits that I believe we should all strive to attain and maintain. I should have made it 11 and added in humour just so I could say "let's talk about six baby!""

1. TEAM PLAYER

For Jürgen, it is all about team. Assistant manager Pepijn Lijnders said in an interview with Dutch paper De Volksrant: "Jürgen creates a family. We always say: 30 per cent tactic, 70 per cent team building."

A great example of putting the team first was his response when captain Jordan Henderson asked his manager to lift the Champions League trophy with him, "I asked him to lift the trophy with us but he said that was my job", Henderson said.

Karen picks out this comment from the club captain to illustrate the managers' attitude of there is no 'I' in team. "I've said this before, this isn't possible without the manager. What he's created at this football club - the team, the atmosphere, the players, everything at this football club he's created is unbelievable and this is impossible without him. We all love him of course. He's got a special relationship with the players. If you ask the players that he's worked with previous they'll say the same.

He's a special manager. It's not only the players he's brought in to make the squad stronger; the players that were already here he's made better. There's such a togetherness in the group. He's created a special dressing room. All the praise, everything, goes to the manager."

2. HUMILITY

Klopp joined Liverpool without suggesting he was "The Special One". He came across as "The Ordinary One" despite his record of success at Dortmund, when he said on his first day: "When I left Dortmund, I said it's not important what people think when you come in but what they think when you leave."

As a leader, it wasn't what he had done in the past that would leave a legacy but what he was to do from that day forward. He had no illusions of grandeur when he arrived and hasn't changed in the four years he's been in charge.

3. EMPATHY

Jose Mourinho, when asked about Klopp's success said it was due to the "fantastic empathy Klopp created with this group of players".

On empathy Klopp said: "But my confidence is big enough that I can really let people grow next to me, that's no problem. I need experts around me. It's also really important that you have empathy, that you try and understand the people around you and give them real support."

4. RESPECT

Klopp earns the respect of his team because he leads by example. Karen picks out one of his comments from an interview when he was asked about his leadership style.

"I try everything to be as successful as possible. I live 100 per cent for the boys, with the boys, what we do for the club. I think that's leadership in the first case. As a leader you cannot be the last who comes in and the first who goes out; you don't always have to be the first coming in or the last going out, but you have to be an example."

5. GROWTH MINDSET

Great leaders allow failure and to celebrate failure as an opportunity for learning and development. In 2015, when Klopp experienced his first defeat at Liverpool he said: "It is not a problem to lose a game, it is football, it happens all the time but we have to learn the right things. If we learn the right things tonight it is very important and then it will be good we lost. At this moment I don't know the reason for why it will be good but we have to learn the right things."

He has also said: "Players make the right decisions when they have confidence, when they don't have it, then they feel 'next pass needs to be the goal' or 'now we are under pressure and need to force it'. No! You stick to what you're doing, try, try and try again. Each missed chance is not a failure, it is information - use it and go again."

6. AUTHENTICITY

Jürgen acknowledges that he doesn't always have all the answers. "That's what leadership is: have strong people around you with a better knowledge in different departments than yourself, don't act like you know everything, be ready to admit, 'I have no clue in the moment, give me a couple of minutes and then I will have a clue probably.'"

Jürgen Klopp's description of himself as "The Normal One" became so popular that Liverpool FC applied to trademark the phrase their manager used on his first day at the club. He is prepared to admit when he has made a mistake. When Liverpool played Arsenal in August 2016, reporting for ESPN, Glenn Price summed up the incident and Klopp's admission.

"Jürgen Klopp accepted responsibility for almost letting his side's "deserved" 4-3 win over Arsenal slip away at the Emirates Stadium. Speaking to Sky Sports after the game, the German admitted he had got carried away after the three points looked to have been all but secured. 'OK, the Premier League has started -- nothing is sure until the final whistle,' Klopp said: 'I have a big, big part in the excitement of the last half an hour because it is not allowed to celebrate a fourth goal when there's still 35 minutes to go. I knew in the moment, but it was too late -- I had Sadio on my back and in this moment we switched off the machine for a second. It was so intense, it was so wrong, it was the first game.'"

7. TRUST

In the Western Union video The World According to Jürgen Klopp, Jürgen says: "I have a lot more information than I give to the players, not because I want to keep that, just because they have to play a football game, and football is a game and you have to play it with freedom."

Jürgen trusts the 'boys' as he calls them to do the right thing, so he doesn't need to dictate the play.

8. RELATIONSHIPS

On relationships Klopp said: "All that we do in life – how I understand it – is about relationships. Otherwise, if you only want to be responsible for the things you do and not anyone else, then live in a forest alone or on a mountain alone. When you enter a room, you have a little bit of responsibility for the mood in the room. As a football team, we have to work really closely together. Each of our players knows the name of each person who works at Melwood."

9. MOTIVATION

The motivational talk he gave his players before the match against Barcelona where Liverpool went into the leg three goals down is legendary. This is what he said: "Believe - put it in your mind that you can do it. Boys, belief. One, two goals. Even if we don't score in the first 15 or 20 minutes. Believe in the 65, 66, 67 minutes that we can score. With Anfield behind, trust me guys, we can do it. We did it once, the Dortmund game, and we can do it tonight. Just show some f***ing balls."

Liverpool won the second leg 4-0 to reach to the Champions League final, when no one thought it possible. That was motivation to win.

10. SUPPORT

Whatever else is being said, the leader supports the team and every individual within it. When asked how he makes his voice heard over the noise from fans, media and the like that can often be loud and unforgiving he says: "This is very important. What we need to create is where they understand completely that the only criticism they need to take is mine - not because I'm the only one that knows anything, but because I'm the one they have to pay attention to. I'm the one giving them the direction together with our backroom and support team. So it makes no sense to trust what people who are not involved in the process think. There needs to be one plan, one voice, one belief. It will not always be perfect, because we are not perfect, but it is our way."

7: THE PERFECT START

THE 30-YEAR WAIT FOR A LEAGUE TITLE brought its own weight of history into the dressing room with Jürgen Klopp making every effort to alleviate that intense burden from his players. James Milner accepted that the expectation of the fans brought its own intensity. "They started getting quite nervous early in the title race last season. It was the first time I had sensed that atmosphere at Anfield. But nothing really changes in the dressing room. The lads are always calm and confident and hopefully winning the Champions League settles people down. I hope they can just enjoy it. As much as people want the trophy, it's the journey that you enjoy most.

"It's so difficult to win the league. I've been fortunate to win it a couple of times [with City] and last year we were so close. We were flying. We were winning every week and felt we should be 10 points clear. And you're still second. Last year, if you'd have said: 'You'll only lose one [league] game all season,' I'd have snapped your hand off. But it wasn't good enough."

Liverpool began their 2019/20 title charge with an emphatic 4-1 thrashing of newly-promoted Norwich at Anfield on Friday Night Football, racing into a four-goal lead at the break with strikes from Salah, van Dijk, Origi and a Hanley own goal. Teemu Pukki gave the travelling fans something to cheer with a consolation on 64 minutes. It took just seven minutes for Liverpool to open their account; Origi's cross from the left cannoned in off the unfortunate Hanley, who got his legs in a tangle. Liverpool lost Alisson to a calf injury just before half-time, the only negative for Klopp on a night The Reds issued an early statement of intent at the start of their bid for a first league title in 30 years.

Klopp said: "It's not good for us. We have to see how serious it is. It's a calf, that's it. He couldn't carry on, that's not a good sign. The scoreline tells the story of the first 60 minutes. We were really sharp from the first whistle, we did what we wanted to do, we scored goals. There's a lot of space for improvement but a lot of things were there today as well. We should have controlled the game more and kept the ball. It is normal when you're not physically at your highest level and you lose a bit of your concentration. The boys were good, and we deserved the three points, which is the most important. I'm very happy with the start, but the Alisson situation is a shadow on that game.'

After triumphing in the Super Cup Liverpool beat Southampton 2-1 on the south coast to secure an 11th successive top-flight victory, equalling their best-ever Premier League winning run - despite a late blunder by Adrian who cleared against the shin of substitute Danny Ings to gift the Saints striker a goal against his former club. Sadio Mane had put Liverpool ahead at the end of the first-half with a delicious arrowed finish from the edge of the penalty area. Adrian, who was passed fit despite an ankle injury in a collision with a pitch invader following the UEFA Super Cup win over Chelsea, had earlier kept out Yoshida's header. Mane turned provider to set up Firmino to double Liverpool's advantage with a clever finish. Adrian's error could have been even more costly for the Reds because in a dramatic finale Ings wasted a great chance to equalise inside the six-yard area.

"Adrian had a swollen ankle and we played too many balls back to him in that period," said Klopp. "The other players have to then feel more the responsibility for the build-up and cannot give all the balls back to him and hope the pain killers still help or whatever. I don't think the goal was because of that, but a few other balls were. He is completely good with his feet."

Liverpool and Arsenal had made perfect starts so something had to give at Anfield in the third game of the season and it was Liverpool that maintained their 100% winning record to with a 3-1 win, their third consecutive win of the campaign, as Matip's header and Salah's second-half brace secured the points at Anfield.

Just before half-time, Liverpool took the lead. A superb outswinging corner from Alexander-Arnold picked out Matip. Salah netted a ten-minute brace, while the Gunners managed only a consolation goal with five minutes left.

Klopp spoke of his side's greater desire, the way they had done the good things from the earlier weeks of the season for longer, but he acknowledged his team need to control games better. "I was really happy with a lot of parts of the game; I think everything we did well in the first four games we did tonight for longer, more precise and better tuned. I loved the desire, the passion, the power and the energy that we put into this game. It made us really uncomfortable to play against, which is what we wanted and so we deserved the first goal."

Reflecting on the goals, Klopp added: "It was a very determined header as well; Joel was there – big Joel – and scored a fantastic goal. In the second half then, there was the clear penalty. We played nice passes and we were there with a lot of good moments, football moments, today – but you need these decisive moments. The penalty was nicely taken and then the third goal is just incredible again – a really, really good goal."

Klopp was keen to point out that his side still had things to work on, admitting his player's game management had been poor at times. "So, pretty much the story of the game; we could have controlled it better, that's probably our real challenge. [When we were 3-0 up] Arsenal didn't really press anymore, they were deep, together, and we passed the ball into their legs and that makes no sense. It was a brilliant game from my side so early in the season. It was outstanding. It was a performance full of power, energy, greed and passion, which I think you need to have against a team like Arsenal. We are still really early in the season and throwing such energy on the pitch is exceptional. The work rate of the whole team was exceptional. Tactical discipline was exceptional apart from maybe 10-15 minutes."

Although Liverpool eased off in the latter stages and allowed Arsenal to score a consolation goal, Klopp was satisfied. "The tempo we put from the beginning was incredible, really incredible. There was no time to breathe. The opponent of the quality of Arsenal, you have to break somehow: break them physically. We should have kept the ball better because they did not attack us really. For 80 minutes we were completely in charge of the game. We are not Disneyland, we do not need to excite everyone in every second. It was intense, and yes our decision making could be better. The boys, though, did what we wanted them to do, and scored wonderful goals. The work rate of the boys was just exceptional. Our identity is intensity and that is how the boys showed up today. We were completely in charge and won the game as we deserved."

Mo Salah was the decisive figure – turning David Luiz to gain a penalty which he blasted home in the 49th minute and then beating Arsenal's former Chelsea defender out wide before scoring an outstanding solo goal.

Liverpool now held a five-point advantage over City, after they had controversially dropped points to Spurs having had a goal ruled out by VAR. They went on to beat Bournemouth the next day to narrow the gap at the top to 2 points with a 3-1 win on the south coast, Aguero scoring twice, with Sterling also on the scoresheet.

There was a moment of controversy in the fourth game of the

season when Sadio Mane reacted to being substituted in the 3-0 win over Burnley at Turf Moor. Jürgen Klopp praised his forward line for helping the club achieve a 13-match winning run in the league, a new club record. They were only the second English top-flight side to win 13 in a row while scoring more than once each time (after Tottenham in 1960). But in the 85th minute with the Reds 3-0 up, Mane walked off making a gesture to the bench and continued to be animated as he sat down, frustrated at Salah's decision not to pass to him in the opposition area moments earlier. Klopp laughed off the incident: "But it's good eh? He was upset, it was obvious. Sadio cannot hide his emotions, I like that. But it's all sorted. We spoke about it and everything is fine. We are individuals, we are emotional. It was a situation in a game. What else could have happened? It was not a phone call."

Mane, Roberto Firmino and a fluke own goal helped the Reds maintain their 100% start to their title campaign. The breakthrough came in the 33rd minute when Alexander-Arnold's intended cross to the far post brushed the back of Chris Wood and sailed over the head of the stranded Nick Pope. Soon after the restart, skipper Ben Mee inadvertently found Reds forward Firmino with a short pass, who found Mane who fired low past Pope. Finally, Firmino fired in from the edge of the area after he was teed up by Salah. Firmino became the first Brazilian to score 50 Premier League goals; the ninth player to reach the milestone for Liverpool overall - no other club has had more (level with Manchester United).

Klopp was surprised the league leaders had extended their winning streak, because none of his front three had a full pre-season as Mane and Salah played at the African Cup of Nations, while Firmino competed at the Copa America. "If you ask me four weeks ago I wouldn't expect it would happen," said Klopp. "We had a tricky pre-season. No pre-season for the front three but they still deliver. So far, so good."

His players went into the international break with as many points and in the same position as the corresponding period last season. Klopp won five Premier League games against Burnley boss Sean Dyche; against no manager has he registered more victories in the competition. Klopp was at pains to defuse the row between Mane and Salah. Liverpool had not lost any of the last 33 Premier League games in which Mane found the net (W29 D4 L0). Since the start of last season, no Liverpool player scored more goals in all competitions Mane (30 - level with Salah).

★

After the international break, Liverpool shrugged off an early scare to sweep past Newcastle and maintain their 100% start with another dominant attacking display and a 3-1 win at Anfield. Mane scored twice in the first half after Jetro Willems' fine first goal for Newcastle gave Steve Bruce's side a surprise early lead, which turned out to be their only shot on target in the entire match! Salah added a third after the break, with the third member of Liverpool's attacking trinity Firmino providing two brilliant assists and stealing the show with a superb man-of-the-match performance from the bench. The Reds had now won 14 league games in a row, stretching back to a draw at Everton in March - the joint third-best winning run in English top-flight history - as they went five points clear at the top after second-placed Manchester City surprisingly lost 3-2 at Norwich in the evening game in one of the shocks of the season so far.

The spotlight was on Salah and Mane after their disagreement at Burnley, but whatever the tensions off the field, there was only unison and joy on it. As Firmino played an hour for Brazil in Los Angeles in midweek in a game that finished at 06:00 BST on Wednesday morning, the plan was to give him some rest as Origi started on the left of the front three. But an injury for the Belgium striker meant the Brazil forward was introduced earlier than anticipated. Mane had already equalised by that point, collecting a pass from Robertson and curling superbly into the top corner. Salah celebrated with a punch of the air, so no animosity anymore for sure.

Firmino then robbed Atsu and slid in Mane with a beautiful pass. The Newcastle keeper Martin Dubravka should have gathered it but pushed it back towards Mane to allow the Liverpool forward to tap-in for his 19th goal in his last 21 Premier League appearances at Anfield. After the break Firmino was even more impressive, laying on chances for both his full-backs before setting up the previously quiet Salah with a wonderful assist. Receiving the ball with his back to goal, the Brazilian dragged the ball back then back-heeled it into the path of Salah, who did the rest.

City's record of 18 top-flight wins in a row remained within sight as did Chelsea's record of nine victories in a row at the start of a Premier League season. Klopp commented: "I started enjoying it after 35 minutes when we arrived in the game. It was difficult, Newcastle did what they did and did it well. They had the speed to go in behind on the break, it was not easy. We played them onside for the goal unfortunately and that made the game not easy. We had some time to set the rhythm, we had to play much quicker and then we had chances. We scored two wonderful goals. I'm not too pleased about coming from behind. We have to learn from the game. The challenge is always after the international break to find a common rhythm again. The boys have played in different ways for different countries and we have one-and-a-half days to work on it again."

Newcastle boss Steve Bruce remarked: "Liverpool are as good as you get. You can understand why they are European champions and lost once last year. They are an excellent, excellent team with pace and creativity and at the top end of the pitch they damage you. They are going to be there or thereabouts."

After a 2-0 defeat in Naples in the first Champions League game, Liverpool bounced back with goals from Trent Alexander-Arnold and Roberto Firmino to secure their 15th straight win with a 2-1 triumph over Chelsea At Stamford Bridge. Alexander-Arnold's thunderbolt and Firmino's free header, either side of a disallowed Azpilicueta equaliser, saw the league leaders open up a two-goal lead inside half an hour at Stamford Bridge. N'Golo Kante's brilliant solo effort set up a tense final 19 minutes in which substitute Batshuayi and Mount spurned glorious chances to earn the Londoners a point. Manchester City's 8-0 demolition of Watford showed the reigning champions would not relinquish their crown without a fight, but another hard fought victory on tricky away territory proved yet again the Reds were more than capable of going toe to toe with their title rivals.

"It was a really good performance," Jürgen Klopp commented, "and we scored two wonderful goals. It was an exciting game and it was intense. You will never win at Chelsea without putting a proper shift in, and I think we deserved the three points. 15 straight wins is exceptional, but what can I say? We try not to think about it, we just do what we have to do in the next game and fight for each ball and it is always really hard work."

A straightforward 2-0 win at MK Dons in the League Cup was followed by a visit to Bramall Lane where Liverpool's next league opponents, Sheffield United, were enjoying a dream start to life among the big boys. In the event Liverpool edged the game 1-0 in a game in which the Blades had their fair share of chances. "We don't think about the 15 wins," Klopp said afterwards, "Thank God we lost from time to time in the Champions League eh, because we still know how it feels. That's really important because we want to change things when we lose a game. We just want to go to Sheffield and make their life as uncomfortable as possible. That's the plan. We are considered as a top team but we don't want to behave like a top team. We want to fight like a proper challenger. Is it allowed that they fight more than us? No. Is it allowed that they run more than us? No. Is it allowed that they just do more than us? No. We must be there, absolutely spot on."

Following a win by the odd goal in seven against RB Salzburg, Anfield witnessed a more tense occasion on the Saturday and needed James Milner's injury-time penalty to earn a dramatic win over in-form Leicester City to maintained Liverpool's flawless start to the league season. Brendan Rodgers' side looked to be on course for a hard-earned point on his return to Anfield after Maddison's low finish 10 minutes from time equalised Mane's 40th-minute strike but deep in stoppage time, a communication breakdown between Schmeichel and substitute Albrighton ended with the latter bringing down Mane, the penalty awarded after consultation with VAR and Klopp celebrated wildly as Rodgers turned away in despair.

This had been the closest Liverpool had come to dropping points, but once again late Anfield drama provided a twist. Mane was not just his usual attacking threat - scoring his 50th top flight goal for the Reds after racing on to Milner's pass and expertly beating Schmeichel in the first half - he also worked tirelessly in his defensive duties to subdue the threat of full-back Ben Chilwell in the first half. The Senegal forward was now regarded as world-class and came to Liverpool's aid once more when it looked like the visitors would repeat their feat of last season and leave Anfield with a draw. Mane, making his 100th league appearance for Liverpool, scored his 50th Premier League goal for the Reds, the 10th player to reach the milestone for the club in the competition, more than any other side.

Liverpool's run of 17 Premier League victories was bettered only by City's sequence of 18 wins between August and December 2017. They were also unbeaten in 44 league games at home - 34 wins and 10 draws - the longest current run in Europe's top five leagues. Milner's penalty was the 34th time Liverpool scored a 90th-minute winning goal in a Premier League match - at least nine more than any other side. Liverpool were the first to win their opening eight matches of an English top-flight season twice, having also done so in the 1990-91 season. Yet Liverpool were not at their fluent best but, like at Sheffield United, they got a break when they needed one.

Leicester City had arrived at Anfield with many tipping them as serious top-four contenders given the crisis at Tottenham and the transitions taking place at Chelsea and Manchester United. A very impressive side, superbly organised by former Reds boss Brendan Rodgers, would, as the season progressed establish their credentials as much more than just a top four contender, so it was imperative to have won this game in the grander scheme of things.

Rodgers left Anfield bitterly disappointed as he said: "It's cruel to concede so late. I am very proud of the team. We're playing against the European champions and we looked like we could get goals. We were always a threat in the game, we had the confidence to pass the ball. We are showing our personality in how we played. We are bitterly disappointed to concede the penalty and it did not look clear and obvious to me. I think Mane made the most of the contact. I don't think if it had not been given by the referee it would have been overturned by VAR. When the referee gives decisions it is hard for them to overrule it."

Klopp commented: "It was a super game. We upped the tempo. The football we played was so important. Leicester's goal really stopped us but then we wanted to go forwards. The penalty was obviously a penalty. We knew it would probably happen, we knew we were going to fight for the win - and we did. Without luck, we cannot win the amount of games we have won, but over the 90 minutes we deserved it - we deserved the three points. Milner held his nerve and that was superb."

Klopp was livid with Choudhury's tackle on Salah when the game was 1-1 and Salah was racing towards the opposition box when Choudhury scythed the Egyptian down. The referee brandished a yellow, but it merited a red. Salah was eventually forced off and needed a scan. "It was just a challenge which I really don't understand. I don't understand how he can do it, because the ball is far away. The player is in full sprint, to bring him down without the ball around, for me there is only one colour card. I might be the only one who sees it like this, but it is dangerous as hell. How can Mo be okay? Mo limped off the pitch. That's hard. It was done to slow Mo down and that is not OK."

Leicester felt they had done enough to earn a point and their frustrations boiled over at the final whistle, with substitute Ayoze Perez involved in angry exchanges with several Liverpool players - who were celebrating extending their lead over City to eight points. Perez was involved in a scuffle with Robertson, with others trying to break things up.

But was the result lucky? No way, at least according to the manager; Klopp dismissed the notion although Brendan Rodgers felt Liverpool were fortunate. Nevertheless, Klopp was full of praise for Rodgers but warned that they will find it hard to play so well if they qualify for European football next season. "This one [win] alone feels already big enough, to be honest, because of how difficult this league is [and] how difficult the life of an LFC player is. I think Leicester at the end of the season will be in the top four and then they will realise how different it is when you play Wednesday, Saturday, Wednesday, Saturday. The quality they have is already good and we all know Brendan, what a sensational manager he is and what he's doing with them. So it was difficult, but for 60 minutes we were the clear better side. We played really good football, we forced ourselves for a proper performance, to be honest, but with a little problem: we only scored once. If you score in the 95th minute with a penalty everybody would say that's lucky but over the full game we had more chances, we were the better team, so I'm really happy about that.

James Milner added: "This season we have a team that can do it. I think there's a calm around the club, both inside and outside, and people are confident we can get it done. But City are so good they're capable of winning every game. The gap is not that big so we have to just keep pushing, and not worry too much about the title. A couple of bad games can happen, and with the amount of games we're playing there might be a couple of injuries. It could be a couple of poor performances and the lead's gone. That's why it's so special to win the league. It's so difficult and the best team always wins the league, no matter what. Hopefully winning that first trophy, the European Cup, as a squad will give us the experience to win the league."

Liverpool had made a blistering start to their Premier League campaign, but it wasn't without its problems. Klopp revealed he had called Sadio Mane into his office to defuse the row between his strikers. Klopp wanted to make sure that there was no ill feeling beneath the surface between two of the club's most important players. Mane and Salah confronted had each other in the changing room after their incident at Burnley. Mane was incensed with his team-mate when Salah failed to square the ball to him when he was unmarked, trying to add a fourth Liverpool goal.

When Mane was taken off by Klopp a few minutes later he was still raging. When the team got back to their dressing room at Turf Moor, Mane told Canal Plus: 'He said to me "Sadio, why are you angry?" I told him, "You needed to give me the ball, Mo", to which he replied, "I didn't see you. You know I've got nothing against you".

"I know that, but his reaction was a bit strange to me. We talk on the phone sometimes, we text each other and we don't have a problem. We talked between ourselves, and then the manager called me into his office and we spoke. I told him it was already sorted and he was pleasantly surprised." Although the pair both publicly denied that their spat was ongoing, the statistics didn't look particularly favourable when it comes to their partnership. Salah hadn't created a single chance for Mane in their opening eight Premier league and a number of cup matches.

Mane played down his angry reaction at Turf Moor when first asked about it. "I feel a little bit frustrated because it is football and you want to score to score more goals," he admitted, adding: "We are really, really good friends." They finished level on 22 goals with Arsenal's Pierre-Emerick Aubameyang for the Golden Boot the previous season, and both naturally wanted to claim the prize for their own. Mane created more chances for Salah than the other way round - 20 to 17 - but Mane took just one of those chances, while Salah took three. Both are natural competitors, both have a goalscorer's hunger for goals, more goals, and both want the Golden Boot. The manager would want to keep a close check that they were not adopting a more greedy approach.

Klopp believed Liverpool were learning from the small mistakes they made in the title race last season. After 20 games last term, Liverpool led City by seven points but four draws and one loss were enough to allow City to capitalise. This time Klopp's side already held a five-point lead after six games and were in a strong position to win their first top-flight title since 1990. Klopp, though, took their title tilt one step at a time. "The next step? I don't know. It is just to stay on this level and make the next steps and I cannot say that means we will be champions, that is not possible. We have the strongest competitors in the world, that is for sure."

He added: "If you put Barcelona, Real Madrid and Bayern Munich in the same league, that would be more difficult, but we have them already in the league, that quality. So that makes it really tricky. If we would have had more luck in a season... I don't say Manchester City were lucky, my God, not at all. But they had it in parts where we didn't, but at the end of the season they had more than we had and it was really decisive with little goals here and there.

"They deserved it, 100 per cent, but if we come to the same situation again, I don't know [who wins]. But learning from your own mistakes or success is the best thing you can do. And so far, it looks like we have taken the right information out of our situation last year and tried to make the next step."

Liverpool's tremendous start saw Klopp named Manager of the Month for the second month in succession. During September, the Reds beat Newcastle 3-1, Chelsea 2-1 and Sheffield United 1-0 to maintain an impressive 100 per cent record. He became the first manager since Kevin Keegan in 1995 to win the first two Premier League Manager of the Month awards in a season, with the former Newcastle boss doing so in the 1995/96 campaign in which the Magpies eventually surrendered a 12 point lead to Manchester United. Now Klopp had won it three of the last four occasions stretching into the previous season. In winning two consecutive awards, Klopp matched the achievement of Rafael Benitez, who managed the rare feat of winning it back-to-back, in November and December 2005. Roy Evans also managed the achievement for Liverpool, in December 1995 and January 1996. In the 14 years since Benitez, only five managers—Carlo Ancelotti (Chelsea, March/April '11), Manuel Pellegrini (Man City, Dec '13/Jan '14), Claudio Ranieri (Leicester, March/April '16), Antonio Conte (Chelsea, Oct/Nov/Dec '16) and Pep Guardiola (Man City, Sep/Oct/Nov/Dec '17)—have won the award in consecutive months.

Eight points clear, after eight games, the Reds were averaging a point a game more than City. Liverpool's experience of the past 29 years cautioned against premature celebrations even as they savoured the most commanding lead a team have held at this stage of a Premier League season. It was a great way to start the latest international break, and mark Klopp's fourth anniversary of his Anfield arrival after defeat for Manchester City (at home to Wolves) on the same weekend left The Reds with a healthy eight-point lead. That inevitably produced an avalanche of pundits predictable claims it was Liverpool's title to lose. But it was still just the first week in October! And if any team could string a series of results together to close that gap it was Pep Guardiola's City.

Liverpool had beaten Leicester with their fourth-choice centre-half, Dejan Lovren, back in the team, illustrating the wisdom of Klopp not to sell him in the summer when offers came in and it might have been tempting for the player. Paradoxically City had only one fit centre-half and were struggling as a consequence of failing to find a successor to departing skipper and losing defensive lynchpin Aymeric Laporte to a serious injury until February 2020 in central defence.

Klopp, though, would have been fully aware that in the first weekend in March failure to beat Everton meant they missed out on the championship with a club record 97 points. Goalkeeping errors and a controversial penalty decision had contributed to the past two wins over Sheffield United and Leicester. But games in which four points were dropped last season, Chelsea away and Leicester at home were this season addressed.

Losing Alisson for eight weeks to a calf injury could have had dire consequences for a team that have had its No 1 issues in the past. To lose the Golden Glove winner might have proved a big handicap, but for the arrival of Adrián, the club's only senior signing of the summer.

Brendan Rodgers remarked before his Anfield return: "What they now have is the confidence of winning. Once you become a winner, that gives you an edge. They have gone close a few times over the last few years in the League Cup, the Europa League and the Champions League final but, actually having won it, that lets them know they can be winners. I think that gives the players great confidence."

Now Alisson was back in full training while Naby Keita remained at the club during the international break. He had several injuries over the past year so Guinea decided not to take him. The 24-year-old started in the win over MK Dons in the Carabao Cup but wasn't brought on in the win over Leicester City. Guinea coach Didier Six wanted the midfielder to regain his fitness, and the Reds didn't want Keita to leave for two friendlies. Six would speak with Klopp about Keita possibly watching one of the friendlies. He hoped Keita would be fit for the upcoming Africa Cup of Nations qualifiers which start in November.

Liverpool youth player Harvey Elliott was banned from all domestic club football for 14 days after admitting derogatory language about Harry Kane in a video. The gifted winger joined Liverpool in July having become the Premier League's youngest player Premier League's youngest ever player in May, appearing for Fulham aged 16 years and 30 days. Elliott's social media video, for which he apologised, was deemed an "aggravated breach" of FA rules. He must complete a face-to-face education course and pay a £350 fine.

Elliott posted the offensive video on Snapchat during Tottenham's Champions League final defeat by Liverpool on 1 June. The player stated that the video was filmed at his friend's house, where he and seven of his friends, all aged 16 and fans of both Liverpool and Tottenham, were goading each other during the match. He was unaware one of the terms he used mocked disabled people.

Liverpool sought to assure the FA that they take a zero tolerance approach to any forms of discrimination and said Elliott was spoken to as soon as the video circulated. The meaning of the offensive words, and how they may be viewed by the general public, was explained to him. In addition, club captain Jordan Henderson, Kane's England team-mate, spoke to Elliott about his conduct. The FA said the fact that the player had only recently turned 16 at the time of the video had been taken into mitigation, as had a previously clean disciplinary record and that he had not intended for his conduct to be viewed by the general public.

The FA added that Elliott "needs to take responsibility for the fact that there was a risk that it would be and that in any event his conduct was unacceptable". The decision of the three-person panel may be appealed against in accordance with the Non-Fast Track Appeal Regulations.

A Liverpool spokesman said: "Harvey's apology was sincere, immediate and unequivocal. He has acknowledged privately and publicly his actions were wrong. Given his age when this indiscretion was committed - in a private setting and prior to signing for us - we will continue to work with Harvey on an educational basis as relates to his conduct. He has already demonstrated to us a willingness to learn and live up to the values and conduct expected of a Liverpool player."

8: END OF THE 100% RECORD

PEP GUARDIOLA REFUSED TO CONCEDE THE title race in October despite City trailing in Liverpool's wake but confessed that the Anfield side looked unstoppable. It was far too early in the season to make any predictions despite the eight-point gap, thanks to The Reds impressive 100% start. City had overcome a seven-point deficit to become champions last term to pip Klopp to the title but Guardiola knew he couldn't guarantee that history would repeat itself. "I don't believe in that kind of thing, every season is different. In sport the only way to do well is to stay in the present. I'm not setting any points targets or objectives at this stage. In April and May you can do that but what we are facing is an opponent who are unstoppable right now. Liverpool are champions of Europe and haven't lost once in eight games. We'll just have to try and do what we can, we have 50 games left in all competitions. I'm not concerned about being the guy who thinks he's going to win every Premier League for the rest of his life. Of course I still want to win, and I still believe we are contenders, but there is a long way to go and all sorts of dynamics, momentums and injuries still to happen. If we don't win I will say congratulations to the team that does. What Liverpool are doing is fantastic but Chelsea and Arsenal are also getting better. The level is rising all the time."

No English team had won back-to-back titles for 11 years and, after setting records for the past two seasons, Guardiola knew there might be a slight drop in intensity. "We tried to avoid it, but sometimes it is normal. We are going to come back like we want to be, we have to be focused on winning our games." City would be helped in that regard by the return of Kevin De Bruyne from injury at Crystal Palace. John Stones and Benjamin Mendy were back in training though may not be fit in time for Saturday's game. Guardiola is looked forward to the return of Aymeric Laporte after Christmas, though not during the packed festive schedule his side must endure first. Because of games being moved for television, City must play two matches in 48 hours at the end of December.

"The broadcasters are the bosses, it is not about us," he moaned, "We have lots of meetings with people but nothing changes. The system does not protect the players. All I can do between the two games [Wolves away on Friday 27 December and Sheffield United at home on 29 December] is to tell my players to get inside the fridge."

A win at inconsistent Manchester United would see Liverpool equal the Premier League record for consecutive victories, but Klopp expected a backlash from the struggling hosts with their manager under pressure as he said: "We have to go there and play the best football we can play, with the biggest 'balls'".

After 17 triumphs the team could match City's total set in 2018-19. Then Spurs would stand in the way of re writing the history books with 19 wins, but the form book would go out of the window in a match that once was billed the game of every season.

Jamie Carragher was sure Klopp would have transformed United. Writing in his Telegraph column , the former Liverpool centre-half said: "I wrote two years ago that if United had appointed Pep Guardiola they would not be waiting long for the title. The same logic applies to Klopp. If he was United's manager, the Premier League table would look very different today. Let's not forget, even amid this vast improvement Liverpool still finished below United in 2016 and 2018. That sums up why for all the crowing about owners and executives and scouts the most important figure at any club is the manager. Get that right and everyone else looks better. The truth is, in the story of the modern Liverpool we will talk about the club before and after Klopp's arrival. The club's transformation quickened after he was unveiled in October 2015. Klopp led Liverpool to its current position by meeting a series of demanding but realistic targets one step at a time. You can spend all the hours you wish detailing the work of owners, chairmen, chief executives and heads of recruitment, but if you want to sum up what Liverpool possess that United lack, really it comes down to this – a world-class manager."

LIVERPOOL'S 17-GAME WINNING RUN

March 10 – Liverpool 4-2 Burnley
March 17 – Fulham 1-2 Liverpool
March 31 – Liverpool 2-1 Tottenham
April 5 – Southampton 1-3 Liverpool
April 14 – Liverpool 2-0 Chelsea
April 21 – Cardiff 0-2 Liverpool
April 26 – Liverpool 5-0 Huddersfield
May 4 – Newcastle 2-3 Newcastle

May 12 – Liverpool 2-0 Wolves
August 9 – Liverpool 4-1 Norwich
August 17 – Southampton 1-2 Liverpool
August 24 – Liverpool 3-1 Arsenal
August 31 – Burnley 0-3 Liverpool
September 14 – Liverpool 3-1 Newcastle
September 22 – Chelsea 1-2 Liverpool
September 28 – Sheffield United 0-1 Liverpool
October 5 – Liverpool 2-1 Leicester

Liverpool were 15 points ahead of 12th-placed United at kick-off and defeat for Solskjaer, following embarrassing performances during losses at West Ham and Newcastle, would turn up the pressure on the Norwegian in the Old Trafford hot seat. Yet Ole used his press conference to tell the world's media that this was the "perfect game" to motivate his young, talented but struggling side. United would take great delight in denying their arch-rivals the chance to equal Manchester City's record of 18 successive Premier League victories. Klopp, however, took issue: "I don't think there are a lot of teams who would love to play against us at the moment. It looks like Manchester United is the only team that wants to play us, and we have to make sure that is a misunderstanding."

Yet Klopp conceded that if his team were targeted in the same way that United players were by the media, with the pundits sharpening their claws, he would use it to his advantage. "In general, the mood that these things create? Yes, I would use it. I would do the same if the situation was the other way around. This is the game [where] we can change the world; that is the way I would prepare [for] it. They have a really good football team there in a situation they don't like so they want to change it. We just have to make sure that if they want to change it, they start a week later and that's all."

United's only victory in their previous five games had come in a penalty shootout win over Rochdale in the Carabao Cup and their form intensified pressure on Solskjaer in arguably the toughest job in the game. Klopp wants every manager to have "as much time in the world", but added that "no club is willing to wait for success". Solskjaer had actually won two more points from his first 29 matches in charge of United than Klopp did after taking over at Liverpool in 2015. Asked about the comparison, Klopp said: "After my 29 games, there was not 100% agreement I was the perfect manager for Liverpool. I have no clue about his position. It's not important what you are writing, really. It's more important what the board are telling him. I don't have an opinion. Man United is a massive club and nobody is ready to wait for success. In my case it was not any different. He has to live with that. If there was any doubt internally, it would be bad. But as long as it is only externally, that is not important really. I know people think sometimes the manager has to manage Real Madrid before he can take over but that is not the truth. He knows what he has to do.'

Klopp refused to aid the 'media circus' surrounding both teams which could be a 'banana skin' for this team. Sky Sports pundit Danny Mills insisted that no United player was good enough to get into a combined XI from both sides. So too did Ian Holloway, Jose Enrique and Stephen Warnock.

"On Sky you made a combined line-up and had 11 players of Liverpool. It's like a joke, like building a banana skin," Klopp said in his Friday press conference. "If you ask me about Barcelona I will tell you the same. I don't want to have any Barcelona players in this specific Liverpool team at the moment. There's no difference - no Bayern player or Dortmund player, nothing. This is the team I have and I am completely happy with it. The world at the moment is like a circus, and we are at the centre. I'm not influenced by it. I am 100 per cent sure of the strength of Manchester United. All these articles look like they have been written by Man United supporters!

"So, yes, that's it and we'll live with it. In the dressing room, that's the one advantage they have at the moment. And playing at home. They [the pundits] are trying to make it as we are the team and they are nobody. That is the situation that everyone creates – that we are so good and they have so many problems, they cannot play football any more, we are flying, all this stuff gets built-up in a week when there have been no other games. It is like we just have to go there and not respect them on the level they deserve. They are all on their toes, ready, they wait for us. They said it already, they said that we are the perfect opponent now,"

Klopp cast doubt on the injuries of Paul Pogba and David de Gea, who were ear-marked to miss the game. "Yesterday, Pogba and De Gea there is 'no chance'. Today it is 'maybe', tomorrow it is 'a chance!" But Klopp was happy to talk about Salah, suggesting he could expect some 'old-school' treatment.

In the event the Egyptian was not selected, not even on the bench. However, in his pre match press conference Klopp expressed his surprise when told Salah had never scored against United. "If someone had told me that he (Salah) had never scored against United, I would have said 'really?' I suppose the more you go without scoring against an opponent there may be one moment when you start scoring. There is a reason for these kinds of stories, just like our history and stats against United away, such as the stadium or the intensity of the game, stuff like that. Yes, it is a big test and sometimes there will be the old school challenges and you have to be ready for them. That is how it is."

Jordan Henderson was the only player left from the last Liverpool side to take three points at Old Trafford when Brendan Rodgers was manager and Steven Gerrard dominated scoring twice, both from the penalty spot, Suarez added to the scoring on March 16, 2014 when United were managed by David Moyes.

"I never really struggled with confidence to be honest," the Liverpool boss commented, "I am quite optimistic they (his players) have a chance. History, in this case, is not really important. We are really looking forward to playing the game. If someone tells us I haven't won there I wouldn't have known. Let's try for the first time and if we cannot win then perform in the best possible way and if they beat us 'Congratulations'. We are not nervous because of the winning streak and the history we could make, we don't think about it really. We are pretty relaxed but very ambitious as well."

December 14, 2014: Manchester United 3-0 Liverpool
September 12, 2015: Manchester United 3-1 Liverpool
January 15, 2017: Manchester United 1-1 Liverpool
March 10, 2018: Manchester United 2-1 Liverpool
February 24, 2019: Manchester United 0-0 Liverpool

★

The focus may have been on United during the build up but there were concerns expressed about recent performances with Liverpool enjoying a large slice of luck in their last two wins against Sheffield United, when goalkeeper Dean Henderson allowed the ball to slip through his legs, and Leicester, with an added-time penalty. Klopp, though, was unconcerned, saying: "Can we play better, yes of course. But first and foremost you have to play better in the moment and that is influenced by your opponent, different situations, last game, next game, whatever. I liked the Leicester game a lot but that's over now and we don't rely on winning a game without performing. I didn't understand that people said we didn't deserve to win. We were lucky in the moment to get the penalty but the game was 100% Liverpool. They had a lot of quality but we deserved to win. It is just about building on things and making the next step. We are not perfect but we are working on getting better. It worked out kind of so far and now the next challenge is a good opponent in a difficult situation and we should be ready for that as well. I am sure they (United) are all on their toes, ready and waiting for us."

Klopp urged his players to take the 'next step' en route to the title by beating United, even more imperative as City had bounced back from their shock defeat by Wolves to win comfortably at Crystal Palace the day before. "That would be a big next step," he said. "It's not a step we have to make otherwise we cannot develop, no. But of course for our own history it is obviously something we have not achieved yet. This team wrote their own story and made their own history and this would be another step but we cannot make it by simply talking about it. We have to go there and play the best football we can play, with the biggest 'balls', being ready for each challenge, fighting for every ball, all that stuff. That is what we have to do. But if we can play our game, we are really an uncomfortable opponent. That is what we have to make sure – with football, not with overly hard challenges. We are not like this. If we can do that, we have one foot in the game and then we can make it."

Ole Gunnar Solskjaer turned all the mind games back on Liverpool with a dig at The Reds long wait for the title. Solskjaer insisted his 4/1 underdogs won't be satisfied with a draw. He also promised that United's current slump will be sorted out quicker than the time since Liverpool were last league champions in 1990!

"I'm sure we will bounce back and win the league and I'm sure it won't be 30 years until the next Premier League that we do win. For this next game, you never take a draw when you're at Man United. I want to go out there and get three points. We need to start winning games, it doesn't matter if you're playing Liverpool, Manchester City or Brighton. A good performance and result can change the players' and mood and perception of themselves. Maybe they haven't believed they are good enough and when you lack confidence you think twice instead of acting on instinct. Because I know these players are good enough, no worries about that.'

In the event, Ole Gunnar Solskjaer won the tactical battle in a Super Sunday clash that exposed Liverpool's weaknesses for the first time in the season. United led through a 36th minute Marcus Rashford goal as Ole's rapid two-pronged attack and 3-5-2 formation ran Liverpool ragged for over an hour. With Welshman Daniel James and the Mancunian Marcus Rashford upfront it was uneasy afternoon for the world's greatest defender, Virgil Van Dijk, who was beaten several times by trickery and blistering pace. In truth United always needed a second to feel secure and a late defensive mistake allowed Adam Lallana to snatch a point for the Reds to spare their blushes.

Jürgen Klopp was understandably unhappy with the outcome and complained that it is "a fact" that United always set up to defend against his side at Old Trafford after the 1-1 draw left him without a win in five visits to United. "This year, last year, the year before, they just defend," he said. "That's how it is. It is okay. It is no criticism. It is just a fact. When you think about Manchester United against Liverpool, you think both teams are trying like this. But it is not. We try."

After eight straight wins, the 100 per cent record ended with a draw at Old Trafford, as Klopp commented: "They defended well and we only played our best for the last 15 minutes. It's never easy after an international break. That's no excuse but it might explain the lack of rhythm. The fight was there to the end and we got a point. You see that character in the squad time and time again. If someone's not in the gym you say: 'Where were you today?' That's the sort of dressing room we have. It's massive.

"We are the one team where everyone is on their toes when United play against us. We don't have to say it is a compliment. We are a good team. When you play against somebody it is normal for them to think about how they can stop us."

The result ended Liverpool's 17-match winning run in the Premier League, one short of matching City's record. Still top, but the lead cut from eight to six points.

Jose Mourinho, then a Sky pundit, and said Klopp's teams "have limitations against teams with low blocks". He explained: "He [Klopp] didn't like the menu - he likes meat and he got fish. United, with the limitations they have at the moment, played with five at the back, were solid and didn't give the chance of transition. Jürgen didn't like the menu. Liverpool missed quality to play against a team with a low block. They can smash opponents that play the way they want to play against. Jürgen clearly has frustrations. It's a fantastic situation for his team but at Old Trafford - which is a special place to win - he never did it."

Liverpool dominated possession, 68% to 32%, had more shots and more shots on target, but had to wait until the 85th minute for Lallana's equaliser after Rashford had given United a first-half lead. Klopp gave Jon Moss, the fourth official, an ear-bashing on the touchline for much of the game following Rashford's opener. Klopp was adamant his side should have been awarded a free-kick by referee Martin Atkinson for a challenge by Victor Lindelof on Divock Origi in the build-up to the goal. "I think most people thought it was a foul. I am sure it was a foul. Mr Atkinson let the game go on because he knew we had VAR. As soon as they scored they checked it but then it was not obvious because with a challenge you cannot always be 100% sure. But without VAR I am 100% sure Atkinson would have blown for a foul. It's great for offside and handball but for these situations we have not got it right yet. I was so confident that it was going to be overturned. It has to change that not many decisions are overturned.

"Look at Manchester City yesterday - it was so clear and obvious that Kevin de Bruyne was pushed [against Crystal Palace] and if I am saying Manchester City should have had a penalty then it must have been a penalty."

United halted the perfect straight win start, and now Spurs, beaten Champions League finalists, were out to become the first team to actually beat them. At Anfield! It was asking a lot, especially as the Londoners were suffering a poor start to their season. Liverpool returned to form in midweek with a 4-1 thumping of Belgian side Genk in the Champions League.

For Klopp there were plenty of midfield options but the one player who had become indispensable was Fabinho. The return to fitness of Oxlade-Chamberlain and Keita allowed Klopp to play an attacking formation in the 4-1 midweek Champions League win at Genk. Fabinho covered the most distance of any player on the night to shore up the open spaces as his team-mates pushed forward but despite his efforts at times they were over-exposed. "The Genk game was a good example of how important he is. Very!" said the Reds boss. "It was clear it was not perfectly-tuned with Naby and Ox around because they didn't play a lot together in this formation, but it is a possible formation for sure. Fabi had a lot to do to sort some little gaps which we left open. In that game he played as pretty much the only midfielder in some moments. The job of the six in modern football is incredibly important and the more offensive the players around you are, the more important it gets. But he is not only a gap-closer and a challenger, he is a very good footballer as well."

After a hesitant start adjusting to his debut season, the Brazil international started 13 of 15 matches this season – one of the games he missed was the Carabao Cup tie against MK Dons when most of the first team were given the night off – and 40 of the last 48. Klopp was delighted that Brazil coach Tite choose not to play him after calling him up for the international team. "He only flies in the international breaks, he doesn't play! That's pretty much how it is. He is somewhere but not playing. It's difficult in my life not to create headlines but I don't want to create a headline in Brazil. So no comment."

Fabinho, though, would need a rest at some point. "There will be a moment when we have to think about that, 100 per cent. But we have replacements; Gini can play the position really well and Hendo played it for a time. No headache, just bigger selection, more players to choose from. If good games from players gave me a headache my life would be really sad.

"We decided the team for that game because of fresh legs and we will try to find the best line-up for Tottenham as well, and of course the last game is always important information – but not the only one. It's no secret how much I like Ox as person and as a player. At the end it's about being ready for specific moments. He made big steps in the last couple of weeks, but my expectation of Ox is pretty high. Goals, incredible! I didn't see a goal like his second maybe ever. It was special. I'm impressed by the goals but know there is still more to come. He knows that, I know that.

"We have more players to choose from and we try to find the best line-up for the Tottenham game. A lot of subs have had an impact for us and that is great for us. I was pleased for Adam and he was so close to start at Genk. We respect all these signs of course. If you show up in a game then you are in a different part of a manager's brain."

In addition, Wijnaldum is Liverpool's perfect midfielder, even though the Dutchman speaks his mind. "Gini speaks on the pitch for the way he plays. It's just so obvious his importance," said Klopp. "And it is in both directions – in attack and defence, small spaces, big spaces, it is hard challenges, fine football, pretty much all of that. Is he the perfect midfielder? Yes, from the skill-set, 100 per cent. He has all that you need. There was his header against Barcelona too. He is not the tallest, but he is good in the air. He is a good jumper with good timing, all that stuff. It all makes him a pretty good footballer. That is how it should be. It is not my fault if he goes under the radar. You cannot ask me why he goes under the radar. I don't set the radar!"

Wijnaldum was furious with Klopp for leaving him on the bench against Barcelona in the Champions League. But, after coming on at half-time, the Dutchman scored twice in as many minutes to help Liverpool catapult Klopp's stars to the final.

Klopp said: "Don't worry, he is a personality in the dressing room. He is not the guy who says yes to everything. He's not really knocking on my door, but, just like any other human being, if there are things he doesn't like, it's normal. Character is what makes you the person you are and sometimes it stops them going a bit further. I don't mind players knocking on my door, but it shouldn't happen too often. It is more about the information. If my information is correct, then hopefully they will accept it rather than making it a more personal thing. The perfect reaction was when I didn't start him against Barcelona at home – and he came on and scored twice. I said to him, 'You scored twice!' He replied, 'Yes, but that's because you didn't let me out from the start'. I said, 'So, who is right now?"

Unbeaten at home in the Premier League in 45 matches, Klopp insisted they would have to 'fight like crazy' to maintain their record, but why were they so dominant at Anfield? Klopp says they always aim to be "ugly" to play against! A high-pressing, hard-running, aggressive style supplemented by their ability, a never-say-die attitude and a passionate home crowd; it was a compelling answer to why they feel so invincible at Anfield.

Klopp aimed a dig at the fans of Manchester United by claiming they went quiet after Liverpool's late equaliser at Old Trafford. He said: "We have this run because we put in a specific mix of attitude and the potential of the boys, plus the crowd. That can make life difficult. We saw last week that the Manchester crowd was really good until we scored the equaliser and then it was [clicked fingers] done. That is something that is different here. Okay, somebody can score an equaliser but it does not mean we cannot win the game anymore. These are the things we have to keep. If you remember the target, I said I wanted us to be the most ugly team to play against. Hopefully for most teams it is like that. We all worked for it and deserve it and earned it all together but cannot take it for granted. Against Tottenham, especially. The numbers are not important, only the next game. We are in a good moment but to keep that moment we have to run a lot, work really hard and fight like crazy.

If we do that it is difficult to play against."

Liverpool hadn't lost a Premier League home fixture since April 2017 while Spurs only won three times at Anfield in over a century and have endured an inconsistent start to the season. But Klopp did not believe they were suffering a Champions League final hangover and expected "a very good" Spurs team when the two clubs go head-to-head for the first time since they met in Madrid despite the fact that Mauricio Pochettino's team suffered embarrassing defeats, 7-2 against Bayern and 3-0 at Brighton, winning only three Premier League games, and languishing outside the top six. Klopp observed, "In the end it is a football match between two really good teams. Their current situation will not make a massive difference. We will not be that confident that absolutely nothing can happen to us... I don't know how many points they have but they will not play like a team with the points tally they have. They are a top side in the Premier League and they will be a top side the whole season in the Premier League. We have to respect that and play the best football we can play.'

Klopp was impressed when he watched Spurs produce an impressive 5-0 home win over Red Star Belgrade in midweek. "I am the most experienced manager in the world at losing big finals!" he added. "I cannot say anything about what happened at Tottenham in the summer so I don't know why it is not going like Tottenham want it to go. What I saw on Tuesday was a very good Tottenham side. That's what we are thinking about, not about why the start has not been as you or they expected. They have not forgotten how to play football. They can't change what happened in the final, but they can use that and that will not be helpful for us. They have quality and are in a situation they don't want to be in."

Asked by Sky Sports' Phil Thompson whether he dreams of winning the title, Klopp said: "No. I didn't dream of the Champions League, we won it. We are in a better position than we would have expected before the season. Are we already through? No. What we created in the last few years was a proper basis to work with and that's what we have to do now. The hardest period ever will come up: November, December. Crazy, the games we play. You need to be lucky in some moments but what we can influence is a specific performance in a specific game. That's what we try with all we have."

Klopp did not mind others thinking of the title. "We know that a lot of people dream around us," Klopp added. "For the boys, time to time they can dream as well, that's no problem. But we have to fight for it. No guarantees."

The weekend had begun with Leicester's incredible 9-0 win at Southampton on Friday evening, taking Rodgers team into second on goal difference, City winning the Saturday midday kick off 3-0 against Villa at the Etihad, to cut Liverpool's lead from eight points to just three, although, of course, The Reds had a game in hand, and it was imperative they should win it.

When Harry Kane scored inside the first minute with a stooping header after Son's shot changed direction hitting Lovren's head, it looked like Liverpool the pressure would grow on the Anfield side but Klopp's team created enough chances to have been 4-1 up by half time. However Son hit the bar early in the second half when Spurs could easily have been 2-0 ahead. Instead Liverpool kept their never as the skipper equalised with a close range volley that bounced in, to make up for losing possession when Spurs broke for their opening goal. Mane won another late penalty which Salah converted for the winner.

"Our mentality has improved. That's grown over the last few years and the gaffer has changed that so much," Henderson said as Liverpool remained unbeaten at home in 45 league games. "We have faced adversity at times. It's not always going to go your own way. After 48 seconds I was thinking it was my fault because I gave the ball away for their goal. Thankfully I managed to get a goal to make up for it."

Rival fans claimed Klopp only does the celebration when the cameras are on him. So when the Sky cameras closed in waiting for his usual fist pump to his adoring fans, he waved the cameras away! He put his hand out to block the camera following him closely behind, then indicated to the crowd that he couldn't celebrate the way he'd want to because the camera was on him, making fun of the long-running joke.

Klopp commented: "I really liked the way we played against really tough opponents. It was a wonderful game of football, it's how you wish games should be. The boys delivered. We had chance after chance and the keeper had sensational save after sensational save. We started well but the way we conceded was a bit unlucky. Tottenham then defended well, their counter-attacks were incredible. But the best thing was that you couldn't see any influence of the goal. We weren't nervous, we just followed the plan, doing everything in the right way. Their goalkeeper made some incredible saves but we stayed calm.

"It was just how football should look, how you should play against a really strong, good, organised side with the threat constantly in your mind that each ball you lose will possibly end up in front of your own goal. The counter-press was exceptional, it was kind of back. That was the plan today – we wanted to be really strong, especially in that department, because it was clear we probably might be dominant but that means you loose balls. You cannot finish each situation off and then the counter-press must be there. I loved that, that was really, really good.

"At half-time we said this game only had one problem, the score. There were one or two things we could do better and adapt a little bit. I wasn't surprised by Tottenham. They have the quality to cause any team in the world problems. We had 70% possession but that's okay for a team like Tottenham because each ball you lose, they have speed on the counter-attack and Harry Kane is so strong.

"But we were in control, we pushed them back and dominated apart from the last five minutes when we felt the intensity of the game. It was a super game and I loved it. We won the game and deserved it."

Klopp praised goalkeeper Alisson for saving his team despite not touching the ball! "They had a big chance in the second half, and I told the boys at half-time the only problem in this game so far is the result," Klopp said. "Their chance was just a long kick, not even a pass. Dejan misjudged it, thinks he can let it bounce and Son is away and Ali made a really special save. He didn't touch the ball but he was so big in that moment he made life really difficult for Son."

Lovren revealed: "We came in at half-time and the boss said: 'Usually I never say this, but I am satisfied even though we are 1-0 down. But we need to continue like that and keep our nerve'. We knew we would have another chance and we did it. It's a massive, massive win."

Liverpool had restored their six-point lead, but Klopp played down any early title talk, as per usual. "We now have 28 points, but you only have to think what would have happened if we lost today, what the questions would have been. We know exactly what we have to do. We have to focus on all the games, next one Arsenal, then Aston Villa, then Genk, then Manchester City. There is a lot to come but so far, so good."

★

The spine of Jürgen Klopp's team were all made in Brazil; Allison, Fabinho, Firmino. Klopp was effusive in his praise of Fabinho after his side's 2-1 win over Tottenham, hilariously nicknaming him 'Dyson' for his aptitude for hoovering up loose balls. His love for Firmino is well documented and the equaliser against Spurs came after a sumptuous dink from Fabinho put his captain in behind the defence. The 26-year-old succeeded in making more tackles (4) and interceptions (3) than any other player on the field, while only Lovren made more passes. Klopp commented: "You saw it, both wings were so strong with the triangles we created there: with Sadio, Robbo and Gini on one side, with Hendo, Mo and Trent on the other side, and then 'Dyson' in the centre, who was there for each ball defensively – what a game he played, unbelievable. Connecting with Bobby in the centre.'

"I said to the boys after the game that I didn't expect it that good, to be honest, before the game. I thought we are ready to show up a little bit again after being away [from Anfield] on tour for a little while, after Leicester I think – that feels long ago. But that was exceptionally good, and necessary because Tottenham was here today to get three points. The way they set up, line-up-wise offensively, really offensive, but set-up-wise just compact and organised and the counter-attacks are incredible. I have to say that's really tough to defend and apart from twice we did it really well so I am really happy."

Klopp faced the dilemma of whether to leave out one of his most influential players Fabinho for the game at Villa Park. Oxlade-Chamberlain was in line for another chance to start as Fabinho was one yellow card from suspension and would miss the vital City clash if booked again. Milner and Lallana were also in contention, but the Ox had the greater goal threat and Klopp continued to encourage him as he said: "I'm going through the process again - he has to remind me again when I get in these areas to shoot. When we are defending I need to be there and here and press more aggressively, so I'm going though that process again. But you can see him clapping and applauding when someone has a shot from 20 yards and it has gone into row Z. It's because he likes us to try these things."

When asked in his pre-Aston Villa press conference if he thought the Ox was setting the bar too high in not feeling he played well yet scored a fabulous goal in the midweek League Cup win over Arsenal in a 5-5 thriller his team eventually won 5-4 on penalties, Klopp responded: "No. He's right, but it's no problem. That's exactly how it is. He had a lot of moments where he was really outstanding, but then other moments where he's not really involved and these things, that's our life as a footballer, we always try to reach perfection. There are so many games where he still needs to find rhythm and stuff like this. But like I said it's no problem. That's for us a long-term injury and a long-term project to coming back from it."

Klopp knew better performances would materialise in time. "It's good that a player thinks like that and doesn't think 'I scored two goals so I played world-class' because a game [involves] more jobs to do and he knows that. I'm completely fine with his shape and form he's in, but we both know there is quite some space for improvement. That's good news. In his best shape ever before he got the injury, it's not about being there. That's something which happens when you are in your best shape, then you have these kinds of performances. It's just being more involved, feeling the spaces better. I don't when, I just know there's still more to come and that's for me really good news."

Despite concerns that Mo Salah's injury was a big problem, Klopp described the issue as more annoying for the player, but was sure he would be fine. Klopp explained: "He has had to do his individual stuff but he will be in training today. I think it is really more annoying for him, not me, that the injury is a bit of fluid [in the ankle] and he has to deal with it. He gets it out and then has to come back out the team. It is not a 'real' injury like this but he should be fine."

Well, who would have believed it? At half time on the first Saturday in November the title race was in the balance as the top two trailed going into the second halves of their respective games. City were losing at home 1-0 to a Southampton side who were had trailed 5-0 at half time only a week before, eventually going down 9-0 to Leicester. Liverpool were trailing by the same scoreline at Villa Park. Both brilliant Brazilian keepers were at fault for the goals!

3:13pm - SOUTHAMPTON TAKE THE LEAD!

Armstrong's low drive spilled by Ederson, James Ward-Prowse, lifted the rebound over the desperate lunge from the keeper to out Southampton in front.

3:21pm - ASTON VILLA TAKE THE LEAD!

At Villa Park, the reigning European champions were a goal down as McGinn's delivery into the box was met by Trezeguet, who found himself unmarked, his close range header squired under Alisson. The strike was referred to VAR for a potential offside check...the goal was given.

3:29pm - LIVERPOOL 'EQUALISER' RULED OUT!

A fantastic ball from Mane set up Firmino to restore parity for Liverpool, but VAR intervened. The lines used to decipher tight offside calls showed the striker in line, only for referee Jonathan Moss to declare 'No Gepitomisingoal!". Southampton lead at half time in a Premier League game for the first time this season and at Manchester City! How did that happen? City had 13 efforts, but only one on target, although nine of their efforts were blocked epitomising the way Southampton defended their lead, by throwing their bodies at the ball.

At half-time the Premier League release a statement saying that Firmino's leveller was disallowed because his armpit was deemed offside!

The gap between City and Liverpool remained six points as a result of the surprise half-time permutations. But the day could have ended with Liverpool's lead cut back to three points, or extended to nine.

Suddenly, out of the blue, the day seemed to take a bizarre twist, as if it was actually the final Super Sunday last game of the season, with so much interest in each game, virtually kick by kick. Gabriel Jesus was on for David Silva for the second half as the home fans sounded frustrated and Guardiola had had enough! Klopp ordered three of his subs to warm up as, like Guardiola, he had run out of patience, as after an hour there was no change - in either game! Mane was two yards out when he gets on the end of Alexander-Arnold's cross but Heaton made a vital block from Mane's header as the ball cannons off the keeper's shoulder.

City had 41 crosses from open play alone in the first hour, but were still waiting for their first shot on target as Saints parked the bus and Aguero headed over from close range. Bernardo Silva bent in a cross for Aguero and he looked certain to bury a header but his effort was over and Aguero slammed the floor in frustration. City had 17 shots on goal but none on target.

4:27pm - MANCHESTER CITY EQUALISE!

Aguero eventually netted the equaliser. Despite Southampton's players claiming that the ball had gone out of play before Walker's delivery, he shot through the legs of McCarthy. City had reduced the gap between themselves and top spot to five points.

But the drama continued at Villa Park, with Liverpool squandering several openings. In Manchester, Guardiola was incensed after the Southampton bench attempted to delay the restart. Klopp threw on The Ox and Orgi, in place of Salah and Wijnaldum. The Ox had three quick shots in succession, all blocked. Mane had his team's 17th shot drilling wide from a central position as he heads into the final 10 minutes. Liverpool had stuffed Aston Villa 6-0 on their last visit to Villa Park in the Premier League. They were minutes away from a first top-flight defeat of the season

4:43pm - CITY TAKE THE LEAD!

City turned the game around through an unlikely source. Full-back Angelino's cross was palmed out by McCarthy into the path of Walker, who steered home his effort to send the Etihad into raptures. The gap on top spot closed to just three points. Seven minutes left, City ahead, Liverpool behind.

4:47pm - LIVERPOOL LEVEL!

A fabulous curling cross from Mane was perfectly weighted for the onrushing Robertson, ghosting unmarked, firmly on target with his header clipping off Heaton into the roof of the net. The gap increased to five points.

4:53pm - CITY'S VICTORY CONFIRMED

The full-time whistle blows at the Etihad, as City fans waited on tenterhooks for the Liverpool score to filter through via the PA system.

4:54pm - LIVERPOOL SCORE THEIR WINNER!

City thought they ended up within touching distance of the league's summit when Liverpool struck four minutes into five minutes of stoppage time. Alexander-Arnold free kick deflected for a corner off the wall, he dashed over to take a near post corner where Mane glances a header just inside the far post to lead for the first time in the 94th minute.

4:56pm - FULL TIME AT VILLA PARK

The final whistle climaxed another pulsating chapter between two Premier League titans going for glory. Villa players collapsed to the floor, The Reds celebrated as if they know they are going to win the title.

Their six point lead in tact, Klopp was on the pitch handing out hugs to his players, a deliriously happy man after his side turned it around with goals after 87 and 94 minutes. Mane scored the 35th 90th-minute winning goal by Liverpool in the Premier League - at least 10 more than any other side in the competition's history.

Klopp's side retained their six-point lead at the top before the mouth-watering clash with City. Their haul of 28 points from the first 10 games has been bettered only by Spurs in their famous Double winning season back in 1961. "We made it hard for ourselves," said Klopp. "Villa was ready to play for a proper fight, a proper battle, defend with all you have, try to find counter-attack opportunities. We conceded a goal and then it is hard to change this wrong path and wrong decisions immediately.

"It is lucky to score these goals of course, but when you look at the game, if either side deserved to win it is us. We still need to learn and get better. Sometimes you need to get knocks and today we got knocks. For really little mistakes we got really big knocks but at the end we could sort it. We had our good moments during the game but were not clinical enough, especially in the first half. I don't always believe we can win every game but I never give up. So when we scored the equaliser I thought, 'that's what we deserve'. We know we can do better, but on days like this you just need to be ready to fight. When you play in a stadium like Villa Park it's fair you might get a little knock. After the first half we realised we were in the wrong path and we made changes.

"I didn't like the body language. We made it difficult for ourselves. We started playing football well but not exactly how we should — Aston Villa were ready for a proper fight, a battle and to defend with all you have. They tried to make space for counter-attacks, they had good set-pieces. We were playful, which looked good but I didn't like it. It was good football but you have to finish it off. In the second half we started more aggressive, our counter-press was better and we could shoot from distance, which Oxlade helps with. Oxlade on the left space meant space for Robbo. It is lucky when you score these goals but if one team deserved to win it, it was us. I can imagine how bad Villa feel as with their hard work they deserved something.'

Klopp gambled by leaving out Fabinho with the looming shadow of the City game on the horizon, he was replaced by Lallana, and it clearly didn't work, and the manager called on his substitutes into the second half. Klopp became a specialist in late goals only matched by Sir Alex heyday at United. But he was scathing about the VAR decision that ruled out Firmino's strike which made it necessary to stage the latest of his team's late recovery. "When we talk about serious moments, very important moments in football, it's not right to sit here and everyone wants to laugh about it," he said. "It is not to laugh about. It is too serious. Managers get sacked for losing football games. They just have to clarify it. I am not saying anyone is doing it on purpose." Even Villa manager Dean Smith admitted he thought Firmino's goal should have stood. "I thought it was a goal, but we've had gnats-hair goals go against us too and it is factual so you can't moan."

Klopp also felt his side should have had a penalty when the ball struck Targett's arm. 'We need to sort a few things obviously. Nobody talks about the Targett handball situation as it was not whistled." Was it a penalty? Klopp insisted there was contact on Mane: "He got the yellow card and when you see it back it was not diving, there was contact but it is a decision we have to accept it."

With 31 points from 11 games, the two clubs with the same tally at this stage of a Premier League season - Chelsea in 2005-06 and Man City in 2017-18 - both went on to win the title.

9: NOVEMBER SPAWNS A MONSTER...

KLOPP ON GUARDIOLA

"He looks good. He has a very nice figure" - 2013

"Johan Cruyff started Total Football, but Pep made it perfect. He's an outstanding manager, 100 per cent. He's very influential." - 2016

"Pep always looks perfect – body, clothes, everything is perfect." - 2019

"Hands down, the best manager I've coached against." - 2019

"I am not too sure if I want to put oil on the fire. I am not interested in these kind of things. And I promise not to mention tactical fouls." - 2019

GUARDIOLA ON KLOPP

"Maybe Klopp is the best manager in the world at creating teams who attack the back four with so many players, from almost anywhere on the pitch. They have an intensity with the ball and without the ball, and it is not easy to do that." - 2016

"If it's up and down quickly they are much, much better – they are maybe the best team in the world." - 2019

"It [diving] has happened many times, what Liverpool have done, in the last few years. Mane is a special talent. Sometimes he's diving, sometimes he has this talent to score incredible goals in the last minute." - 2019

The clash of the titans - Liverpool v Manchester City - was billed as a global phenomenon, watched by billions: the English Champions against European Champions. But the suggestion that the fixture was now the ultimate clash in English football, brought a typical response from Jürgen Klopp on the eve of the clash: "That is obviously bollocks!"

Wind back a tad and the build up actually began instantly after the last round of Premier League fixtures when Guardiola stepped up hostilities accusing Sadio Mane of diving, and Liverpool of often crying about how unlucky they had been to lose the title to City the previous season by one point. Mane scored Liverpool's winner in the fourth minute of stoppage time at Villa Park, but was booked for simulation in the first half. City's match finished several minutes before Liverpool's and Guardiola said: "We arrived in the locker room and it was 1-1 and after it was 1-2. When we won, Liverpool still didn't and at the end, again they won. What happened has happened not once, twice, it happened a lot of times - it is because (Mane) is a talent. Sometimes he's diving, sometimes he has this talent to score incredible goals in the last minute. He's a talent. If it's one time, two times, "we were lucky, we were lucky", but it happened in the last two seasons many, many times they won many games in the last minutes, they have a special character to do that. We look at ourselves, we know which team we face, I think they have won 10 and drawn one. Next week we go to Anfield to try to play them."

Klopp took a swipe at City's tactical fouling as he responded to Guardiola's jibe that Mane is a diver. Klopp did not want to become embroiled in a spat but got dragged into it. "I couldn't really believe it. Do I like that he says this about one of my players? I am not sure if Pep spoke in that moment about Sadio or the team — both is not too nice. I am not too sure if I want to put oil on the fire. I am not interested in these kind of things. And I promise not to mention tactical fouls. That is maybe already too much — but that is the only thing I'll say about it. I do not know how he could have known about the incident so quickly after the game."

Klopp wanted to stress that Mane "is not a diver". Klopp explained: "Yes, there was a situation in the Aston Villa game where he felt contact and went down. Maybe it was not a penalty, but there was contact. It's not like he jumped over a leg or something. All the other penalties were penalties because he was there. If something like that had happened for Manchester City, I'm sure they would have wanted a penalty, too."

Klopp's focus was on the midweek Champions League tie against Genk but the media only wanted to discuss the clash with City. But until that was the next game, Klopp said: '"I'm not really in a Man City mood at the moment. Do I get asked as much about Man City? I don't know. When I came into the interview after the Aston Villa game, I had no clue what the other Premier League results were. That is the truth. It was 45 minutes after the game when I heard the results of the other matches. I didn't ask anybody. I had to speak to the players, I had to speak to a lot of people and then I went into interviews. I didn't think for one second about the other games. Then, after the interviews, 'By the way, how did the other teams play?' Someone told me City had won in the 86th minute and all this happened. I don't understand these types of things. My brain is not big enough to think about another team as well. I have enough to do to think about us and deal with all these things.

"We play Genk and that deserves all my attention — and gets it. That is the only way I can do it. After that, we can speak about Manchester City... we have to! We will internally speak a lot about them, then we will prepare the game. Before then, not at all."

Sergio Aguero confessed that Klopp's side were the only team who could 'hurt' them. "It may be the Clasico for television, but for us, the Clasico, it's the match against United," he told France Football. "Liverpool have always been a tough opponent. But when I arrived, the team we were fighting for the title was United. Initially, it was something strange in [Manchester] that City competes against United. Then there was Chelsea. But these last four seasons, Liverpool have become a very strong team and are now fighting with us to win the Premier League. They are the only team in the league that can hurt us. They have been chasing a new league title for years. Last season, they didn't go all the way, so they are very motivated. This year, they are in front of us and will try to go to the end."

Pep continued to add to the intensity by suggesting City didn't have to win at Anfield. Since Boxing Day 1981, City had played 31 times at Anfield and won once – when Kevin Keegan was manager. Despite an injury to the influential David Silva, the City boss was adamant they were going there with the attitude to win, but he added that it wasn't "necessary" to do so. Pep said: "How long is it since they lost at Anfield? Last season we did not win there and we won the title.'

Meanwhile Jürgen Klopp suggested that Guardiola was becoming increasingly obsessed with Liverpool, and the City boss responded as he prepared for his Champions League tie against Atalanta at the San Siro, "I didn't listen to what he said so I don't know," Of course he did listen! He added: "I don't put oil in the fire." Guardiola also clarified his 'diving' accusations against Mane. 'My son and my daughter, all the times when Liverpool win in the last minute, ask me how lucky they are. I said to them at the time it's not lucky, what Liverpool have done last season and this season many, many times is because they've this incredible quality and this incredible talent to fight until the end. Against Leicester, it was a penalty it was "wow, like this or like that". That was the intention for my comment. Far away from my intention to say Sadio is this type of player because I admire him a lot. For Jürgen it (the Leicester decision) is a penalty, for the referee it was a penalty, for the VAR it was a penalty. I was the wrong guy - or maybe not, I don't know. So it was a praise for Liverpool, not just about one action. To say it's lucky again? No. It happens many times at Anfield and away (from home) because they push and they push. That's why it's nice to face them and try to compete with them. Hopefully I can clarify everything for Jürgen."

Sadio Mane refused to change his style, sarcastically responding: "If it could be a penalty for sure I will 'dive' again," adding "if the 'dive' will give me a penalty then I will do it! Why not? But what Jürgen said is correct. I do not dive." Mane thought it was "clever" of Guardiola "to get the attention of the referee".

When Jürgen Klopp was asked about Guardiola and the fall out over Mane, he tried to side step it, "I'm in exactly the same situation as him. We constantly get asked questions, and sometimes we say in that second what is on our mind, without thinking of anything else - that we're in public, that there's a camera. He explained it well, saying when he speaks to his kids, it's like this. It could be a penalty or not, and that's a discussion they had at home. I'm completely fine with it, and I couldn't have more respect for Pep Guardiola. I know him for so long, and for me it's still a big thing to be his contender. For me, he's the best manager in the world, and we have the chance to win against his team which is very difficult but possible which is enough for me. From my side, there is nothing but respect. Of course, you can't leave it completely without a comment, but I'm not interested. There's enough to write about before the game. It's not necessary for us to make it bigger by the things we say."

Jamie Carragher wrote in his Daily Telegraph column: "I had an immediate thought when I heard Pep Guardiola and Jürgen Klopp exchange barbed comments ahead of Liverpool against Manchester City this week: 'about time'. There was something unnatural about the Premier League's two leading managers competing for the title without an extra edge to their relationship. Until the past seven days, the mutual respect was denying us a feud to match the early years of Sir Alex Ferguson v Arsene Wenger or Jose Mourinho v Rafa Benitez. Manchester City's extraordinary run at the end of last season denied Klopp and Liverpool what, in any other year, would have been a deserved title. Whatever the appearances publicly, and whatever the consolation of being Champions League winners, this was a cause for despair on Merseyside and there is a determination not to endure a repeat. Equally, it is not hard to imagine the annoyance at The Etihad when Liverpool won the Champions League and the global coverage dwarfed City's achievement of an unprecedented domestic treble. City's last couple of title wins filled the new cycle for 24 hours. Because of Liverpool's size and popularity, a first title in 30 years at Anfield will undoubtedly generate much more media attention.

"I do not believe I am exaggerating when I say the hierarchies of Liverpool and City cannot stand each other, resentments which are reflected in the fan bases. City appear to suspect Liverpool of lobbying governing bodies to investigate the legality of their transfer spending, while they make no secret of their belief that the positive coverage of the Klopp era is disproportionate when compared to Guardiola's trophy haul, and City's in general since the Abu Dhabi takeover. Within Liverpool, eyebrows are raised when stories emerge about fears of another attack on City's bus as happened in the Champions League quarter-final in 2018, and there was incredulity at Guardiola's comments about Sadio Mane's diving. As Klopp suggested, it certainly feels like Guardiola talks about Liverpool more than Klopp does Manchester City, and City generally seem preoccupied with how Liverpool are portrayed in the media.

"The Liverpool manager's reference to City's 'tactical fouling' was a shot back, echoing comments by Ole Gunnar Solskjaer last season. Solskjaer's remarks angered City so much they rushed out statistics to the press in an attempt to show they commit fewer fouls than their rivals. Guardiola seemed to acknowledge his miscalculation by refusing to comment about Liverpool in midweek. Some suggested he was being cynical and deliberate with his earlier observations about Mane. They struck me as more emotional than calculated."

Klopp acknowledged the rivalry was "getting bigger and bigger" following a string of close games. "It's a big game, two really good teams facing each other at Anfield, under the floodlights. The last three games we played 0-0 at home, then lost 2-1 at the Etihad where we nearly scored a goal and then the last one was a draw in the Community Shield, before we lost the shootout. It will be a good football game - I'm not sure whether it will be just from a coaching and tactical point of view or a spectacle for supporters. But everything is on a plate and no one hides anything, we cannot only be offensive but you have to be brave against Manchester City - even for a point. I take enjoyment and fulfilment from how my players have improved and grown together to bring us to the point that we are involved in great occasions like this. I take enjoyment from the fact these players and this team have earned their status as being one of the best football sides in the world in this moment. I take enjoyment from knowing that these players have total belief in themselves. I could not be prouder of what this squad has done and continues to do.

"Liverpool Football Club is so blessed to have this remarkable group of people together in this moment representing and competing for the club. They are so special, each and every one of them. We cannot and should not ever promise an outcome. We can't promise a specific result today or that in May we will achieve anything specific either – that would be foolish. What we can promise, and what they constantly deliver on, is that this team, whichever players feature on the teamsheet, will give their all. These players don't know any other way – it's all of themselves and nothing less when they compete for Liverpool."

Fully focused on City after a narrow 2-1 home win over Genk, Klopp brought the biggest game of the season so far into context: "We are at matchday 12 so obviously there are some games to come. We know about the City situation last year where we only lost one game and that was decisive in the end. That's maybe how people see it, but you have to play all the games. There is so much to come, and the most intense period of the year in November, December and January is still coming so we have to be ready for all these games. At the moment we are focused on preparing for this game, but we don't think too much about what influence it might have on the rest of the season.

"This season is different to last season, and we don't know how it will go. We pushed each other on a really high level. The previous season, there was the real pressure of the 100-point season and I could not have more respect for them that they had 98 points the year after - but for sure we were a reason for that as we pushed them really hard. In the last couple of years, we both gave a lot of respect for each other. City's performance at Liverpool last season was probably the biggest show of respect one of my teams ever got. That's how it is. They played differently to what they usually do - that's true. But, that's football. We all have to make a plan for one game, and in this specific case against one of the best sides in the world.

"We play at home, and last season we played a game at theirs where we lost by 11 millimetres otherwise the ball was in [John Stones' clearance on the goal line] and it was another draw. I think that would have been deserved, so there are tight games and that's how it is when high-quality teams face each other, so I expect another tight game."

So was this a 'must not lose' game? "Maybe there are people who are smarter than I am and see it like this, but I don't. For me, it's 100 per cent a 'want to win game' - 100 per cent with all I have. I've never understood 'must-win' games because that doesn't change the chances. For us, as a team to prepare a game like this, you have to do the right thing again and again: being brave, playing football, defending for your lives. All the stuff around the game doesn't really affect us. We want to win, and we'll try everything to make that happen - which is difficult enough. The season will not stop after this, but it's a big one, we know that. The whole world will be watching it, 100 per cent. Everyone I know will. I'm really looking forward to it, but the discussions around, I'm not part of."

City goalkeeper Ederson had came off at half time in City's Champions League midweek win against Atalanta with Claudio Bravo red carded and Kyle Walker ended up in goal to end a farcical game. Klopp felt Guardiola would risk Ederson: "If he did not play, it would change. Ederson is an important part of their game, 100 per cent. Claudio Bravo can do similar things, but I expect Ederson to play 100 per cent. He's an ever-present player."

Klopp emphasised the magnitude of the game by suggesting even the hot dog seller needed to be on top of his game, let alone his players! He observed: "City in the last three years have been the team in the Premier League and it has always been our plan to get closer. In the last three games we have drawn once and lost twice, but the guys are showing improvement. Everyone has to be in top shape in the stadium on Sunday, even the guy selling the hotdog. Everyone has to be there from the warm-up and be there. That is what I wish for - that before we even know whether we are going to get something that we invest all our emotions for the game and let's play football. The best news is that it is as Anfield, under the floodlights. Everything is on a plate nobody hides anything, if you are not brave against Man City you don't have the chance of even a point. You have to create, but your positioning and protection must be perfect. It is a lot. It is an interesting game! From a sport's point of view this rivalry is getting bigger and bigger. We live in now and obviously Man City are a pretty good football team and thank god there is a rivalry because it means we are a pretty good team as well. Raheem Sterling is always a big threat, and he is always improving. He is a fantastic footballer, I can't say anything bad about him, outstanding. He is not the only threat unfortunately. That is the problem we have."

Liverpool's 10 points from 12 in games against the top 6 included matches with Arsenal, Tottenham, Manchester United and Chelsea, while City's 2-2 draw with Spurs in August was so far their only fixture against the elite clubs. City did not look quite as formidable as in the previous two seasons when they won back-to-back titles, contending with injuries to key defenders. Klopp was not having it, he was far from sympathetic as City had the far stronger squad to cope with such set backs. 'We all have problems. Last year De Bruyne couldn't play against us, one of the best players in the world, and they still got results."

When these two heavyweight managers had met 13 months earlier, with the clubs level on 17 points, City set up more conservatively than at any other time in Guardiola's reign and left with their first goalless draw and clean sheet on the ground since 1986. They would have snatched a deserved victory had Mahrez not missed an 85th-minute penalty. Liverpool hadn't lost a game at Anfield since April 2017 when Crystal Palace beat them 2-1. It was a remarkable record that led Guardiola to compare Anfield to the Camp Nou and the Bernabeu, but he was undaunted. "It is never easy to win against a good team on a big stage," he added. "Everyone knows how hard it is to win away at Camp Nou or Madrid or Juventus, and at present Liverpool is probably an even tougher place to go. But I also know that last season we had a great chance to win, when we missed a last-minute penalty. So sometimes it can happen."

He welcomed the fervent scenes inside the famous arena. "I love it," said Guardiola. "I didn't like what happened in the bus outside the stadium but, in the stadium, when they support the team, it's perfect, it's lovely. That's why we're involved in this business, to be involved in this kind of experience, in these stadiums. They're an exceptional team and the stadium makes an influence. The history speaks for itself, it's something special, but I think it's more for the quality of the team and what they do, the quality of the players and the manager they have. I would say, right now, it's the toughest stadium in Europe to go to."

Added to their formidable record was Liverpool's incredible run of form in 2019, they hadn't lost a game in the league since that 2-1 defeat at the Etihad Stadium on January 3 and lately they became masters of late goals. Forget Fergie time, ran the headlines, now it was KLOPPAGE TIME! The Daily Mail graphic of the stats was impressive reading for Reds fans. They had assumed the mantel of Sir Alex Ferguson's great United teams, seemingly getting results in the last minute of games as and when required. It was the hallmark of champions.

★

Sunday, November 10 was a bright chilly day and following Saturday wins for Chelsea and Leicester, City lay fourth in the table, an unfamiliar sight under Guardiola. But it emphasised City's inconsistent start to the season having already dropped points to Spurs, Norwich and Wolves. So a win was imperative for City at Anfield while a defeat might be terminal for their chances of emulating those great Liverpool and United teams of the past by winning three titles in a row.

Large crowds greeted the City bus as it pulled off Anfield Road into the stadium; there was jeering, gestures and the odd red flare but nothing untoward. The team news revealed one expected change for Liverpool - Fabinho in for Lallana. Klopp resisted the temptation to start in-form Oxlade-Chamberlain, who made a habit of scoring against City at Anfield. In fact Klopp made four changes from the Champions League win over Genk with Robertson returning at left-back, Henderson coming back into midfield and Firmino and Mane rejoining the forward line. Claudio Bravo would make his first Premier League start for City in 18 months with an intense focus on the 36-year-old Chilean. Rodrigo returned from a hamstring injury to replace David Silva, Angelino gets the nod at left-back.

In a pulsating first half that lived up to its hype, City were often spectacular going forward, but Liverpool were clinical on the counter. The visitors dominated the opening few minutes, penning Liverpool into their own half and a cross looked to have struck Trent Alexander-Arnold on the arm before the ball was cleared downfield and found Mane, his cross was only half cleared by John Stones and fell to Fabinho who fired in from 25 yards. It was a smash and grab raid that highlighted City's weakness at the back and their uncertainty over stand-in keeper Bravo. City protests about the potential handball were turned down by VAR and Liverpool led against the run of play. On 13 minutes Liverpool broke again, Andy Robertson's cross finding Salah who headed home. Again VAR checked for a marginal offside against Salah but again the technology favoured the home team. Conspiracy theories abounded on social media but there was no denying the fact that Liverpool were 2-0 up.

Klopp's team then managed the game, letting City have the ball and limiting them to very few chances although Angelino struck a post and Aguero missed a good chance. It promised to be a gripping second half with City looking quite capable of scoring plenty of goals, but Liverpool looked even more threatening on the break. The next goal would be critical and Liverpool added a third when Henderson's cross from the right deceived Bravo and Mane dived to head home. Yet City carried on pressing and there were multiple penalty claims for fouls and possible handballs all turned down by VAR.

Bernardo Silva did manage to score a consolation for City but in reality Liverpool had played their opponents to perfection, exploiting their weakness on the counter and their uncertainty at the back.

Of the first goal, Trent Alexander-Arnold told Sky Sports: "I think it might have hit my arm but it hit Bernardo Silva's first. You have to carry on playing, they complained but you have to keep on playing."

Former City captain Kompany, a Sky pundit for the evening, argued play should have been stopped in the Liverpool box, regardless of the final verdict. "You can argue about Bernardo's handball before - I don't think he knows anything about it and it's a natural position. But [Alexander-Arnold's] is a handball, that's not a natural position. Stop the action then and make a decision. You go which way you want to go, but my interpretation is that Bernardo's hand is in a natural position and Alexander-Arnold's isn't."

These games are often decided by millimetres and split second decisions and so it proved again. Back on 3 January, as Liverpool arrived at Etihad Stadium looking to open up a 10-point gap over City, and with the game goalless, Mane struck the post and Stones' attempted clearance rebounded off Ederson, forcing the defender into a dramatic last-gasp clearance. Goal-line technology showed the ball was 11.7mm short. Guardiola's side went on to win 2-1 condemning Liverpool to their only defeat of the season as City eventually claimed the title by a single point.

Clearly unhappy about the incident that led to the first goal Guardiola said, "Ask to the referees, don't ask me. Ask to Mike Riley and the guys in VAR". During the game he had been furious as there was a second Alexander-Arnold 'handball' claim. Guardiola leapt up and down with rage wagging two fingers at the fourth official Mike Dean. The call not to award City a penalty was, according to the Professional Game Match Officials Board, because the appeal for handball against Alexander-Arnold "did not meet the considerations for a deliberate handball".

"What a load of rubbish! Absolute drivel," said Radio 5 Live pundit Chris Sutton as he was read the statement. "If I was a Man City player I'd be furious. In games that are decided by such tiny moments, that was a refereeing howler. There will be controversy. It did look like Trent's arm was in an unnatural position. I think Alexander-Arnold is a lucky, lucky boy. It should have been a penalty. I don't understand why it wasn't given. His arm was out, it hit him on the arm - it's a penalty. I just don't get it, with what we have been told about the handball rule that has to be the definition of a penalty. Why on earth does Michael Oliver not take it upon himself and look at it on the monitor? Later on he will see that decision and know that he got that wrong."

Robbie Savage, also speaking on BBC Radio 5 Live, added: "How on earth is that not handball? It's absolute nonsense. Go and use the pitchside monitor - it's a big error."

Guardiola had confronted Michael Oliver with sarcastic 'thank yous' at full-time as the pressure of a title race he was clearly losing seemed to be getting to him. Meanwhile Jürgen Klopp was having his own meltdown on the pitch! He refused to play to the Sky Sports cameras, clearly wanting a close up of his famous fist pumps to the fans, and beating his chest, waving them away, saying "not while you're here... I'm not a clown".

When the dust settled, the champions were fourth behind Brendan Rodgers' Leicester and Chelsea and the big question was could anyone prevent Liverpool from claiming their first Premier League title? Guardiola claimed he "does not know" as City's quest to become the first side since Manchester United in 2009 to win three consecutive titles was in tatters and it was still only early November!

"I am not a magician; I don't know the future," Guardiola said. "We have Chelsea at home next. We will try to beat them." He offered no comment on the big penalty beyond saying: "Ask Mike Riley and his people please" but then added, "Congratulations to Liverpool, they scored three, we got one but I'm so proud of my team, few teams can come here and play the way we did. We started incredibly well, we showed incredible bravery, they are the champions of Europe and it is the most difficult stadium in the world. We played like back-to-back champions. We cannot deny how good Liverpool are but the way we played, the personality, it was good."

Klopp called the frenetic game "incredible...really wild". Fabinho's opener met with a muted response but he explained: "The problem was the VAR. I saw the discussions before the first goal and I was just waiting. It is not the same any more but it is no problem. I can celebrate tonight. It was so tough to play, the intensity of the game was so clear. It was all worth it, really great."

Klopp was determined not to let any negative thoughts enter his player's head, with the inevitable 'it's yours to lose' stigma, and hoped this result gave his players the the confidence to go on after the latest international break. 'We don't feel any pressure, to be 100% honest. The things that will now come up – we know about it. If you are with us, then nine points is a positive. There's a long way to go. Other people will 100% say – and have said already – that from now on Liverpool can only lose it. That's a very negative approach, but you can see it like this. But we don't care. I can promise you that we don't care. We were completely focused on this game – not the situation in the table and how many points we are ahead of City in the table. That's crazy. Nine points ahead of City, you cannot imagine that something like this would happen. But it's not important because who wants to be first in November? You want to be first in May. It's only November. We all know that but don't have to say it as it's clear. We will try and see what happens in the end. The pressure or whatever is not there yet. It will come, but, at the moment, it's just opportunity and go for it and do the work, throw all in what you have and let's see what happens. Each point we have we need to go through the most intense period ever."

Klopp was ecstatic with the quality. "The second goal we scored, I don't think I've ever seen a goal like this. A right full-back with a 60-yard pass to the left full-back, two touches and then a cross over 40 or 50 yards and a header. That's pretty special. It was a good moment to score a goal like this. The third goal was very, very good as well. Sensational cross (from Henderson) and Sadio in the right position. All around these three goals it was the hardest work. The boys deserved these three points. Great."

"They're [Liverpool] in great form. I'm not a betting man, but I think it's done," admitted Sky Sports pundit Roy Keane. "It's not supposed to be easy. If it was easy everyone would win league titles. But it's not, it's meant to be tough and demanding, and that's why when you get there it's absolutely fantastic. If you're in the Liverpool dressing room you'll be thinking bring it on. We're talking about them ripping teams to shreds," the former Manchester United captain continued, "they've been doing it for the last two/three years. The way they're playing is fantastic. And on top of everything they've got, they look like a fit team. Energy on top of quality gives you a great chance.'

Jose Mourinho agreed: "From my position I think it's done. Unless something dramatic happens in terms of an injury that breaks the team, but I think the team is a complete puzzle. It's adapted to the quality of the players. What they did tactically to leave Mane and Salah in those positions, the work that Firmino does for them, the puzzle is really, really good. City are capable of winning seven, eight, nine matches in a row, but I don't see how Liverpool can lose their advantage over them."

Phil McNulty, BBC's chief football writer, was sure: "Liverpool's confidence and self-belief has been gathering ominous momentum throughout manager Jürgen Klopp's remarkable rejuvenation, but Sunday's victory over reigning Premier League champions Manchester City may just be the moment when they began to feel unstoppable."

Liverpool legend Phil Thompson was convinced The Reds were on course to break their top-flight drought, "This is one of the best Liverpool teams in the club's history. In my time we always lost three to four games [at this stage of the season], but this team leads by nine points and lost only one game last season. This season they have beaten everyone, except for a draw at Old Trafford. They are doing something great."

Peter Crouch joined Alan Shearer on Match of the Day 2 as he explained what makes Klopp's side so formidable, but why Liverpool fans were not celebrating anything yet. "I got loads of texts from family and friends at the final whistle on Sunday, saying they are absolutely buzzing and that it is a massive, massive win. But, when it comes to the title, all the Liverpool fans I know are trying to keep a lid on their feelings as best they can. I totally understand why. I was up at Anfield for the game near the end of the 2013-14 season when they beat Manchester City 3-2, meaning the title was in their hands with four games to go. The place was buzzing, and everywhere you went in the city it was the same - absolutely electric, with people telling you they were going to win the league. Then came Steven Gerrard's slip against Chelsea in their next home game, and they ended up throwing it away. A lot of people were burned by that and that has left them thinking 'we are not going to make that same mistake again'. That is still true now, even after beating City. I know loads of Liverpool fans and they are all saying the same thing to me - 'it's not over'. None of them are talking about winning the league yet; they are saying there is a long way to go. I think some of them might secretly be thinking differently, but none of them will say it. It will be the same with everyone connected to the club at the moment. It has been 30 years since Liverpool were last champions, which is a long, long time

- they know what has happened in their most recent title bids, and they don't want the same to happen again.

"From the outside looking in, I have to say I cannot see Liverpool losing the three or four games between now and the end of the season that it would probably take for them to be overhauled by City or anyone else. So you have to say that they are huge, huge favourites now. No-one inside Anfield will have been saying that at the final whistle on Sunday, but Liverpool are the best team in the league and I think they proved that against City. There is so much to admire about them, and the way they play. It felt like they were just ruthless against Pep Guardiola's side and every single player is pulling their weight."

A few days later Klopp amused watching reporters running away from Guardiola at a UEFA coaches summit in Switzerland, when they attended the Elite Club Coaches Forum the day after Klopp's Liverpool beat Guardiola's City. Massimiliano Allegri, Carlo Ancelotti, Unai Emery, Rudi Garcia, Maurizio Sarri, Ole Gunnar Solskjaer, Erik ten Hag and Thomas Tuchel attended along with Klopp and Guardiola. Klopp reiterated that they have no problem with each other in a hilarious interview that saw him dashing away from his 'adversary'.

Klopp was asked by a reporter, "Did you speak with Pep?", but didn't understand his question after the journalist mispronounced the Spaniard's first name.

Klopp replied by saying: "Pepe? Who is Pepe?" He laughed and said: "Of course we spoke, why shouldn't we speak?" At that moment he spotted Pep coming round the corner and whispered: "Pep Guardiola is coming!" He jokingly ran off camera much to the amusement of the reporters.

Klopp and Guardiola were in agreement at the summit in Nyon how VAR was not working. Klopp said: "With VAR, handball, offside, it is clear there is a process where we have to keep on improving. There were good ideas from UEFA how we can sort things from the referees, so everybody is in on it. There is still space for mistakes. These things are done by human beings and none of us is perfect. But it is about improving it. Nobody is asking for perfection, you just want to have the right decisions." When asked whether VAR could be made right, Guardiola commented: "I don't know."

★

The aftermath wasn't quite so convivial within the England camp where Raheem Sterling apologised after an unseemly bust-up with Liverpool centre-half Joe Gomez at England's training base. It followed their altercation on the pitch toward the end of the Sunday evening game. Team-mates had to pull them apart in the canteen at St. George's Park. Gareth Southgate dropped Sterling when the Three Lions played their 1,000th game and confessed he thought about sending Sterling home. In fact Sterling was in his car on his way back to Manchester when he got a late reprieve. The players suggested he could stay in the squad if he offered a personal apology. Jordan Henderson also intervened, even though he wasn't in the squad, calling both players suggesting a handshake. Gomez was sporting a large scratch mark under the eye as Sterling issued a public apology: "First and foremost everyone knows what that game means to me. Everyone knows that I am not that way inclined and more to the point. Both Joe and I have had words and figured things out and moved on. We are in a sport where emotions run high and I am man enough to admit when emotions got the better of me. We move this is why we play this sport because of our love for it. Me and Joe are good, we both understand it was a 5-10 second thing, it's done we move forward and not make this bigger than it is. Let's get focus on our game on Thursday."

Elsewhere it emerged that Liverpool "might have considered" signing Zlatan Ibrahimovic in January if he hadn't already played for Manchester United. The Sweded, now 38, came to the end of a two-year spell in Los Angeles after the Swedish forward announced his departure from the Major League Soccer club via social media and Klopp commented "If he had not played for Manchester United before, then we might have considered him but I'm not even sure he wanted to play here. We're a pretty intense team," Klopp laughed. "With that said, I couldn't have had more respect for Zlatan. I love his whole career, love his efforts, love his confidence. While it may not always be right, it is entertaining anyway. He's a fantastic character and I really hope he doesn't stop playing football. The world will miss him too much."

Speaking to LiverpoolFC.com, Klopp confessed even he was surprised by what his team achieved so far: "It's just the start, that's how it is, everybody knows that. If you would have told me that you can have 34 points [at this stage of the season], wow!" To maintain momentum, it was imperative his players did not return injured, as City's big hope was a long line of casualties outside the Liverpool medical room! He observed, "It's pretty much impossible but we did it but now the boys go for the last international break of the year. They have to come back healthy. You saw it how intense it was [against City]. Hopefully they all come back healthy and then we go to Crystal Palace. I think the last games are somewhere on the planet on Tuesday in the week that we play on Saturday against Crystal Palace. So they will fly back on the Wednesday, Thursday have a recovery session and Friday, Saturday 'Hello, Crystal Palace!' That's the situation so nothing happens so far but it's still the best situation we could have asked for so let's hope we can carry on.

Virgil van Dijk said Klopp had urged his players to stay grounded despite their eight point advantage at the top as they bid to continue their unbeaten start against Crystal Palace, "Of course I can sense how much winning the title is spoken about. For our fans, winning the championship has been way too long, so they place the Premier League title now above everything. No competition is more important than this one, but we need to keep the fever outside. Klopp tells us every week, 'Focus on the next match'. We are doing alright, but it is only November. The hardest months of football are still waiting."

Van Dijk had pulled out of the Netherlands squad ahead of their upcoming European Championship qualifier against Estonia. He captained Holland to a 0-0 draw against Northern Ireland as they sealed qualification but he then left the squad due to "personal circumstances". Salah, Robertson, Gomez and Henderson also left their respective international camps.

Klopp hated international breaks because when his players are away representing their countries it 'kills' him as does not know what's going on with their fitness. He specifically mentioned Mane going off for Senegal: "I hate the internationals! From a personal point of view, I just hate it. Sadio Mane played in Swaziland (for Senegal). You know nothing about games like this. He went off straight after half-time and you are thinking 'oh'. These are the situations that kill me, to be honest. It's just not knowing about what is exactly happening, trying to find out what we can do, what we have to do. As soon as Sadio got a phone we could get in contact but he's the player, he's not the guy who organises everything else around it. Dealing with things like this is not cool. That's why the last game before an international break is always difficult for me. The final whistle goes and then I'm thinking 'now they leave'. That's the biggest problem in my working life."

Liverpool were often accused of 'luck' in securing all three points with a stoppage time goal but Klopp knows it's a reflection of the players mentality. Klopp's team had won 10 points from losing positions, the most in the Premier League this season and in total dropped just two points in 12 games. In the last seven games where they conceded the first goal, Liverpool went on to win six and draw the other, making them one of the game's most resilient teams. Klopp is often asked his secret is to grinding out results. Klopp and his players worked on the psychological aspect for years. "Of course it's all about that," Klopp told The Athletic, "but you can't just order it and then assume the boys will deliver it. If it was that easy then you could just tell them in the moment when you are 1-0 down with 10 minutes to play, 'you still have to believe'. You have to create something and what we have created all together started long ago. People now talk about it but I already feel uncomfortable talking about it because I don't take it for granted, not for one second. It's not that I'm thinking five minutes before we go 1-0 down "no problem, you can score". It's happened more often than not that we've come back which is good, very good, but [we are] not allowed to take it for granted. It's just that because it's happened so often, psychologically it's clear. If you do something good then it's absolutely likely that the next time you do it, it's likely that it will work out again."

For Klopp, talent was important, but it's inseparable from mentality. "You can have the best technical ability but if you aren't ready to show it then you can't make the best of it. It's no different in football than it is in normal life. The first step is to think you can do it. You want to do it, you want to achieve it, then you have to find a way to go there. It's constantly like question and answer, question and answer. Right, not right, trial and error. That's how we do it and in football it's no different."

As if to prove his manager's point, Roberto Firmino scored yet another late winner as Liverpool maintained their eight-point lead at the top of with a hard-fought victory over Crystal Palace as Leicester maintained the pressure in second place with an away win at Brighton. Klopp was preparing Salah, already stripped and ready to go on the touchline, to come off the bench just as Firmino scored, the manager then put his star striker back on the bench, and sent on Joe Gomez instead. Salah could only smile as he put his training gear back. Liverpool stretched their incredible run to 30 games unbeaten in the Premier League. Firminio poked in from a corner five minutes from time to restore his side's lead three minutes after it looked as if Zaha had rescued a point for the Eagles. Zaha's 82nd-minute goal was his first of the season and cancelled out Mane's 10th goal of the season just after half-time. Zaha wasted a great chance to score a second equaliser late on when he blazed over from close range. Tomkins had a goal ruled out in first-half stoppage time by the video assistant referee after Ayew was adjudged to have fouled Lovren.

Klopp hailed his teams 'exceptional' start to the season but made it clear they are only interested in winning titles, not breaking records. Should they remain unbeaten against Brighton, they could break their own record during the Merseyside Derby against Everton. "I have no clue about records," Klopp said. "We are not out there to break records but we are really there to get the best result in the full season. If on the way we break one of two records then good but winning the next game is much more important than people saying in 10-15 years that was the record set by this team. We really have a bigger job to do."

Guardiola needed to avoid his side being distracted by Liverpool although he felt one more defeat for City might be the end of their lingering hopes of a third in a row title. After coming from behind to beat Chelsea at home, he said: "Liverpool look unstoppable. I know it's far away with these numbers. My teams always try but we accept other teams can be better. So [if] we are going to lose the Premier League, we are going to try the next season. It's not the first time Manchester City in 100 years of history lose the league. If we don't do it, I'm not going to retire but I'm going to be disappointed.

"In these three years and a half, people can say we play good or bad but give up? That is not going to happen. My teams, always we try but I accept that the others can do better. If we lose, it's done. The line is so tight. I know we are winners and losers and that's all. But I think it's not a good message for society, for our kids, for our teenagers, showing them that just the winner is perfect. We are creating a depressed people, loser people. What is important is the effort, the commitment, the situation. In football I know we want to win but just win once and the other is disaster? It's not. It doesn't work in that way. That's why I said to the players relax, do your job, we will see in December, January, February, March and we will see what position we are in. If the position is far away, okay it's far away. We are going to try again next season."

Guardiola joked about Klopp's "beautiful smile" after giving a speech just after the Liverpool manager at the Football Writers' Association dinner. He enjoyed some friendly banter with the watching Klopp, even suggesting the two clubs swap their trophies, a reference to City pipping Liverpool to the Premier League title, while Klopp got his hands on a trophy Guardiola and City crave – the Champions League.

Klopp insisted other teams run more than his own including Brighton. Known for their relentless pressing under Klopp, the manager pointed out that they do not run as hard as others. "If you look at the numbers we are not the most intense team in the league. Teams run more than us. We are pretty high in the sprints. Brighton run much more overall than we do. It's not always the same, there are games that are very, very intense. We don't feel it in the last two or three years. We have to be 100 per cent for the next opponent. Other teams have difficult situations as well. In this moment we want to play the best football we can and usually that's a pretty good one. And we have to against Brighton, because they are brave and organised. It took a while until Leicester scored a goal. In all the games they were there. That's our job not to think about intensity.'

Liverpool had kept just two clean sheets despite winning 12 out of their 13 league games. They had not kept a clean sheet at home but only Leicester (eight) conceded more than the Reds (11) in the league. Brighton manager Graham Potter was confident his players will embrace the challenge at Anfield. Potter's young side had already upset Tottenham and Everton this season. 'We'll have to embrace the challenge and everything it brings. Teams like Barcelona will go there and they'll tell you that it's a big atmosphere. The supporters get properly behind the team - there's a real history and tradition to it which makes it a special place. The environment can be really powerful, but that's one of the big challenges for us to rise to. It's all part of what we have to do to get a result. You have to deal with everything that surrounds the game as well as what happens out on the field. We have to play well and hope they have an off day - but we can influence that and we certainly have to be better than we have been in the last couple of weeks. I have no idea who'll win the league and it's hard to say in November who'll do what, but clearly they've been fantastic up until this point of the season. Their points record over the last few years has been amazing - to maintain that and fight for the Champions League is incredible from them. I think whoever wants to win the league will have to get themselves above Liverpool.'

Guardiola conceded City could not afford to lose many more games as they headed to Newcastle having lost three matches already this term. 'I know we cannot lose games. I'm not thinking about winning the Premier League right now. The target is the next one when you have games every three days.'

But as Liverpool embarked on 11 games in 34 days, including two games on two different continents in 24 hours, Klopp had to manage without Fabinho and Matip as he reckons the biggest football culture shock when he first arrived in England was the madness of a Premier League December. Shaking his head still in disbelief at an impossible fixture list, Klopp recalled a conversation with Gareth Southgate. "I was in Manchester and I was next to Gareth Southgate and he told me in 1993 they played on the 26th and 27th. That is not 50 years ago! So, obviously you (England) have always liked these funny schedules. In the beginning, it was surprisingly intense. It is not easy, but as long as someone decides we have to do it, we do it. You need a bit of luck with injuries - that is very important - and I have a lot of decisions about who is ready and not."

Klopp thought that it might be January that determined whether his team can break the club's 30 year hoodoo, and finally lift the league title again, rather than December. "The worst December since I arrived? Yeah, always a tough period. We have had wonderful Decembers, but very average Januarys! So it is about going through that and getting as many points as you can. That is it. It is for all of us. It would be hard if we are the only team with that kind of schedule, but it is all OK. We cannot change it, so we don't think too much about it."

For all the ground-breaking data and science, the boss revealed that gut instinct had always played a big part in his team selections as well as all the information as his disposal. "It starts with my pure thoughts and then I get all the information on top of that. So many factors decide on who we will use and rotate, that we don't have enough time to talk about it to be honest! It is the opponent, it is the system, the tactics and it all comes together. The data, medical? Oh yeah, of course, that is the information around that and talks with the boys, too. They say one thing and look like the other, 'I'm ready...' but then we have to see. I have no clue if we are more advanced in sports science, because I don't know how the other clubs are. I hope we are not behind. It is important."

In the Saturday midday game Newcastle came from behind twice to snatch a 2-2 draw as City dropped more points. Klopp could equal the club record of 31 games unbeaten, set by Kenny Dalglish from May 1987 to March 1988 but he was more interested in stretching his lead over Guardiola to 11 points. Wijnaldum was making his 200th game for an English club, Gomez his 50th in a Liverpool shirt, and Klopp's team made no mistake romping into a two goal lead thanks to Virgil van Dijk enabling the manager to bring off Mo Salah, still recovering fully from his ankle issue, needing game time to regain his rhythm at the same time needing a break, a difficult balancing act for Klopp who brought Lallana in his place. A little later he also took off Firmino to send on Origi. Then, a red card for Alisson! From a long ball and with the keeper outside his area, probably intending to head clear, Trossard got the better of Lovren as Alisson jumped up and palmed away the lob – it was a straight red, the first Liverpool goalkeeper sent off in a Premier League game since another Brazilian Doni against Blackburn in April 2012. Alex Oxlande-Chamberlain was sacrificed to send on reserve keeper Adrian, who immediately conceded from the resulting free-kick. Quick thinking Dunk takes it early, as Liverpool's players are still organising the wall. Adrian stands and watches at one post as the low strike goes unchallenged into his bottom right corner. From cruising to victory, Liverpool now faced 10 nervous minutes with 10-men and a one goal lead.

Brighton continued to press as Mooy nodded into the path of Burn but he smashed it wide from a tight angle inside the box then Lovren jogged over to do up Adrian's shoelaces! The defence needed to pull their socks up as well! All I want for Christmas is a clean sheet, one fan tweeted. But he should have been grateful as Adrian pulled off a decent save to his left as Mooy was left in space in the box. And what a let off as Adrian gave every Liverpool fan at Anfield a heart attack as he spilled a routine save following a header from Gross in the box, Maupay was alert, ready to pounce on the rebound, but Adrian recovered just in time as it headed backwards toward the line; a fumble from a keeper who didn't look as though he had warmed up properly!

The crowd whipped up a rendition of "Allez, allez, allez" to rally their players, clinging on with four minutes of stoppage time as Brighton threw everything into trying for a last gasp equaliser. The fans held their breath when the board went up with 4-minutes left. Klopp on the edge of his technical area, looking at his watch, and looking as nervous as any supporter as Liverpool saw it out, the final whistle greeted as if they had won the league, and they nearly had - 11 points advantage. The players celebrated with their fans who were singing deliriously. Klopp and Robertson were the last to head down the tunnel.

Klopp felt it was "unnecessary" for the game to come to an edgy conclusion. "It was unnecessary, of course, because we had unbelievable chances. Their keeper made some good saves. It was difficult this game because Brighton are a good football side. They put players between the lines. They put so many players there so it's difficult to defend. They had a lot of possession and we had to work really hard. I loved that the boys were prepared to do that after a busy week. We then had the red card for Alisson. Adrian comes in with cold feet and cold hands but made two really good saves. I think it was handball but I haven't seen it. There was no offside and then it is a tricky situation. He wanted 100% to head the ball but the other player got there earlier so we can't change that.

"Of course, life became more complicated with the red card and the change we had to make. We brought on a frozen goalkeeper, pretty much. Everybody sitting here is probably not really warm yet, and then you imagine you go on in shorts, a really thin shirt and some gloves which are not made for keeping you warm, and then, some people let the free-kick happen. You look a little bit silly in that moment, but that's what you have to accept. We kept on fighting and Adrian, especially, helped us a lot with two really, really good saves and crosses he caught... although with his cold feet he obviously couldn't [kick] the ball as far as he wanted. That kept it a bit interesting, but in the end it's only important that we won the game and that's what we did, and I'm really pleased about that. I'm very, very happy with the effort the boys put in again. I'm really happy and proud of the desire the boys showed. The red card made it a really special win, to be honest."

Klopp added: "Virgil was probably man of the match with the two goals but Adrian is for me - to come in to a game like this and make two saves." The manager was quick to point out that Lovren played well as well at the back. When asked again by his two goal hero, he said: "Oh come on, do we have to talk about individual players? He scored two goals, that's the story itself. He's good, really good, outstandingly good. But he has to be, he's a very talented boy, so he just has to use that talent and it would be a shame if he doesn't. So yes, incredibly important but if Virg plays the last line alone it would be pretty difficult. I think Dejan Lovren, who maybe doesn't have the headlines like this, but what he's playing since, he has all my respect, to be honest."

There was still no clean sheet, though. And Klopp was far from happy with the referee allowing the free kick to be take as his players were still in the process of organising the wall. "I think in a situation like this, when you have sense for human beings, you don't do it like this. It was very clever from Brighton but the keeper has just come on and is trying to set the wall. They are trying to get used to each other and the referee lets it go like this. We cannot change it but for me it's not 100% right."

With City dropping points and Chelsea also losing at the Bridge to West Ham, their first win there since 2001, it left only Leicester challenging Liverpool! The Premier League table even before December took on an incredible appearance. Not for Klopp though, any time to reflect. "It's how it is. But if Leicester win tomorrow we are eight points ahead. We don't think about these things. It was just to win this game - not that I don't think Everton can win there. We have one more day between now and the next game so we have to use that and then we try again. Results-wise, it's an incredible period, for sure. But we don't want to think about the last 14 games. We are concerned about the next one, that's next Wednesday against Everton, so that's a big one. We have to make sure that we are prepared for that because that will be another big fight, whatever result Everton get tomorrow.'

10: A PERFECT CHRISTMAS

LIVERPOOL WENT INTO THEIR FIXTURE challenge with the biggest lead at this stage in Premier League history with a record-equalling opening to a season, but Jürgen Klopp demanded total focus and continued mental strength.

Alex Oxlade-Chamberlain had never played in a team which believed it can win every game. "I'm going into it (a game) with the mindset that we're going to win. I think that's how we all feel. We're going into the games expecting to win and anything else we're disappointed with. I think that's credit to the good work that we've done as a team over the last few years to be in that position. There's times in my career where I definitely haven't gone into all games 100 per cent confident that the team's going to come away winning but with this team, I have that sort of belief in us. I think that's the mentality you need to be successful, to have those high standards that nothing else is acceptable. Then you've got to let history take its course. Obviously it might not happen every time but when you're going into games with that sort of mindset and belief it simplifies everything else."

Pundits had already declared the 11 point gap at the top as unbridgeable but the former Arsenal man didn't agree, "I don't live under a rock so I hear what people say and the predictions that people make. You can't not take notice of other results that are going on around you and the table from time-to-time. When Man City were out in front for a while a couple of seasons ago they would've had all of these sort of things to come up against. You've got to just keep going out and churning out results. There might be a time where results don't go so well and people maybe close the gap a little bit. We've got to be also ready for those moments mentally as a team to just keep going and see what happens."

The Ox explained how Jürgen Klopp looked to experienced leaders in the dressing room to maintain a desire to look no further than the next game, the derby with Everton, "The manager insists that the leaders in our team, Jordan Henderson, Milly, Adam Lallana and Virgil van Dijk, demand the most from all of us, themselves first and foremost. It's the sort of expectations that we have on each other and that's the mentality you need to be successful. Then you've got to let history take its course."

Klopp thought Everton had a "really good" squad but did not know "why it's not clicking so far". Klopp felt for under-fire Everton boss Marco Silva, "Of course I have sympathy because I know how difficult the life of a manager can be. But the last thing Marco needs now is that I feel sorry for him – I don't. But I am really on his side because I know about the job. The table tells the truth at the end of the season, but if you go through the Everton squad, nobody denies that it's a really good one. They've had difficult injuries, especially the Andre Gomes one. Fabian Delph, too, is a very important player for them. There is a lot of pressure, of course, as Everton are an ambitious club and rightly so. They are not the only ones in this situation, this league is really difficult for everyone.

"Are managers given enough time? For me, yes. Generally, I don't know, I can only speak about me, I have never felt in doubt. And in my job or others, there is pressure to deliver. If it doesn't work out then they try something else. In general, the pressure and the decisions are made too quickly, of course. It happens because people think they cannot reach targets anymore."

Klopp, who has won five and drawn three of his eight derbies in charge, believed a win at Anfield could be the 'silver bullet' Everton were hoping for. "Remember we don't have to speak about quality and quality differences. Are we in a better moment in the table? Of course, that is obvious. But the stats, from my point of view, help Everton more than us because they want to strike back. They want do show they can do differently. They can solve a lot of problems in one game. It is a very important football game for us but that must be enough for us. We expect Everton at their best. It is a standout game for both teams. We have to make sure we are ready.

"For both teams it is a hugely important game. My first (Merseyside) derby we won 4-0 but I think they had a red card in that game but most of the time since I have been here the derbies have been tight results. We know we have to work extremely hard because all I saw against Leicester was them making life really difficult. That's what we expect. In the first few derbies there were some harsh challenges. Hard tackles are normal in football, but they were kind of over-forceful. That didn't happen in the last two or three games and as long as we can keep it on this level, everything is fine. Fight for it with everything you have in a football way."

And what about drawing the Toffees in the third round of the FA Cup? "I didn't run through my living room celebrating!" Klopp joked.

"I think for both it is not exactly what you look for, playing Everton is a big game, no problem. It's a tough game for our first round and for Everton."

Last year's fixture at Anfield was memorable with Origi scoring a winner in an added-time after Pickford's catastrophic error, prompting Klopp to run 50 yards onto the pitch to celebrate with goalkeeper Alisson. Klopp was fined £8,000, so had no intention of repeating it. "In this game Joe Gomez saved off the line. Everton were good that night, it was an intense game and there were a few winning moments before finally there was a strange goal and my celebration, which I said sorry for," Klopp recalled. "It will not happen again – not even in a derby – but in that moment it was a pretty cool moment. That was a year ago so it has nothing to do with tomorrow night and we have to be focused on the important parts of the game – and they are on the pitch."

Without Alisson the defensive organisation again fell on the shoulders ofVan Dijk, and following City's comfortable 4-1 at Burnley that cut the lead to eight points, the same as Leicester, it was all the more important to win the derby, and the media seemed to focus now on the strikers, rather on the lack of clean sheets, no doubt bored by that repetitive line of questioning.

Klopp was unconcerned that Jamie Vardy was setting the scoring charts alight rather than his own strikers, who had the monopoly last season. Klopp felt Vardy's electric form was due to the 32-year-old retiring from international football and not currently being involved in the Champions League. "I'm not concerned, not at all. You guys (journalists) always confront me with these kind of things and I'm like 'wow, really?' I don't count goals, I don't look at these numbers. Jamie Vardy is an exceptional striker, but he has Tuesdays and Wednesdays off and is sitting on the couch watching international football so you cannot compare this. It's a big, big plus for Leicester with the quality they have and all the rest. Yes, we have to score goals. I was completely fine with scoring two after set-pieces in the last game with Virg. We could have scored much more in the early part of the game when we played some unbelievable football. We couldn't keep that throughout the game, but still had big changes - the one with Alex Oxlade-Chamberlain for example. I start being concerned when we don't create chances anymore, so that's the moment where you really have to think. We know we could have played better in some games, but we cannot usually - the derby is different - isolate games. We have to think 'OK, it's because of...'

and it is good that we didn't do more and kill ourselves in the game that we can't walk, when we have the next game to play. So we have to be smart as well."

Leicester and City had better goal differences by four and six respectively - although Guardiola's men had played a game more. "Both teams City and Leicester have had these big scorelines (City 8-0 Watford and Southampton 0-9 Leicester) and they are only (a few) goals ahead of us. It's not that it is a massive difference. Our goal difference is good and I'm really fine with it. The most important thing is we win the games, who scores - I don't care."

Speculation was rife that Klopp was now favourite to sign Borussia Dortmund's Jadon Sancho, also a target for Manchester United and Real Madrid. Klopp refused to be drawn on January transfer speculation. "It's not important, for us it's always the same. We don't speak about it. We are pretty much always ready but the January window is maybe more difficult than the other window. But the summer window only hurts English clubs, not help them, because of the different moments it closes in Europe."

During the week Lionel Messi won a record sixth Ballon d'Or, while Virgil Van Dijk was second, a mere seven votes behind. Klopp said: "I see it slightly different and a lot of people see it slightly different but that's absolutely no problem. I have seen Lionel Messi so many times, probably 500 times in my life already, and he is the best player I've seen in my lifetime. But I can't remember a more impressive season by a defender ever. Honestly. So, it would have been right if Virgil had won it and I heard it was pretty close."

It was a proud night for Liverpool and their manager with three players in the top five and seven nominated overall. A review of how the votes fell show that Alexander-Arnold established a fan base in Sri Lanka, as they chose him as the best player in the world; he ranked19th, two places behind Salah and Mane's attacking partner, Firmino. Wijnaldum came 26th, Alisson seventh. The nation of Bhutan voted only for Liverpool players - Mane, Van Dijk, Salah, Alisson and Firmino.

Van Dijk was magnanimous, paying tribute to Messi, "To be absolutely honest I never thought that I would be up for a Ballon d'Or until I was actually nominated," said the Dutchman at the ceremony in Paris, "It says a lot about how my career has been, it's never been easy. My career has been different than let's say the winner here, I came late but I never gave up on my dream so I had to work very hard for every step of the way.

Unfortunately there are a couple of players like him who are unnatural, I think they are fantastic. Look, six times the Ballon d'Or, we need to respect greatness as well. I was close but there was just someone a little bit better. I'm very proud of what I achieved last year with Liverpool and with Holland and hopefully we can do that again this year, but you know it's going to be tough as long as these guys are around.'

Klopp's team selection caused quite a stir, leaving out Salah, Firmino, Henderson and Oxlade-Chamberlain. Five changes in all. The big surprises were Shaqiri, Lallana and Origi. Alisson was suspended following his dismissal against Brighton so in came Adrian, Fabinho was injured so Milner was called up. Xherdan Shaqiri had managed just 11 minutes in the Premier League this season.

While Everton were delighted not see see Sala and Firmino, they would have been apprehensive at the sight of Origi, who scored a freakish 96th minute winner to give Liverpool victory in last season's derby at Anfield. Everton hadn't won a league game against Liverpool at Anfield since September 1999, courtesy of Kevin Campbell's strike. The Toffees had drawn nine and lost ten of their visits since. They hadn't won a Merseyside derby anywhere in their past 19 attempts when David Moyes' Everton beat Roy Hodgson's Reds 2-0 in October 2010. Klopp explained his reasoning just before kick off, knowing his team had eight games in December: "We can do it. I have to show the respect for the boys. I like the squad so we have to use it. That's the line-up for the day because we think it will be really intense so for this we need fresh legs. With the first whistle, it's a derby. It's an important game for both sides. In games like this you just try to fight as hard as you can and get the three points. That's what we will try. Thank god we are not into these kind of stats. I don't feel a little bit about the last game or the game before. I don't even know about my record against Everton. It's a very difficult game that's all I need to know. We are not thinking about the situation of the opponent. We need to show character. You know about the importance of a game like this but there are different ways to show it. It's to show that you are ready to give your all."

Klopp had a word of praise for Everton supporters: "I don't believe too much in coincidences. One of my first moments when I met Everton was at the Hillsborough memorial and the respect they showed. I appreciated it a lot. In difficult situations the people of this city stand together. That's a part where we are 100% united."

All three of the players Klopp selected out of the blue were magnificent and some of the goals were world class as Liverpool were majestic racking up a 4-2 half time lead and eventually running out 5-2 winners, as records were sent tumbling. On recording a 32-game unbeaten record, Klopp said: "I would love that this number is in one season. That would be great! Last season we were nearly 38 games unbeaten but it was not enough. Nice number but not really interested in it."

Klopp had won 100 of his 159 Premier League games, he was the second fastest manager to reach 100 wins in the competition, after Jose Mourinho (142 games) and would become the third fastest after Pep Guardiola recorded his 100th win in 134 games before the end of the calendar year. Jürgen Klopp was the fastest ever Liverpool manager to reach 100 wins, but he was more interested in going for the next win to maintain the title push: "I can't remember one game in the 100 [of his PL wins] where we shouldn't have won it. It feels like we have to win each and every game. All the wins are necessary. It's a good start, that's it - maybe a perfect start. We sleep twice, maybe three times then we play Bournemouth. They are in the moment and will go with all they have so we have to recover and go again. It is just a number, 43, but three is the next number when we play against Bournemouth. They are not happy with their situation (having lost four in row). They want to strike back so we have to be ready for that. That is the only thing I am really thinking about. Stats are cool after the season, but in it, I'm not interested.'

As for the quality of some of Liverpool's football, it was of immense pleasure for a manager who had been grinding out results at times, but this time it was of the highest quality: "All the goals were incredible, outstanding. Wonderful goals, sensational passes, super pieces of football. I loved it a lot. We needed fresh legs and I had to show my respect to the boys in the squad, that's all. They proved it. It is much more fun making changes, all of the boys are ready to deliver performances like this. It was a massive moment in my first season when Divock Origi got injured in the derby. It changed his career for a bit."

Sadio Mane was man-of-the-match creating two goals with sublime passes, and scoring himself, although he might well have managed a hat-trick but had to be content with just the one. Mane was the only one of the famed front three to start and added a fourth as the first half finished 4-2 after Keane and Richarlison kept Everton in it with two goals. Wijnaldum applied the finishing touch in the 90th minute as Everton's winless run at Anfield extended beyond 20 years and left Marco Silva's job hanging by a thread, he would be sacked before their weekend fixture against Chelsea. Mo Salah was able to have the night off, Firmino and captain Jordan Henderson were introduced as late subs.

Klopp was delighted with Shaqiri's comeback. "He scored one goal, and it was exactly the same as with Divock. He looked completely fresh, physically strong. It's important players train after they are injured. He had twice this calf thing this season. He is back in training a couple of weeks, completely normal, understood the situation in the squad. When you win a lot of games you don't make 20 changes but this period you need all the boys. I hope they will be in the shape of Shaq or Divock or Adam [Lallana] tonight. It gives us the feeling we can do it more often, and we will do it more often. Incredible performance, his set-pieces were outstanding. There is more to follow."

Shaqiri emphasised that the manager ensures that the players are "grounded", and irrespective of how boring it might sound the manager insisted "we take it game by game and that's the most important thing". The emphasis is "we don't need to think about winning titles". But he added: "My biggest dream is to win the title with this club and give it to the fans. So we will try everything. We have to focus on the pitch, stay grounded and work hard every day. If we win, it will be amazing but we still have a long way to go."

Leicester beat Watford to return to three points ahead of City, making the imminent clash with Liverpool all the more intriguing

★

Bournemouth would be without Liverpool loanee Harry Wilson for the game on the south coast the following Saturday and the manager said. "I'm happy Harry can't play against us. His free-kicks are a proper threat. There has never been any doubt about his shooting, but Harry is at Bournemouth to improve the rest of his game."

There was a suspicion in some quarters Klopp's changes to his front three, by resting Salah and Firmino was a subtle message that nobody's place is sacred. However, Mane was the go to striker as Klopp believed he was challenging Messi for the next Ballon d'Or. The Senegalese striker had won Messi's vote in FIFA's Best awards, finishing fourth in the Ballon d'Or stakes behind Van Dijk and Ronaldo. "The first three in the Ballon d'Or was Messi, Van Dijk, Cristiano and then Sadio. That's a nice row. Having two players there shows a lot. Mo was fifth and Alisson was seventh. We obviously played a good season and they had to respect that. Sadio is in incredible shape. Since the first day he came in he has been an incredibly important player. I can still remember his first goal, the Arsenal goal: running down the line, cutting inside and with the next step left-foot into the far corner. An incredible goal. And each year he made big steps and is in a good way. For an offensive player when Messi says something like this... Sadio, especially against Barcelona at home, was very impressive, it was like we had three of him on the pitch. If he stays healthy he will have an incredible career in front of him and I think he can climb in that Ballon d'Or table. But then some other people make decisions - not even Lionel Messi can decide that."

Mane, top scorer with 13, was sensational against Everton, and a win at struggling Bournemouth guaranteed top billing at Christmas. The Reds had been top on December 25 three times previously but remained the only club never to have gone on and win the Premier League from that position. "I've told you often enough I am really not interested in these numbers and this history but that is part of the deal when you are in a good position. There are a lot of people who celebrate already, a lot of people who worry still and a lot of people who hope that you will still fail. I don't listen to any of them. What that means for Christmas I never thought about. We need to be lucky that players stay fit and healthy. These are all things which worry us much more than who will be first at Christmas and what it means."

Then, as if to buck the trend, one minute Mane is top dog, the next he's benched! Klopp continued to rotate his squad, making seven changes from the Merseyside derby. Alexander-Arnold was rested, while the forward line was benched as Firmino and Salah returned up front. Alisson returned from suspension, while Keita, Gomez, Henderson and Oxlade-Chamberlain started.

Liverpool retained their 11 points lead at the top with a comfortable 3-0 win at the Vitality Stadium. Oxlade-Chamberlain opened the scoring after a brilliant long-range pass from Henderson. Keita made it 2-0 before the break, slotting in with the outside of his foot after Salah set him up with a sublime back-heel. Keita then turned provider for Salah to extend the club record unbeaten run to 33 league games, winning 15 of 16 Premier League matches this season, as Klopp's team developed an air of invincibility.

Salah scored his 63rd goal in his 100th Premier League appearance - only Alan Shearer (79), Ruud van Nistelrooy (68) and Sergio Aguero (64) scored more in their first 100 games in the competition. Salah scored more Premier League goals against Bournemouth (seven) than any other opponent, and has netted in all five of his appearances against the Cherries.

Even more pleasing for Klopp was their first clean sheet in 14 games and new Premier League goalscorers in Oxlade-Chamberlain and Keita - the 15th and 16th players to score in the competition for Liverpool this season. Oxlade-Chamberlain scored his first goal in 25 Premier League appearances for Liverpool. He last netted in the competition against Manchester City in January 2018, one year and 327 days ago.

Mane was an unused substitute alongside Origi. Klopp observed: "People were shouting for Divock and I understand that, but to bring him on to say 'thank you', we just have so many games. It was wonderful we didn't have to use Sadio Mane, but he's been playing all the time in the last couple of weeks. Ask the players if they are upset, but it's not difficult for me. I don't speak to Sadio, I didn't speak to Divock. I didn't speak to Hendo. I don't ask, I just have to make decisions and then next time everyone knows someone else will play. The boys are a really smart group who look at the schedule. They know how it is. If someone is angry or concerned that they are not starting, I can't help that. Next time everybody knows somebody else will play and then it's the next game and the next game so that's what happens now. Today we had 14 adult players plus Curtis and Harvey. That's our squad for today. The only players who are maybe back for Tuesday are Gini Wijnaldum and Adam Lallana to make it 16. We'll see how we start on Tuesday, I have no idea about that now. But we could give these two, plus Gini (Wijnaldum) and Adam (Lallana), so four players kind of a rest and hopefully they are all fit again for Tuesday and we will make decisions'

Speaking at his post-match press conference, Klopp was interrupted as one of the phones in front of him recording his responses began to buzz. Queue hilarity as he removed his famous spectacles to look at the phone and was amused by the name, Princess Leslie Lou that had flashed up on the screen. Klopp made light of it, "I like it, sorry, never heard for the name before, congratulations My Lord!" He had a laugh, along with the gathered media, before handing over the phone. He was in an extra good mood by the way his side had just secured a 3-0 win over Bournemouth.

Klopp never doubted Keita, who cost £52.75m from RB Leipzig in the summer of 2018, but had managed only 17 Premier League starts since. "I ask myself why he is not playing week in, week out; when the team is in really good shape, so do you change? Naby had injuries, we had two really good seasons, the team is in really good shape, so then do you change? If something is really working you ask whether you can squeeze five per cent more out of them with another player, but the players who were playing were playing really well. It was just unlucky and in life you always need luck."

This was Keita's first Premier League start of the season and he marked it by scoring the second goal, before setting up Salah for the third. "We are not flying, it's not like we won all of the games 4-0, or 5-0, so we had to bring on a player who helps us with defending set-pieces. Then Naby is sitting outside thinking, 'why don't I play?' I get all that. So we stayed in contact, we talked and we spoke a lot about it. But in the end of course a player needs to have this evidence that the manager still believes in you. I was never in doubt about that."

Klopp enthused about the performance: "It was a mature and professional performance - controlled, scoring wonderful goals. It was a super performance. It was what we needed. We didn't want to make it exciting again, so we wanted to control Bournemouth, absolutely, so nothing really happens any more. The players didn't like it too much, but I didn't want to see any unnecessary risks. We've hd so many games where we've had to chase to the last second because we were 1-0 down or it was 1-1. Then you have this really rare comfortable situation. The most used word in the dressing room at the moment from the boys when I came in afterwards were 'clean sheet, clean sheet, clean sheet, '...finally! Everybody was desperate for that. Now we have it, let's have it more often. [The injury to defender] Dejan Lovren was hopefully cramp but apart from that it was a perfect game. All round, nearly perfect day."

Liverpool were confirmed as the Christmas No1, and Klopp was asked if he was going to be Scrooge like in giving nothing away as he pragmatically shut up shop when 3-0 up, but he joked: "Christmas is after Qatar. I'm sorry but I can't think that far ahead."

The day got better as the evening wore on as United won the Manchester derby at the Etihad to leave the Citizens 14 points adrift of Liverpool. Guardiola admitted that it was "not realistic" to think of catching Liverpool after a performance that further underlined his team's fall from dominance. "It is not time to think about that, we have to try to continue. There are many things to play for." City would need to win all their remaining 22 games to reach the 98-point mark that secured them title last season, and rely on a significant dip in form from Klopp's side. "We think about what we have to do and the next game - it is not realistic to think about catching up. Obviously it is so difficult because the opponents have had 16 games with 15 victories and they are on an incredible run and sometimes we have dropped points. But our duty, and what you have to do, is continue."

Leicester picked up a record-breaking eighth straight top-flight win with an impressive 4-1 at Villa Park but the lack of acknowledgement from pundits that his side were in the title race didn't annoy manager Brendan Rodgers, as he was quietly going about the business chasing down his old club. "You saw the game yesterday after Manchester United won at Manchester City, the caption comes up about how far Manchester City are away from Liverpool. For us, we respect that, we just get on with our work and try to improve our performance level, just keep developing as a team. I don't think anyone expects us to be anyway near the top. We'll take it game by game and look to improve in our training and see where it takes us. It's just natural, Man City and Liverpool are both incredible teams in the league and showed last year how good they were. For us we know we're constantly looking to improve and close the gap."

Rafa Benitez believed his former club would finally end their 30-year wait for the title. He is one of four Liverpool managers in the Premier League era to lead them to a second-placed finish, back in 2009. "They are very consistent so normally you win games and lose some games but it is very difficult for them to lose games. I think they have been signing the right players the last years but spending in the right positions and they have a good balance. It is not just they have good defenders, but they have the balance, the keeper, the defenders, the full-backs, the strikers have the ability and the midfielders have the balance. It is very difficult to counter-attack or create something. We tried with Newcastle United but we couldn't go behind them, they were faster than our players."

THE PERFECT CHRISTMAS GIFT

Jürgen Klopp's future was settled as Liverpool fans received the perfect Christmas gift, as he signed a new deal to run until 2024. Having joined the Reds in October 2015, he signed a new six-year contract in July 2016 and that was extended. Klopp once said he could never be Liverpool's Sir Alex Ferguson or Arsenal's Arsene Wenger believing that such longevity for managers at one club was no longer feasible. However, he would be the new Bob Paisley, with his new contract making him the club's longest-serving manager since the three-time European Cup winner retired in 1983. If he fulfilled the two-year extension he would become the joint-fourth longest-serving boss in the club's history. "This club is in such a good place, I couldn't contemplate leaving. For me personally this is a statement of intent, one which is built on my knowledge of what we as a partnership have achieved so far and what is still there for us to achieve. When I see the development of the club and the collaborative work that continues to take place, I feel my contribution can only grow. People see what happens on the pitch as a measure of our progress and although it is the best measure, it's not the only measure. I have seen the commitment from ownership through to every aspect and function of the club you can think of.

"I must also highlight the role of our sporting director, Michael Edwards, in this journey so far. His input and collaboration has been just as important as anyone else's in getting us into a position to compete for the game's top titles. For anyone in football who aspires to compete in an environment where every element of the organisation is at its very best – from the support of the supporters to the vision of the owners – there can be no better place than this. When the call came in autumn 2015, I felt we were perfect for each other; if anything, now I feel I underestimated that. It is only with a total belief that the collaboration remains totally complementary on both sides that I am able to make this commitment to 2024. If I didn't, I would not be re-signing."

Assistant managers Peter Krawietz and Pepijn Lijnders also agreed new deals. Klopp praised the pair: "It was so important to me that my staff also agreed these new deals with the club. Without them being prepared to make the same commitment, quite frankly I would not have been able to do this. I am blessed to be surrounded by so many amazing staff; honestly, I feel the luckiest manager in the world in this regard. Peter and Pep have contributed just as much as I have to the development of this team and although as the manager, many may see me as the face of the club, their input and expertise is invaluable to what we're looking to achieve. I have worked with Pete for many years now, going back to my time at Mainz and Dortmund. And even now I am still amazed at the things he spots during a game. He has an incredible talent and one that is priceless for us. It has been one of the best professional experiences for me to see him grow and become the coach he now is. He's always been essential to me, but his own personal development since arriving at Liverpool has been outstanding. He is so smart, so insightful and so important to us.

"Pep, what can I say? What this guy doesn't know about football isn't worth knowing! I have never met a guy more passionate and dedicated about the game. I only got to know him when I first arrived at Liverpool, but I instantly fell in love with his infectious commitment and knowledge of the game. He left for a period and came back – but he came back in a more senior capacity and he's flourished since. He is every inch a top manager of the future, but in the meantime, I am thankful we have him with us. But going beyond Pete and Pep, these new deals are a mark of not only our collective belief in our project, but also a sign of our development so far. We always say it is a collective effort at Melwood; it's not just about me, the players or my coaching team, everybody who works here contributes in their own way to what happens on the field and how we have progressed as a club – that's why we have everybody's names on a wall in a corridor here. We all share the same vision and we all share the same belief in the way Liverpool FC continues to move forward. And that's why today is such an exciting day for myself, Pete and Pep and why I am delighted they will be alongside me for the journey still to come. Both view this decision to extend exactly as I do: a fantastic opportunity to do what we all love at the best place in the world we could do it."

Principal owner John Henry, chairman Tom Werner and FSG president Mike Gordon issued a joint statement, "We are absolutely delighted we have been able to reach an agreement with Jürgen – as well as Peter and Pep – on extending their time with the club. As we are sure our supporters would agree, it is truly wonderful news and we are all extremely thrilled, not only professionally, but personally too. We feel this represents one of the big moments of our stewardship of Liverpool Football Club so far as we believe there is no better manager than Jürgen. The decision also keeps with the club's overall strategy of building from a position of strength. It means Jürgen will oversee the ongoing transition from Melwood to the new Kirkby training base as the club continues to pursue a vision of being elite in all facets of the industry. It also provides us with continuity with the existing football operations management structure, overseen by sporting director Michael Edwards, whose input into the project cannot be overestimated. He has been – and will continue to be – as indispensably important as anyone else to the direction of Liverpool Football Club. In Jürgen and Michael we are blessed with world-class leadership. This is a collective partnership that has seen the club reach and then re-establish itself as an elite performer at home and abroad.

"Back in 2015 we used the phrase 'ideal fit' when we appointed Jürgen. This continues to apply today and, if anything, the circumstances make it more pertinent. We consider him to be the best there is. If Liverpool Football Club were looking to appoint the most outstanding, elite manager for our current status today, Jürgen would be the first choice – no question. We believe this deal cements a relationship built on trust and mutual benefit: Jürgen has delivered for LFC and LFC has delivered for Jürgen. Both parties have come to the conclusion that by continuing to work together and build on the work of the last four years, the opportunity exists to maximise each other's potential."

Was it sheer coincidence or perfect timing that news of Klopp extending to 2024 came within a few hours of Rangers confirming that former Liverpool captain Steven Gerrard extended his contract as Gers boss...until 2024.

Jose Mourinho, now Spurs manager, commented: "It is great news for the Liverpool fans because they love him, for the players, because it looks clear that they like each other and the relation is very good. It is also good news for the Premier League because we want to have the best players and coaches and he is one of the best. It is positive news for everyone. I think it means that they are all happy. Jürgen is happy because if he's not he doesn't sign. And they are happy because if they are not happy they don't give him a new contract.'

Frank Lampard said, "Liverpool are a huge rival. What Jürgen has built has been incredible. Congratulations on the contract, it is fully deserved. We have so many great managers in the Premier League. I love going up against the top managers so I'm pleased, not disappointed. It is a challenge for us to bridge that gap."

By the way Klopp also won Manager of the Month, so not bad for a Friday the 13th before Christmas. The announcement was a massive relief to Liverpool fans as Klopp had cast doubt on his future at Anfield when owners Fenway Sports Group were keen to tie him down to yet another extended long term deal after winning the Champions League. Klopp created a new golden age in Europe, but ahead of their opening Champions League defence in Napoli there was a reminder from his representative, Marc Kosike, there was no rush to commit his future beyond his current contract that expired in 2022. "It is an open secret that the club would like to extend so we still have a little time for that," said Kosike, who joked if climate change in Britain improved weather conditions it might help. Ulla [Klopp's wife] and Jürgen get up in the morning and it's dark. When they meet again in the evening, it is also dark and there is drizzle. During the winter break in Germany, if the weather is really bad, the clubs go on vacation for two weeks, then come back and fly directly to the training camp in the sun for several days. During this time, coaches in England are already exhausted." Asked about his agent's remarks in the pre-match press conference, Klopp said it was a gag that misfired. "It was German humour and nobody got it," said Klopp. "The weather is never a reason for me to pick a city. There is nothing in that story. Nobody got his joke. That is how it is." Klopp also told German sports magazine Kicker that he had no idea what the future held for him in a few years time, and if then he decided to take a break, he would, and return refreshed.

Meanwhile, Pep Guardiola announced it was "not true" he has a contract clause allowing him to leave Manchester City in the summer. "No. It is not true. I spoke a few weeks ago about my intentions with the club." He said in November that he was "happy at the club" and "wants to stay to live and work in Manchester".

James Milner was free to open talks with foreign clubs from January 1, but he also signed a new contract that will keep him on Merseyside until June 2022, in a busy day for some big announcements. "I've been lucky and privileged to play for this club for four-and-a-half years now, it has been an amazing time seeing how the club is changing and developing. I just enjoy coming into training every day, working with this group of players, this manager and coaching staff, and being part of this football club. We had discussions with the club and this was obviously the ideal for me, this was what I wanted to do – stay and play at the highest level as long as I can. Liverpool is an unbelievable place to be and we're a very, very good football team and hopefully we can keep improving."

"Boring Mr Milner" never ceases to bring a smile into the dressing room. He added, "Obviously the gaffer waited to sign his dependent on whether I signed mine, so that makes me a feel bit more important!"

In his usual pre match press conference, Klopp elaborated on his new contract and how that will impact on the club's ability to sign new players, "The club was asking for a while already if we could talk about an extension. In the specific moment I thought it makes sense before things are getting a bit intense. Not now, obviously, it was completely calm, as it should be, but maybe in the summer we would have started again talking about things like that. New players, when you want to bring them in, they ask 'how long is the manager here?' and stuff like that. We all wanted to avoid that, it's now done, and I'm really happy about that.

"I couldn't imagine I would leave. That was the moment I thought we can start thinking about how long do I want to stay? I have no clue how long it will be in the end, but it was not possible for me to imagine that I would leave in 2022 because of the people we have and what we have created here.

It was not that I went to the club and said, 'Come on let's have a new contract'. The club started the talks and then we realised – together with my family – that it is it the right thing to do. I liked the idea more and more."

Looking to the future, but also to the short and medium term, Klopp named five young players in the club's academy close to breaking through. "In the moment we have four fantastic players really close to the first team: Rhian Brewster, Curtis Jones, Harvey Elliott and Neco Williams, plus we have Caoimhin as a goalkeeper. That's five boys who I would have no problem to line up tomorrow if needed. Curtis now had his first [Premier League] minutes and of course they have time as well to develop, but that's four or five and we want to increase that number in the future. I know the boys already who are in now like Curtis Jones and Harvey Elliott. Harvey turns 21 when my contract ends! That is all great news for these boys. We want to use them. We want to involve them in the team and all that stuff. Understanding the culture of the club more and more made the decision at the end really sensationally easy. Just to say, 'That's right — let's do it!' I feel the club is in a good place and we have the chance to develop. It's done and I am really happy.

"With Brexit and stuff like this then things will change, and for the youth departments as well – where can we get the players from? So these players need a perspective and they need to feel 'if I go to Liverpool then I have the best chance compared to all the other top six clubs', for example, to make my first steps in the Premier League.'

Before the game against bottom club Watford, Liverpool honoured their greatest ever manager Bill Shankly 60 years to the day that he took charge. It was a fitting tribute, but also incredibly well timed with Klopp's new extending contract. Shankly's face adorned the match day programme with one of his famous quotes: "Liverpool was made for me and I was made for Liverpool". The same might now apply to the current boss! Klopp's message to his supporters appeared in the programme, "In a dressing room you don't look at someone and see colour, creed, sexuality or anything of that nature. You see a friend, a teammate, someone who you can help and someone who can help you. Someone that by working together, you can have better collective experiences than if you tried to do it on your own.' It was the mantra of a manager who relied on the players who were not selected as much as those who were.

Again, Klopp might have tinkered with his line up, but the outcome proved to be just what he wanted, perhaps, though, not in the manner he would have liked. Mo Salah scored two vital goals, one just before the interval and one moving into added time to ease the team's nerves after a gutsy display by the bottom team under new manager Nigel Pearson. Salah's opener was a curler into the far corner. The second was dubbed the cheekiest goal of the season as his back heel flick nut-megged the defender near the goal-line. Salah scored eight Premier League goals against Watford; more than against any other team in the big 5 European leagues but none as unusual as this one.

Watford missed simple chances in both halves, Van Dijk almost passed into his own net following a mix up with Alisson and Alexander-Arnold was caught in possession on the right. Mane had a header ruled out for offside following a review by VAR, as The Reds worked hard for their victory with Alisson making smart saves after the break. Salah squandered other opportunities but Liverpool did enough to pick up their 16th victory of the season to open an 11-point gap at the top ahead of second-placed Leicester City, who faced Norwich later in the day.

VAR changed Klopp's touchline behaviour. In the second half, with the score at 1-0, Mane's header from a Shaqiri cross was ruled out for a marginal, but correct, offside decision. Although he did not contest it, Klopp does not celebrate goals anymore, in case they are ruled out. "I had no clue where it was offside, to be honest. I don't celebrate goals anymore because you have to wait until somebody says it is a goal. I thought there was one pass before where maybe it was offside, but that Sadio was offside, I couldn't see."

Klopp confessed it was "not the prettiest game" but once again he was delighted with the attitude and application that has made Anfield such a fortress. He enthused: "At this stage you have to show resilience and I believe we did that today. We have so many games but we are happy with this. Watford had their chances but we scored ours. We could have made the game easier for us but it's intense to be constantly in charge of the game. We have to defend with passion not organisation sometimes and that was sometimes now, right? We have many more games than our opponent, who had a new set-up, Nigel Pearson, in the short time he's had with the Watford squad, did an exceptional job. This game was the next step for them.

"They had their chances but we had Alisson. We scored our goals but apart from that we had to fight. Could the game have been easier for us? Of course, if we had kept the ball smarter and moved it around a little bit. The boys are not tired but it is intense to always be in control of games, so I get that, we have to defend some moments with passion rather than organisation because that was not always perfect. But we did that. When we didn't Alisson was there, that is why we have 11 players. Ali was for 85 minutes of the game really doing warm-up exercises, but in these [other] five minutes he was really important and just showed what a goalie he is; he is unbelievable and helped us a lot in these situations. We had to fight, that's what we did and that's why we won. All good."

Leicester dropped two points to Norwich as the gap at the top widened to ten points. It ended Leicester's impressive run of eight straight wins that had made the pundits sit up and take notice. But no sooner had that happened than the pressure got to them. Chelsea were even worse, losing at home to Bournemouth, to leave Lampard's team an astonishing 20 points behind Liverpool in fourth place. Fellow German and ex-Borussia Dortmund reserve manager Daniel Farke was expecting a message from Klopp after Norwich extended Liverpool's lead with a 1-1 draw when Pukki scored his 16th goal of the season for both club and country to ensure his side earned a share of the spoils at the King Power Stadium. "Perhaps Jürgen has already sent me a message, I will check my phone later," Farke said.

Pep Guardiola went into City's game at Arsenal confessing his side were struggling "behind an opponent that doesn't drop points", although he also worried about Leicester. "I should think about Leicester before Liverpool," the City boss admitted, "unless we can catch Leicester there is not one thought in my mind about Liverpool. In the last years we were incredibly consistent at home and away but this time we have dropped points. It is not about the performances, I would be really concerned if I thought our game was not there but we have been allowing opponents clear chances and we have to work on that.

"When I arrived here the normal standard was 85 points to win the league; now you almost have to reach 100, and that seems to be what Liverpool are aiming for. We have helped them make that step, they have bought some incredible players and now it is the level you have to reach.

All the teams behind Liverpool know they have to make 100 points if they want the title. Before it didn't happen and we have been the reason why. I would have preferred to be closer to Liverpool at this point – to Leicester even – but maybe after four titles in one season we believe we are something we are not and the reality of sport is to ask questions of you again and again. All I can do now is hope the situation we are in will help us in the future."

As for Liverpool, "Well, they have maintained last season's standards for this season. This is their second season at such a high level and I think it helps that they haven't won the league since a long time ago. They are keen to win it, you can smell that.

★

Trent Alexander-Arnold voiced the gratitude the players felt for four-and-a-half more years to work with Klopp. Trent has been brought through the Anfield ranks and had flourished under his management, "he has showed he is a world-class manager, if not the best in the world. He has done special things for the club and obviously the fans all love him. He fits perfectly. He has brought players in, he has moulded players into world-class players. We're grateful to have a manager like him and obviously the more years he can spend here, the better it is for the club. So it's really good for us to get a few more years out of him."

The tributes continued: "You know when Jürgen Klopp said he is the 'normal one'? Well, he is – and it's his greatest quality," Robbie Fowler said in his Sunday Mirror column. "I've been lucky enough to see him up close, I was at the Champions League final victory party in Madrid in June with my son, and he's just such a decent guy. He was with his family, having a beer and a laugh, not talking about football, just relaxing and enjoying the moment. He's got time for people. There's no airs and graces, no edge to him. The way you saw him on the bus parading the trophy with those beers, well, that's him. A fantastic manager, no doubt up there as one of the best in the world, but someone who can let his hair down, be with people and just chat about anything. Not just normal... but f ★★ normal!

"I think everyone assumed he would do seven years and then take a break in 2022. So to get him for another two years after that is massive. It gives everyone a lift, the fans, of course, everyone around the club and I can tell you the players too. They see him like I do - he's just normal with them too. I've seen him give them b★★★★ckings, he can lose his rag in training. But he loves them too – all of his players – he loves it when they click and get it. What they see is someone the same as them – someone with real ambition, belief and passion. You don't get to play for Liverpool without ambition, and, when they see it matched and outstripped by their manager, it makes them give more.

"It's big for many reasons. For a start, what a season to get such a lift in. It's like the club signing one of the best players in the world – because he's right up there at the very top. He is also a competitor. He inherited a pretty poor team at Anfield – there are only a handful of them left. But he got to two finals in his first season, in the top four in the second, then a Champions League final. Every year they get better and there's no sign of it stopping. That's a real competitor. The two extra years, though, are a massive bonus for the club because it offers continuity. This team is so exciting, there's a reason they're huge favourites for the title."

★

After two games in two days, in two different continents and two different tournaments with two different teams, Jürgen Klopp's new generation of young stars produced something that not even the Liverpool boss expected, involved in a spectacular 5-5 Carabao cup tie with Arsenal and winning 5-4 on penalties - a game with 19 goals! Yet by reaching the last eight of the League Cup it threw up an unprecedented situation where the next round clashed with the World Cup Championships in Doha and the prospect of an incredible dilemma of when to play, who to play and where to play, with Klopp initially insisting he would refuse to play two teams on the same day in two different continents!

Liverpool featured a number of their brightest youngsters in the as they comfortably saw off MK Dons 2-0 in the League Cup, and Klopp was impressed. However, the club were nearly slung out of the tournament! The EFL Board fined Liverpool £200,000, £100,000 suspended until the end of the following season for breaching the rules of the Carabao Cup fielding an ineligible player against Milton Keynes Dons. The EFL announced that the breach hinged on failure to receive international clearance for Pedro Chirivella Burgos when his loan agreement expired last season with Spanish club Extremadura Union Deportiva. The League accepted "it wasn't appropriate to expel the Club from the Competition because of a number of mitigating factors". The Board noted the Club sought the assistance of the FA in securing the return of the International Clearance prior to the start of the season, and the Club had been able to include the player on team sheets for Premier League Two matches (under Premier League Rules) and one Trophy match, which resulted in the breach not being identified until the Club reported the issue to the EFL and Premier League following the MK Dons match.

Liverpool were found guilty of misconduct in relation to the same breach for fielding the player in the defeat against Oldham Athletic in the Trophy on 7 August, with the sanction incorporated into the financial penalty.

Klopp was pleased to be able to give his bright new kids another chance in the cup, when he announced that the youngsters' 'ability is not in question' and wanted them to show other qualities in a big tie against Arsenal. "Tonight we select a team to win. Winning is our first, second and third motivation – the only motivation always," Klopp wrote in the official matchday programme.

Liverpool had secured a good victory against MK Dons thanks to goals from veteran James Milner and 17-year-old Ki-Jana Hoever and Klopp pointed to the atmosphere at Anfield and urged the crowd to help the youngsters against Arsenal. He said: "It is the job of all us to help them and nurture them and give them an environment to grow, develop and flourish. I am confident we are doing this. And on that theme, again on the assumption there are some Anfield debuts for our young players this evening, it is critical that the atmosphere is one that encourages and inspires. I know our crowd will get this – they are world-class when it comes to recognising their job also."

Liverpool's penalty shootout victory sealed a last eight place in the Carabao Cup after Caoimhin Kelleher, just 20, saved Dani Ceballos' penalty and the celebrations were wild from Liverpool's players at full-time as teenager Curtis Jones coolly thumped the final penalty in off the post to make it five from five in front of the Kop.

Divock Origi's 94th-minute scissor kick had sent the game to penalties after Liverpool had twice come from behind in one of the most thrilling and unusual cup ties in the competition's history. Willock looked to have scored the winner, when he put Arsenal 5-4 in front late in the game, after The Red were 4-2 down, but clawed their way back to 4-4.

Liverpool led just once after five minutes when Mustafi slid in and diverted the ball into his own net. Saka's shot was rebounded in by Torreira to make it 1-1. Martinelli continued his impressive goalscoring form, pouncing on a loose ball at the near post before slotting in from Saka's pass to make it 3-1. Liverpool cut the lead to one goal on the stroke of half-time through Milner's penalty after Harvey Elliott - who became the youngest Liverpool player to start at Anfield (16 years, 209 days) - went down in the box under minimal contact from Martinelli. The goals continued to flow in the second half, when Milner gave the ball away in his own area with a half hit back pass, and Ozil teed up Maitland-Niles for a tap in before Oxlade-Chamberlain fired in an excellent long-range effort and Origi's smart turn and powerful finish made it 4-4 - all this before Willock and Origi's late goals left the teams level at 5-5.

Liverpool comebacks have become a speciality of Origi who secured legendary status among Liverpool fans with the winner on aggregate against Barcelona in their Champions League semi-final second leg. He then secured Liverpool's victory in the final against Tottenham, putting his side 2-0 up with three minutes to go. The fans sang his name again as the players prepared for the penalty shootout.

Klopp had selected four teenagers to start, the youngest in any competition since January 2017 with an average age of 23 years and 122 days. Sixteen-year-old Elliott won a penalty, academy product Neco Williams, 18, set-up Origi's stoppage-time equaliser and fellow home-grown teenager Curtis Jones netted Liverpool's winning spot-kick in the shootout. Klopp was euphoric afterwards, "We made some mistakes, we played some average passes. We were too open at times. We can talk about tactics but who cares on a night like this? I hoped for the boys they would have a game to remember. What they did tonight, I lost it really. It's like a dream to play for the first time at Anfield, but things might not be going right and you have to stay on track. All our goals we scored were wonderful. Kelleher is an outstanding talent. The crossing from Williams, he might not thought he would play tonight. Jones... it was not my decision in the end for him to take the last penalty.

"You need to be born in Liverpool probably to do that. It was not my idea. When I saw the list the last time, Divock was on five and Curtis on four. When I saw the number four coming and it was Divock then I thought, 'OK, obviously they changed it'. Good situation. Curtis has no issue with self-confidence, he absolutely doesn't struggle in that department. It's good. It's absolutely nice. I cannot say more about it really. If you don't win nobody remembers it in three years, if it works out the boys will remember it forever."

Curtis Jones would not be forgetting this night in three years, or indeed 30 years. He reacted as one might expect, "Being a local lad it's always been my dream to get an appearance at Anfield. To get an assist to give us a chance and then to score a penalty is just a dream come true. I was calm, I picked my spot and I was fortunate enough that the winning penalty went in. The team played great, they showed character and belief. The fans were unbelievable too, they helped us through the game and we're glad we paid them back. We knew regardless of the Arsenal team it was going to be a tough game. We knew we could match them and that's what we did tonight. This is just the beginning, I'm just a young lad and I've still got a long way to go. Any opportunities I'll take with both hands."

Liverpool had won more penalty shootouts in the League Cup than any other team in the history of the competition (eight). But the quarter-finals of the Carabao Cup clashed with Liverpool playing in the Club World Cup in Doha. Klopp threw out the challenge that his side might not be able to play both! Within an hour of the final whistle Klopp said, "If they can't find the proper date for us and I don't mean Christmas Day 3am - then we can't play the game - our opponents will progress. They have to make that decision. You have to think about these things. If you have a fixture list where one team cannot be part of all the games, then you have to think about the fixture list. Hopefully it starts now. I really think that's fair, and this problem is obvious now. We will not be the victim of this problem. We play tonight, we wanted to win it, we did that, and if they don't find a proper date for us, then we cannot play the next round and whoever is our opponent will go through. Or Arsenal play them. We will not be the victims of this problem. I think a lot of people from the PL were watching on TV hoping Arsenal do it…" Klopp smiled broadly, looked straight down the camera lens and added: "Sorry!"

After the draw paired Liverpool with Aston Villa, the Premier League refused to allow Liverpool to move any top-flight games after their league game at West Ham United had already been postponed. The Anfield club and the EFL were in talks over an alternative date but Klopp said there was "no final decision yet". Liverpool already had eight fixtures scheduled for December - five in the Premier League, their final Champions League group match and two Club World Cup games. There was a midweek window after the FA Cup third round on the first weekend in January - but that would mean playing the Villa tie when the first legs of the EFL Cup semi-finals were due. Another midweek slot was potentially available in the week commencing 13 January, before the second legs take place in the week beginning 27 January. The EFL Cup final is on 1 March and Klopp questioned the logic of the competition having two-legged semi-finals. "After a very busy schedule in December, there is two [legged] semi-finals," he said. "It is an easy decision for me to say: 'OK, if you keep that competition, why have two (legged) semi-finals?'" The EFL was not planning any change to the format of the two-legged EFL Cup semi-finals.

Pep Guardiola had sympathy with Klopp, agreeing that there were too many games for top-flight players. "If we have bigger squads, how do we pay them? We need less fixtures, less competitions, more recovery, but I have been in meetings and it's always the same. We just talk about it. I'm completely with Jürgen when he makes these statements - it's too much. I had to prioritise Ilkay Gundogan for the last game - no Kevin [de Bruyne], no David Silva. Other clubs do the same."

The outcome was that Liverpool would field different teams in two separate competitions within 24 hours after the EFL announced the date of their Carabao Cup quarter-final with Aston Villa would not be changed. The Reds played at Villa on 17 December at 19:45 GMT and compete in the Club World Cup semi-final in Qatar the following day at 17:30 GMT. The EFL said keeping the date followed a "request from the club".

Liverpool now had nine fixtures in December; including a league match at home to Watford on 14 December, the EFL Cup tie with Villa three days later, a first Club World Cup game the following day, a final match in the competition on 21 December, back for an away game Leicester on 26 December.

It was certainty a kick in the teeth for Liverpool fans who try to get to every game to support their team. The fans who turn out at Villa Park had two flight options to give them any hope of making kick-off in Qatar. A flight from Birmingham Airport at 07:50 GMT on 18 December would land in Doha at 17:30 local time, leaving three hours to get from the airport runway to the stands at Education City Stadium. The cost of that flight was £614 one way at 22:00 GMT on 5 November. The journey from airport to stadium is around 30 minutes, so getting to both games was possible. There was one leaving London Heathrow at 08:00 GMT on 18 December, landing 17:45 local time, costing £509 at 22:00 on 5 November.

So why worry? In April, Venezuelan club Deportivo Lara played two games in six hours, one of which was in the Copa Libertadores - and won both. On the same day, Venezuelan side Zamora played two fixtures 4,000 miles apart, losing 4-0 at Deportivo La Guaira in the league and 3-2 at Brazilian side Atletico Mineiro in the Copa Libertadores. Arsenal and Manchester United played on consecutive days as recently as November 2001. The Gunners lost 4-2 to Charlton in the Premier League on 4 November and on the same day United were beaten 3-1 by Liverpool at Anfield, also in the league. On 5 November, Arsenal beat United 4-0 in the League Cup.

While it looks farcical, and such a headache for Klopp, in reality, Klopp revealed his side's Carabao Cup win over Arsenal was his favourite game of the season so far.

Speaking in an interview with The Athletic, Klopp admitted he doesn't actually get that much enjoyment out of a lot of Liverpool's games, despite some thrillers! Klopp praised the Anfield atmosphere that night. "You know the best game of the season so far for me to enjoy? It was Arsenal in the Carabao Cup. When we were 3-1 down I was thinking 'come on, don't give them a knock, don't lose 4-1 or 5-1 as that wouldn't be nice'. Then we started scoring again. That was my game to enjoy. I don't have that a lot. The boys made it a special night and I loved it. The atmosphere was brilliant and buzzing. We've had a lot of good moments at Anfield."

Now Klopp wanted his young stars bursting with excitement, running for their lives to cause an upset. Under-23 coach Neil Critchley would lead out one of the all time most an inexperienced Liverpool sides in any competitive game. Klopp would watch on television in his team's hotel in Doha, along with his players, after first taking in the first World Club Cup semi-final between Flamengo and Al-Hilal.

Unusually Liverpool were underdogs, but Klopp wasn't ruling out an upset. "I know how a lot of people in the public see it, but if all the football games would be decided before we start, only because of the perception of the people, then most of the games wouldn't be played. I believe, I'm a big believer in everybody has a chance. From the boys' point of view, if I would be in their boots I would be excited like hell, looking forward to it like hell, run for my life, all that stuff." Klopp urged Critchley's squad "to give it a proper try" as they cheer on from afar. "All our thoughts are with them, the more experienced players are looking forward to it, to watch the game and shout them forward from here.

Whatever we can do we will do, but Critch and his staff and the boys, I'm sure they're really looking forward to it and will enjoy it. You can only enjoy football if you work hard and go for the result – whichever result it will be. Aston Villa is the big favourite, that's clear, but who cares? It's football and the ball rolls in each direction, that's pretty cool."

Five debutants, an average age of 19 years, six months and three days, Liverpool fielded the youngest team in their history, and although the mixed bag of youth team and reserves looked impressive they were eventually overwhelmed 5-0. Villa had also made 10 changes from their Premier League defeat at Sheffield United, but their vastly superior experience and extra muscle took control after Liverpool began brightly but conceded two freak goals in the space of three first-half minutes to allow the hosts to settle. Hourihane's free-kick from the right deceived Caoimhin Kelleher, and the Reds keeper then saw an Elmohamady cross deflect off Morgan Boyes and loop over him into the left corner. Kodjia added Villa's third with a cool finish before sweeping in Elmohamady's cross from the right for a 4-0 half time lead. Wesley completed the scoring.

At an average of 19.48 years, it was the youngest line-up in Liverpool's history, eclipsing the 21.81 in an FA Cup tie against Plymouth nearly three years earlier. The starting side had a mere 16 previous first-team appearances for Liverpool between them while their shirt numbers added up to 737. None of the Liverpool players were alive the last time Villa won a trophy, when they beat Leeds to win this competition in 1996. This was Liverpool's heaviest League Cup defeat, eclipsing a 4-1 loss to West Ham in 1988 and 6-3 by Arsenal in 2007. Harvey Elliott made his first EFL Cup appearance, he was so young he had to get changed away from his team-mates on child protection grounds as he was yet to reach his 16th birthday. He was still not old enough to drive and couldn't turn professional until his 17th birthday in April. Elliott's early shot forced Orjan Nyland into a one-handed save when the game was still goalless and he provided a terrific pass that allowed Isaac Christie-Davies to go close later in the half.

Critchley was proud of the boys as he said: "I thought we were magnificent. We were fantastic from the start, we had a couple of chances from the first whistle. We were really unfortunate to concede and then find ourselves 2-0 down. It was an incredible night and no-one wanted it to end. The support we had was unbelievable. The conduct of the Villa players was first class. For Dean Smith and John Terry to come in to our dressing room after the game and say the things they said...

They said 'keep going, good luck' and wished us the best. A moment I will remember and the players will remember for the rest of their lives. Some of them showed the potential to one day play for us, or in the Premier League. They will know it was just part of their journey. My overwhelming feeling is one of immense pride."

Liverpool's defeat was their first in 20 games across all competitions (W16 D3), Villa becoming the first side to beat them since Napoli in the Champions League back in September. Liverpool suffered their biggest margin of defeat in any competition since September 2017, when they lost 5-0 against Manchester City in the Premier League. Liverpool conceded four first-half goals for the first time in any competition since May 2015, against Stoke in the Premier League. Liverpool's youngsters actually had more possession and shots than Villa.

Klopp had instructed Liverpool's youngsters to continue playing with 'bravery' at half-time. Klopp sent a message of support to them telling them to continue fighting until the final whistle. Critchley revealed: 'I was incredibly proud with how those players played. We were part of it and with them and I'm fortunate to have shared something special tonight. The support we had showed what a special club this is. We had information from Jürgen Klopp at half-time to carry on being brave and carry on playing the way we were playing. He was out there watching with his staff and the players. I hope, and I'm sure, he will be proud of the way they played tonight. One or two may be sneaking off to join up with that group and I'm sure they will be well received."

11: THE GREATEST LIVERPOOL MANAGER?

THERE HAS ALREADY BEEN A GREAT DEAL of debate about where a title win would place Jürgen Klopp in the pantheon of Liverpool managers. Some younger fans already view Klopp as a God on Merseyside, in the same way that Bill Shankly was viewed during the 60s and 70s. The thirty-year wait for the title may have heightened that feeling but older, wiser heads counsel caution. One such is former Liverpool goalkeeper Ray Clemence who played at Anfield for 14 years, half of them under Shankly. Because of his close relationship with the legendary manager and his methods, Ray believes it is impossible for anyone, not even Jürgen Klopp, to usurp Shankly's position as the club's greatest ever manager.

In a rare and exclusive interview for "The Boss", Clemence says, "I hear it said that Klopp is the new Shankly and I can fully understand why people say that. Klopp is a fantastic manager, a fabulous manager, but there can only be one No 1 Liverpool manager and that's Bill Shankly.

"I have only met Jürgen Klopp the once, when we shook hands on the pitch at the Community Shield when I was the guest of honour, and like everybody else I can say he is an outstanding Liverpool manager, hugely inspirational, although I can only make a judgement from what I see in his press conferences and the way he conducts himself on the touchline, but I can imagine he is just as inspirational inside the Liverpool dressing room.

"The job Klopp is doing at Anfield is just amazing, and it will be interesting to see where he finishes up in terms of what he achieves, but he has already won the European Cup and the title is within sight, and he could even end up with four trophies this season, and that would be something for sure, simply incredible.

"But no, I am not going to compare Klopp to Shanks. I lived with Shanks for seven years, worked with him every day for all of that time, lived in his company, and then played under Bob Paisley. I knew what made Shanks tick but haven't had that intimate knowledge of Klopp, of course.

"But for me there is only one founding father of the modern day Liverpool, and that's Shanks. He built the foundations of everything you see today. He built teams, carried on by Bob Paisley that was winning things for fun for more than 20 years, and that is beginning again under Klopp.

"Bob Paisley won more than Shanks, but it was Shanks who laid those foundations and built the club from there. Bob was the opposite to Shanks. While Bill liked the media and the limelight, Bob didn't really enjoy the public part of the game, and only enjoyed the football. Bob had some great players and he knew how to handle them."

Pushed to make his judgement on his top three, which are clearly Shankly, Paisley and Klopp, but in which order, he said: "It would be wrong to categorise them, as they are all different. Shanks, though, was the best motivator that I have ever come across, although I am sure Klopp is also a great motivator, that comes across.

"It's the same when asked to compare great Liverpool teams under Shankly and Paisley to the current great Liverpool team under Klopp. It is difficult, if not impossible, to do so, because there are vastly different situations, different pitches, different balls, different boots, different rules. So it's not right or even possible to make such comparison. All I can say is that I spent 12 wonderful years at Liverpool in which time we won just about everything."

Ray Clemence

1. Shankly 2. Paisley 3. Klopp

Alan Kennedy

1. Paisley 2. Klopp 3. Shankly

David Fairclough

1. Shankly 2. Paisley 3. Klopp

Jürgen has been fantastic, nobody has had the connection with the fans since Shanks. His playing style is how we like to watch football, fast and exciting playing in the opposition half.

However in my opinion, it would be almost impossible to overtake Shanks. He was the man who created the modern Liverpool, arriving at a time when the club was in the doldrums for so many reasons; training ground, training methods, team selection. And in doing that set so many processes in place and anyone who came through the apprentice system was influenced for life and still hold and maintain those values today.

So while Jürgen has been an incredible appointment and for all the success he might achieve in the future his influence is unlikely for me to equal as much by the many who have been touched and inspired by Shanks.

Steve McManaman

1. Paisley 2. Shankly 3. Dalglish

Craig Johnston

1. Shankly 2. Klopp 3. Dalglish

To be a greater manager means to me …to lift the Scouse brand up above the trophies, the players and the city into a kind of immortality. That's what Shankly did. That's what made him great and the club great. Part of his legacy was actually educating Paisley and Dalglish. Klopp maybe has that in him, but he would have to stay for another 5 or 6 years and win everything there is to win …including doubles and trebles to be the No 1. To be immortal to make the club immortal."

John Barnes

1. Shankly 2. Paisley 3. Dalglish

Give Klopp a few more years, and who knows ... but as of today not enough to overtake Bill or Bob!

Steve McMahon

1. Shankly 2. Paisley 3. Dalglish

For Klopp to have any chance of reaching No 1, well…. certainly a few more trophies might help.

Michael Owen

1. Shankly 2. Paisley 3. Klopp

Jimmy Carter

1. Shankly 2. Paisley 3. Klopp

Nigel Spackman

1 Paisley 2 Shankly 3 Klopp

A measure of Jürgen Klopp is that he is the manager any club, other than Liverpool of course, would want as their manager. The biggest thing I like about him is that he comes across as such a good bloke, very likeable, someone you wouldn't mind going out to the pub with to have a drink with.

On top of that, he talks very well even though English is not his first language, which you don't always find with foreign managers. He handles the press very well.

But as a manager he gets his points across to his players, he motivates them, and his man-management is outstanding. It's all slotted into place right now and it all stems from the top - and that's him.

He has a great eye for a player and how that player can fit into his team. Tactically he is very astute and you need to be to win the Champions League. He keeps himself motivated, his players motivated, but also buys into the Liverpool Way and keeps the supporters motivated.

However Bob Paisley has won more than anyone and would therefore have to be No 1, Shankly No 2 for starting it all off by setting the foundations, and although Kenny won the Double I would put Jürgen third. What does he have to do to be No 1? Win back-to-back titles, and that is tough in modern day football.

John Scales

1. Shankly 2. Paisley 3. Klopp/Dalglish

Just like Johann Cruyff laid the foundations at Barcelona for the likes of Pep Guardiola, I would say that there can be no escaping what Bill Shankly achieved for Liverpool by laying the foundations at Anfield with the iconic Boot Room, the entire philosophy of the club. It is something that transcends generations, it lives on.

When I arrived at Liverpool there was no mistaking that attitude of the relentless pursuit of the next trophy, the next success, that you were defined by the next game, not the last achievement. In many ways the club back in my time was absolutely amazing, yet so unprofessional in many ways, yet retained a very simple but effective approach that you as a player did not go beyond your station and that you lived up to the expectations of the clubs and its supporters. This Liverpool team is just incredible, and primed to be successful for the next few years and when the time comes to reflect it will look even better as time goes by. They have reached a point where they have got themselves a swagger about them, which very few teams ever achieve no matter how good; its a swagger and confidence yet they never stop putting in the hard work and commitment which takes them to a different level.

As for Klopp… I love him. He is the architect of what we now see, and football is all about the here and now in so many ways. Klopp was described as the best manager in the world, and I would agree with that, but is he the best manager in Liverpool? No, I don't think so. I'm a purist, and I would put Shankly top for building the foundations and Paisley next for achieving more than any other manager. Yet, Klopp is achieving even doing things Paisley didn't do, but one of my all time heroes is Kenny Dalglish and for that reason I cannot put anyone above Kenny. I have such a high regard for Kenny, not only because he brought me to Liverpool, but for the way he conducted himself after Hillsborough.

Using a point system of 3 points for first choice down to 1 point for third, the results of this former player straw poll is as follows: Shankly - 29; Paisley 24; Klopp 10, Dalglish 4.

Bill Shankly built Liverpool into 'a bastion of invincibility' during a 15-year reign at Anfield

BILL SHANKLY OBE

"For a player to be good enough to play for Liverpool, he must be prepared to run through a brick wall for me then come out fighting on the other side."

"Liverpool was made for me and I was made for Liverpool."

"Although I'm a Scot, I'd be proud to be called a Scouser."

1959-74 - Honours: Second Division Champions 1961-62; First Division Champions 1963-64, 1965-66, 1972-73; FA Cup Winners 1965, 1974; UEFA Cup winners 1972-73, FA Charity Shield winners 1964, 1965, 1966.

JÜRGEN KLOPP IS LIVERPOOL'S TWELFTH manager since the late great Bill Shankly; the man who managed the club for 15 years and transformed it from a forgotten backwater into a powerhouse of English football. After winning the FA Cup in 1974, Bill Shankly stood on the steps of St George's Hall, opposite Lime Street station, before 100,000 supporters, the crowd was hushed into absolute silence. Then, with one hand in his pocket, and his team standing behind him, he started talking: "Since I came here to Liverpool, and to Anfield, I have drummed it into our players time and again that they are privileged to play for you. And if they didn't believe me, they believe me now." As the crowd chanted his name, Shankly raised his arms and turned to his team, before facing his crowd again, arms still aloft. Little did anyone know that within weeks his tenure as Liverpool boss would be over in a resignation that stunned the city even more than the day the Beatles called it a day.

Shanks has been immortalised for several famous phrases, most notably, "Some people believe football is a matter of life and death. I am very disappointed with that attitude. I can assure you it is much, much more important than that." More importantly for his legacy at Liverpool, Shankly developed the Boot Room system that became synonymous a coaching dynasty that ruled the game for decades. It was Shankly's greatest gift to his beloved Liverpool and meant that the club were still churning out trophy winning sides years after his death.

Th day Shankly stepped down as manager in July 1974 many were in tears as they jammed the club's switchboard hoping it was all a hoax. A local factory threatened to go on strike if he left. Shortly afterwards he received the OBE. The Queen said to him: "You have been in football a long time." He replied: "It's been 42 years."

It's hard to believe now but Liverpool were marooned in the Second Division for most of the 1950s and didn't earn promotion to the top flight until 1961-62, in an era dominated by Spurs Double winning team under Bill Nicholson. Upon promotion Shankly, who had been appointed in 1959, thanked his assistants, "Without the help of Reuben Bennett, Joe Fagan, Albert Shelley and Bob Paisley, we could have achieved nothing," he said told the Liverpool Echo.

There are parallels with Jürgen Klopp as he also acknowledges the crucial role his coaching team makes to the club suggesting that he is "nothing without them". The pair have a lot in common; Shankly, like Klopp, works with a group of trusted assistants. And like his predecessor it took a few years before their coaching, tactics and selections bore fruit – time being essential for any manager starting at a new club.

Shankly's team were relative unknowns. Albert Shelley was anonymous to anyone outside Anfield, he was not involved in coaching but had been around the club for some time as an odd-job man. "He was a volunteer, he wasn't even on the payroll," says Peter Hooton, author of The Boot Room Boys, "his love of the club had become an obsession and he wanted to be there and just be involved, and no one ever questioned that" so Shankly included him in his close-knit team. Another key member of staff was Reuben Bennett who was obsessive in improving player fitness, while Joe Fagan was the tactician and confidante to the players. Bob Paisley had already been directly involved on the coaching side for a couple of years before Shankly's arrival, he had a keen eye for potential transfer targets. Shankly had played with and against Paisley and was a fellow devotee of American boxing but then Shanks had personal connections with all the men on his staff; he knew Bennett through his brother Bob as they had played together at Dundee; he had tried to sign Joe Fagan for Grimsby when Fagan was playing for Manchester City, and he told Shelley, who had cleaned the dressing rooms for years, that he was a legend in the game.

In Stephen F Kelly's biography of Shankly the author writes: "On that first morning Shankly was to make the wisest decision he was ever to make in his entire Anfield career. He guaranteed every man their jobs... at a stroke he had Paisley's supporting role and tactical knowledge, Fagan's psychology, Bennett's Scottishness, Shelley's loyalty; all of them, including Shankly, had been forged in the same hard-knocks school of life... and had all learned the lessons of common decency, honesty and pride." Shankly sat them down that morning. "Fellows, your jobs are safe. Some managers bring their own people with them. Not me. I have my own system and it will work in co-operation with you. I will lay down the plans and gradually we will all be on the same wavelength. I demand only one thing: loyalty. Nobody must carry stories about anybody else. If anyone tells me a story about anybody else, that man with the story will get the sack, and I don't care if he has been here 50 years. Every one of us must be loyal to each other - and every single thing we do must be for Liverpool football club."The ethos of the Boot Room was conceived there and then.

They often gathered in the cramped space, packed full of training gear, known as the Boot Room. There the brain storming sessions began as the club began its assault first on English and later European football. The Anfield back room team, plus the odd bottle of hooch, grew to be considered an inner sanctum where strategies were conceived, discussed and refined as Liverpool went on to dominate the domestic and European game. As a result Shankly became one of the best-loved and respected figures in British football.

As an illustration of Shankly's modus operandi, Ronnie Moran recalls the moment he joined Shankly's backroom staff. "When I came to the end of my playing days I was in the reserves and he called me into his office one day at the end of the season. I thought he was going to tell me my days at Liverpool were over, but he said 'Sit down, son! How would you like a job on my staff working with the youngsters?' So then I was working with the kids for three years while Joe Fagan was in charge of the reserves. Then he asked me to help him with that so Joe moved on to the first team in 1971 and I took the reserves. In 1974 I joined the first team set-up when Bill retired to work with Bob [Paisley] and Joe. One of the reasons he was so popular with our supporters was because he told the truth all of the time."

★

In the early autumn of 1981, he suffered a heart attack and was rushed to Liverpool's Broadgreen Hospital. The former Liverpool manager was 68 years old and had been in good health; he neither drank nor smoked, and exercised daily. "When I go, I'm going to be the fittest man ever to die," he promised, but he was thought to be invincible. Three days later, on 29

September, he had a second, massive heart attack and died that morning. Bob Paisley, who had been Shankly's deputy for 14 years, said: "Bill was one of the greatest managers there has ever been."

By the time of his death Shankly cut a tragic figure, he could not live without football, but Liverpool had became an even more formidable force since he had left the club. The Anfield board later banned Shanks from their training ground at Melwood, where the newly retired Scot had tried to rediscover some of the camaraderie that once filled his life. "It was," said Kevin Keegan, "the saddest, saddest thing that ever happened at Liverpool." Shankly was a fit man; but he died, in the words of the former Leeds player Johnny Giles, of "a broken heart".

Not only had Shankly turned Liverpool into one of the most successful footballing sides in Britain under his own management but he left a legacy that was unrivalled in the game as the club went on to win more after his shock retirement.

★

Born in Ayrshire, one of ten children, in 1913 Bill played his first football in the Scottish junior league. He turned professional with Carlisle United in 1932 and the following year was transferred for £500 to Preston North End. He won an FA Cup winner's medal as a wing-half and five caps for Scotland. Even as a player Shankly's destiny seemed to be in management. Preston legend Tom Finney says that he made a big impression on himself and the younger players. "He was always a football fanatic, you could tell from the moment he left playing that he was going to be a manager."

A qualified success at Brunton Park, he managed in the lower leagues for a decade, with spells in charge of Grimsby, Workington and Huddersfield, however none of Shankly's team finished higher than 12th in the Second Division during this time. Yet his infectious personality and knack of developing outstanding young players, such as Denis Law and Ray Wilson, got him noticed by bigger clubs. In November 1959 Shankly was approached by two men at the end of a Huddersfield game. One was Tom Williams, the Liverpool chairman, the other Harry Latham, a director. "How would you like to manage the best club in the country?" asked Williams.

"Why?" Shankly replied, sharp as ever. "Is Matt Busby packing it in?" A few days later, Shankly was unveiled as Liverpool's new manager.

On Tuesday December 1 1959, the *Liverpool Echo* announced that Shankly was to be the manager of Liverpool FC, then languishing in the Second Division where they had been since 1954. The article stated that the new man would begin duty on New Year's day because his current club, Huddersfield Town, had demanded he work a month's notice. The paper said the 46-year-old had beaten future Everton boss Harry Catterick, Manchester United Assistant Manager Jimmy Murphy, Doncaster player-manager Peter Doherty and legendary coach Jimmy Hagan to the job. The Echo stated his annual salary as £2,500 which was £500 more than he was getting at Huddersfield. Within days of his resignation Huddersfield relented on the month's notice. Early on the morning of Monday December 14 1959 Shankly parked his Austin A40 in the tiny car park behind Anfield's main stand. He had bought a new suit. He announced himself at the front office - "I am your new manager, lassie" - and was told to go upstairs where chairman Tom Williams and club secretary Jimmy McInnes awaited him, as well as a photographer from the Echo who posed the trio shaking hands and "sharing a joke", although Shankly was not smiling. "Now we'll show you around," said Williams. "No need," said Shankly, "I saw all I needed on Saturday after I watched the reserves play," Liverpool reserves had beaten Manchester City's 5-0. "Did you know you've some useful players in the reserves?" he told them. The pair were already thinking they had made the right choice.

Liverpool FC at that time, recalled Bob Paisley, was a "happy-go-lucky, slap-happy" place, with the directors content for the club, then below Shankly's Huddersfield in the Second Division, merely to get back to the top flight "and go along three or four places off the bottom". Anfield and the training ground at Melwood were dilapidated; directors meddled in team selections and funds for transfers were rarely forthcoming. As Keegan put it, Shanks put "his character into the club in every facet from the bottom to the top". He instilled pride, discipline, loyalty and a relentless work ethic. He bought astutely and galvanised the new players, he made everyone believe Liverpool were the best team in the world!

Success wasn't instant but following two seasons in the Second Division everything finally clicked in 1961/62 as Liverpool topped the table from the first weekend to the last. Within two years of promotion the glory days were back at Anfield as the club won the title in 1964, and again in 1966, although perhaps of more importance to fans of the time was the club's first FA Cup success in 1965.

It wasn't just about trophies. Shankly built a family at the club; Tommy Smith had joined Liverpool as a 15-year-old in 1960 and was made captain in 1970. Shankly became like a father to him – Smith's own father had died shortly before he signed, and Shankly "took care" of him. John Toshack, who was signed as a 21-year-old striker from Cardiff City in 1970, was in awe of Shankly from the moment he met him. "He inspired us in every way," says Toshack, "his belief in Liverpool Football Club, the standards he set for himself and for the club, the intensity that he went about his job. His quote about football being more important than life or death, he really felt that way. He rammed it into us how important it was to be playing for Liverpool, how privileged we were to be playing for these people. We really believed that. I remember Bill Shankly calling me aside and saying, 'Never be frightened to miss. You must always go into the penalty area. If you go in and miss one, you go in with more determination the next time.' I think it's probably the best bit of advice I ever had as a forward player."

Having triumphed in the mid-sixties with one team, Shankly wasn't afraid to rebuild his team around outstanding youth team players and hungry unknowns, such as Kevin Keegan and Ray Clemence, plucked from the lower leagues. "He looked at people and wanted to see himself: in terms of self-motivation, wanting to win, wanting to play football," says Brian Hall, the midfielder Shankly signed in the late 1960s. "If you had those sorts of character traits you were good enough for him."

The re-vamped team helped Shankly win his third league title in 1973, and they narrowly missed a league and cup double a year later, when they finished runners-up but won the FA Cup with a 3-0 win over Newcastle. At the end of the Final a fan ran onto the pitch and threw himself at Shankly's feet so that he could kiss his shoes. Nobody knew it, but the great man had just managed Liverpool for the last time. The board had grown tired of Shankly's constant threats to resign, and a 1967 resignation letter still sat in Peter Robinson's filing cabinet. In the summer of 1974, Shankly insisted that he was quitting. "I think that perhaps it was tiredness, that football had taken its toll on him," says his granddaughter, Karen Gill. Peter Robinson initially played along, thinking he was crying wolf, but as he realised that Shankly was unmovable he started to search for ways for him to stay – in any capacity.

At a press conference on Friday 12 July Shankly made public his decision. "It's one of those moments in time, like when Kennedy was shot," says Brian Hall. "I couldn't believe it because he was so besotted with the game, with Liverpool Football Club, and with the fans." Hall believes that the pressures of being not just a manager but an icon had taken their toll on Shankly. "He put enormous pressure on himself," he says, "because every time he stood up in front of people, whether it be the media boys, or fans at a dinner or a school function or whatever he did, he had to produce a performance that was Shankly-like. It had to be dramatic, it had to be poignant, it had to hit nails on heads. I just have a sneaky feeling that the pressures of football management and the pressures of who he was and how he had to perform in front of people became too much in the end."

"He was always on stage," says John Keith, who as the Daily Express Merseyside correspondent, knew him well. "We were all Boswells, waiting for the words to drop out of his mouth."

Fairly quickly Shankly realised that leaving Liverpool had been a terrible mistake. "Retire is a terrible, silly word," he said. "They should get a new word for it. The only time you retire is when you're in a box and the flowers come out."

When the Liverpool players reported back to Melwood for pre-season training, days after he had announced his retirement, Shankly was there to greet them, dressed in his training kit as if nothing had happened. He had come to join training with his former colleagues to stay fit but the players still greeted him as "boss", while his successor, Bob Paisley, was just "Bob". Paisley's initial pleasure to see him soon turned to polite embarrassment as it became clear that he was being undermined by Shankly's presence. "He started taking the training," says Tommy Smith. "Prior to that, as a manager, he didn't actually take the training, he'd walk around and talk to Reuben Bennett, Joe Fagan and Bob Paisley and tell them what to do. But he started taking the training! In the end Paisley, if only for his own sanity, had to say to him: 'Bill, you don't work here any more. This is my team here, I've got things I want to do.'"

"It was difficult for Bob, having him hanging around," says Toshack. "We're not just talking about any member of the coaching staff who's retired, who just came to Melwood to have a bit of jog around and a shower and that was it. Shanks was Liverpool; he was an institution."

Eventually, with Paisley threatening to resign, Shankly was asked to stay away by club chairman, John Smith. It was a decision Shankly bitterly resented. Shankly drew a contrast in his treatment by Liverpool and Matt Busby's at Manchester United. When Busby retired in 1969, he was given a place on the Old Trafford board and continued to play a role in the running of the club yet Shankly's relations with the Anfield board had frequently been acrimonious. However while Liverpool went on to win trophy after trophy in the wake of Shankly's retirement, United were relegated just 6 seasons after winning the European Cup with the shadow of Busby a very real presence at Old Trafford.

Shanks' contempt for club officials was well documented, one of his favourite maxims went as follows, "at a football club there's a holy trinity – the players, the manager and the supporters. Directors don't come into it. They are only there to sign the cheques." He was supported in this belief by his experiences with the Liverpool board. In 1962 Johnny Morrissey had been sold to Everton without Shankly's knowledge and went on to star in two title winning teams with the Toffees and more than a decade later Shanks was still furious about it. That 1967 resignation letter was written after he lost out on the signing of Howard Kendall to Everton, another title winning star. This time Shankly blamed the board and stormed out of Anfield, he stayed away for a few days before returning, and even then sullenly refused to retract his resignation letter while carrying on his work. "I used to fight and argue and fight and argue and fight and argue until I thought, 'Is it worthwhile all this fighting and arguing?'" Shankly reflected later. "It is bad enough fighting against the opposition to win points but the internal fights to make people realise what we were working for took me close to leaving many times."

Episodes like this may have been pardoned by Robinson, but other board members were less forgiving. "When he finished he thought he was going to become a director, but the directors got their own back," says Tommy Smith. "I don't think they were out to get him, but I think there was an opportunity whereby Bill Shankly had retired and they said: 'Right, that's it, we've got rid of him at last.'"

Smith says that Shankly's predicament was an accumulation of mistakes by the board that stemmed from their inherent misunderstanding of football matters and their treating him as a mere employee. "They didn't realise that he was a god on Merseyside because they didn't mix with the fans," he says. In retirement Shanks presented his own chat show on the Liverpool station Radio City, interviewing such figures as Harold Wilson, Freddie Starr and Lulu. Sometimes he worked for the station as a match pundit alongside commentator Elton Welsby.

John Toshack said he was great help when he went into management with Swansea City in 1978. "He was in the dressing room with us at Preston when we went up that first year. Whenever we played in the north-west I'd invite him and he'd come along to the hotel, he'd have lunch with the players and give them a boost. I can remember him walking into a room, and saying 'Jesus Christ, John, who you going to leave out, what a team you've got.' And of course some of the local lads, the Swansea lads that didn't know him, hung on every word he said."

The club erected the Shankly Gates, 15-foot high cast-iron gates which stand in front of the Anfield Road stand which were inscribed with "You'll Never Walk Alone". They were "unlocked" by his widow Nessie at a low-key ceremony 11 months after his death.

Kevin Keegan suggested that the only fitting memorial would be to rename Anfield 'The Shankly Stadium', "That stadium wouldn't be what it is now if it wasn't for Bill Shankly," he said in 1995. "They might still be a club with no direction as they were when he joined. The gates are not enough, nowhere near enough and the club know that." In 1997 a seven-foot tall bronze statue of Shankly was unveiled outside the Kop funded by club sponsors Carlsberg.

Elsewhere in the city, there are tributes galore. The Shankly Hotel opened in 2016 aimed at fans of the Reds and their legendary former manager, it was a temple to the memory of the great man, adorned with memorabilia, photographs, programmes, a pair of boots in the lobby, and Shankly clan tartan and crests. Behind the reception is one of many Shankly quotations: "Liverpool was made for me and I was made for Liverpool." The Shankly Experience is everywhere, on the way to your room there is a mural charting his career, inside one of the themed rooms is a bust of him on the table and on the ceiling above the bed a long homage to him penned by his grandson, Chris, who is the hotel manager. Owner Lawrence Kenwright fits out all his properties and the Shankly is a £20m project with 57 bedrooms over three floors; a fourth floor has apartments. Breakfast is in the Bastion restaurant (from a Shankly quote about LFC being "a bastion of invincibility"). Other themed hotels in the city include one to the ubiquitous Beatles and the Titanic. One wonders quite what Shanks would have made of it all...

Bill Shankly: "The socialism I believe in isn't really politics. It is a way of living. It is humanity. I believe the only way to live and to be truly successful is by collective effort, with everyone working for each other, everyone helping each other."

Jürgen Klopp: "My political understanding is this: if I am doing well, I want others to do well, too. If there's something I will never do in my life it is vote for the right. I believe in the welfare state. I'm not privately insured."

Bob Paisley became the most successful manager in Liverpool history averaging over 2 trophies a season during his 9 year reign.

BOB PAISLEY

1974 – 1983 - Honours: Div 1 Champions: 1976, 1977, 1979, 1980, 1982, 1983, League Cup 1981, 1982, 1983; European Cup: 1977, 1978, 1981; UEFA Cup: 1976; European Super Cup: 1977, FA Charity Shield 1974, 1976, 1977, 1979, 1980, 1982.

BILL SHANKLY WAS SUCCEEDED BY HIS assistant, Bob Paisley, who continued the work of his predecessor between 1974 and 1983. Since Paisley's nine-year reign, no Liverpool manager has managed longer than the six years Kenny Dalglish managed the club between 1985 and 1991.

Just looking at that list of honours, it is easy to see why Bob Paisley is the doyen of Liverpool managers, it is a sublime record that would take some beating. Yet, it is remarkable to think that he didn't actually become manager of Liverpool until he was 55 years old and then he almost reluctantly succeeded Bill Shankly in the summer of 1974.

New chairman John Smith offered Bob a new contract on an increased salary to step up from Shankly's inner sanctum to the role of manager, but it wasn't about the money. Shankly was an impossible act to follow, so it seemed at the time, a daunting task to take the reins of Mr Liverpool himself, who had been at the club for nearly 15 years and who didn't really want to leave Anfield. In his autobiography Bob suggested to the Board that 'the only way to make the changeover was to promote the rest of the staff'.

Paisley had actually been at Anfield twice as long as Shankly, having signed as professional in May 1938, he was a one-club man, although he had to wait until after the Second World War to make his debut. Bob had played as an amateur for Bishop Auckland, before joining Liverpool where he played almost 300 games until retiring at the end of the relegation season of 1953-54, in his mid-30's. He then served as assistant trainer, chief trainer and assistant manager before taking over from Shankly. There was a seismic change in the personality of the new Liverpool boss, he was the polar opposite of Shankly, Bob even found the task of dealing with the Press a tiresome and daunting 'task' whereas Shankly relished being in the limelight.

Paisley observed that Shankly 'used to wear steel tips on his shoes so that people would hear him coming'; Bob was more at home in slippers! Bob actually had a slight limp from of an old injury to his left ankle, which he would bandage up in a figure of eight before leaving the family home for Anfield and sometimes wore slippers around the club to ease the pain. Bob only cared about 'doing his talking on the pitch', and during his nine-year reign as manager Liverpool embarked on a run of success at home and abroad of enormous success.

Shankly's retirement coincided with the signing from Arsenal of Ray Kennedy on the same day. While forging a prolific forward partnership with John Radford in Arsenal's 'Double' season of 1970-71, Kennedy only scored a hugely disappointing five in 25 League appearances in Paisley's first season as a manager. So Paisley converted Kennedy into an effective midfield player and one of the key men in his team for the rest of the decade.

Without Kevin Keegan for the early weeks of his first season in charge following a lengthy ban following a punch-up with Billy Bremner in the Charity Shield at Wembley in August, Paisley's season ended with a whimper when defeat at Middlesbrough on the penultimate weekend of the season ended their challenge for the title. There was disappointment in the cups and the only highlight was their biggest-ever competitive victory with an 11-0 thrashing of the Norwegian part-timers from Drammen in the opening round of the Cup Winners' Cup but conceding a last-minute equaliser at home to Ferencvaros in the next round, they went out on the away goals rule. But that was to be Paisley's only season at Anfield with no silverware, over the next eight years he won the English championship six times, four European trophies, took the League cup more seriously achieving a hat-trick of victories in his last three seasons as manager.

Paisley outdid Shanks in Europe; leading Liverpool to their second success in the UEFA Cup in 1976 and became the only man to coach teams to the European Champions' Cup on three different occasions. During Paisley's reign, Liverpool set an all-time record of 85 home games unbeaten in all competitions, including 63 league matches stretched over three years from 7th February 1978 to 31st January 1981.

Paisley integrated slowly but surely some wonderful additions; Terry McDermott arrived from Newcastle in 1975, David Johnson from Ipswich in 1976, Kenny Dalglish from Celtic to replace Kevin Keegan in 1977 and a year later Graeme Souness arrived from Middlesbrough, followed by Alan Kennedy. Paisley was reluctant to use his substitute as much as Shankly had been, but young David Fairclough came off the bench to earn the title 'supersub' with a knack of scoring timely goals.

Liverpool became a relentless winning machine under Paisley but also winning in style, scoring 85 in 42 league games in the 1978-79 season with Ray Clemence conceding just 16.

By the time Bob retired in 1983 he had been associated with Liverpool Football club for 44 years. He continued to offer advice as a director, especially to Kenny Dalglish when he took over in the aftermath of Heysel and led the club to the League & FA Cup 'Double' in his first season in charge. The FA Cup was the one domestic trophy that had eluded Bob as manager, just as it had as a player when, after scoring in the 1950 semi-final against Everton, he was replaced by Laurie Hughes for the final with Arsenal which they lost.

The 1983 League Cup final was the last time Paisley led his team out as manager at Wembley, so the players allowed their boss to climb the famous steps to collect the trophy on their behalf. Later, he walked out at Anfield for the last time as the man in charge to be presented with the championship trophy yet again. Bob Paisley had the daunting, near impossible task to follow the clubs' greatest ever legend, only to become one himself. Twenty trophies in nine seasons was the silverware haul of a man loath to make the step up into football management with the unenviable task of succeeding the Shankly.

Yet, the shadow of Shankly was never far away. When Paisley appeared with his players at the St George's Plateau in the city to parade the European Cup won in Rome, the fans still sang the name "Shankly", who stepped forward to take a microphone and respond to the adulation. Young coach Roy Evans, summoned up the courage. 'Boss,' Evans said. 'It's Bob's turn first.' Paisley spoke briefly before handing over the microphone to the 'Boss.' But Paisley hated the limelight, especially the adulation and media attention, unlike Shankly. He also lacked the sort of ego some modern day managers possess which would have made such an episode impossible for them to fathom.

Paisley's nickname was 'the Rat' due to serving with Montgomery's Desert Rats, perhaps some of the players thought of him in that way, as players often have unkind images of their bosses. But the humble Geordie's knowledge of the game and his ability to spot a player, meant Liverpool were never short of quality in their ranks as the of Kenny Dalglish, Alan Hansen, Graeme Souness, Alan Kennedy, Ronnie Whelan,

Ian Rush and Mark Lawrenson to the team were acquired as the team dominated the late 70s and early 80s.

Bob Paisley became recognised as one of the greatest football managers of all-time. His ratio of 1.5 trophies per season eclipsed Alex Ferguson's 1.03 and Brian Clough's 0.61. Bob died on 14 February 1996 at the age of 77 and was honoured by the club with the opening of the Paisley Gates at one of the entrances to Anfield, complementing the existing Shankly Gates.

"There was only one Bob Paisley and he was the greatest of them all. He went through the card in football. He played for Liverpool, he treated the players, he coached them, he managed them and then he became a director. He could tell if someone was injured and what the problem was just by watching them walk a few paces. He was never boastful but had great football knowledge. I owe Bob more than I owe anybody else in the game. There will never be another like him." - Kenny Dalglish

JOE FAGAN

1983-85 - Honours: League Championship 1983/84; League Cup 1983-84; European Cup 1983-84; Manager of the Year 1984

JOE FAGAN WAS BORN IN LIVERPOOL ON 12TH March 1921. He signed for Liverpool in July 1983 but manager George Kay said he wasn't good enough, but he went on to be a dependable centre-half with Manchester City. Joe returned to Liverpool on 30th June 1958 as a coach, and took charge of the reserves in July 1971. Following Bill Shankly's surprise departure as manager he was promoted to first team trainer in July 1974 and by 1979 he was right-hand man to Bob Paisley.

On 1st July 1983, Fagan succeeded Paisley as manager. For Joe it was as tough to replace Paisley as it was for Paisley to replace Shankly, yet he wrote his name in the record books by becoming the first British manager to win three major titles in one season; the League, the Milk Cup and the European Cup.

His response on securing the league title was typically understated: "Not bad is it?" he said. "I don't know how we did it. Well, I do really. It's the players."

The title was secured on May 12, 1984, more than two weeks before Fagan's greatest triumph in the 1984 European Cup final against hosts AS Roma. The Italians boasted Brazilian midfielder Falcao, and World Cup winners Bruno Conti and Francesco Graziani but they were defeated by the mastery of Anfield's coaching staff and players. It began the day before, Fagan disarming fretful Italian journalists with his outward joviality. "Our team talk will be longer than usual for this one - about five minutes," he said.

Souness recalled Fagan addressing his players on the day of the match. Fagan informed them of the time of their coach departure, his views on Roma were succinct. "They must be a good team to get to the European Cup final, but they're not as good as us." Fagan earlier advised his players of a new UEFA edict, banning players jumping over advertising boards to celebrate with fans. "Be careful with the first two goals to keep UEFA happy, but do what you like when you score the third!" was his solution.

His thoughts on leading Liverpool to a fourth European Cup were recorded in his diary. "Well what can I say? We won 'The Big One', and rightly so," he wrote. "Alan Kennedy made us the champion with the best penalty he has ever taken. Well done the lads."

However following that triumph in Rome, skipper Graeme Souness, one of the club's most influential players, left for Italy at the end of the season and the most promising player of the 1983-84 season in the First Division, Luton Town's Paul Walsh, was bought in May for £700,000, Jan Molby from Ajax for £225,000 and midfielder Kevin MacDonald from Leicester. To cap it all, Fagan's signing from the previous January, John Wark, burst into form and was the season's top scorer in 1984-85.

Fagan endured a bad start, missing Souness and with Ian Rush injured until October by which time the European champions were languishing in 20th place, only two places from bottom with just two wins, five draws and four defeats. Liverpool rallied to 10th in December, but in the end couldn't catch Everton who won the title by a distance, Liverpool finished second but reached the European Final again.

The Final was a massive occasion for Fagan as he decided it was his last match in charge. He told his players before the game that after the match they could call him Joe not Boss. Hooliganism destroyed the great occasion and ensured that Joe's career ended on a tragic note following the death of 39 Juventus supporters. When he disembarked from the plane Joe cried on Roy Evans' shoulder. Joe was 62 when he took the job and he had only intended to stay for two years. The tragedy meant that English clubs were banned from European competition for 5 years with Liverpool banned for an extra year due to Heysel.

A TV interview with the BBC's Barry Davies a day after the final is a reminder of the horrors. "I wanted to leave with my head held high," said a distraught Joe, "I can't...".

One of Fagan's signings, Republic of Ireland international Jim Beglin said: "He was just a very genuine nice man. He was a very humble, down to earth person. He had a lovely way about him and was very gentlemanly. Underneath that soft exterior, there was also a hardened professionalism. Joe had authority and when strong words were needed, Joe could produce them."

"He is very much overlooked, probably because he was in charge only two years," says Ronnie Whelan, a member of Fagan's European Cup-winning side. "But this is how he wanted it. He was the archetypal father figure, living in his little house down the road, walking into work

Joe Fagan was the next Boot Room figure to assume command at Anfield and won a treble in his first season

every morning. That was Joe. He wanted to have his club close, go into training and then back to the family. You would never have guessed he was the manager of Liverpool and so instrumental in everything that happened through the Shankly and Paisley era. He was a down-to-earth fella who loved his football, loved his family and loved Liverpool.

"There was a meeting in 1981 when he was first-team coach, which was hugely important to the club. I had just got into the team with Ian Rush and we lost to Manchester City to drop to 12th. Joe called the meeting on his own with the senior players and tore into everyone. It was the right time. He intuitively knew when it needed shaking up. Joe was quiet, but you knew he was there. It was not often he lost it, but when he did it mattered. We won the league that year [winning 20 of the next 22 games]."

Elsewhere in his diaries, Fagan explained why he declined to confuse his players with opposition strength. "Too much can bog your own team down and make you forget to let them worry about you," he wrote.

The Boot Room was Joe's preferred venue for dissecting performances but also for welcoming visiting guests, initially because the cubby-hole-sized space stored the post-match 'refreshments'. Fagan's relationship with a friend connected to Guinness Exports ensured guests were suitably entertained sitting on upturned beer crates. "It's just like popping down to the local," was Paisley's recollection. Elton John, then Watford chairman, requested a pink gin. "We've brown ale, Guinness or whisky lad," Fagan replied.

SIR KENNY DALGLISH

1984-1991 - Honours: First Division: 1985–86, 1987–88, 1989–90; FA Cup: 1985–86, 1988–89; FA Charity Shield: 1988, 1989.

IT WAS MY PLEASURE AND PRIVILEGE TO HAVE interviewed Kenny Dalglish exclusively for a series for the articles of the *Daily Mirror*, so I know the guy on a personal level. Meticulous would be the one word that I would use for the Anfield Legend –Kenny made sure he approved and authorised every word, even it meant two or three drafts before he was fully satisfied.

Working so closely with him, it was easy to see why he was so obsessive in his career, both as player and then as manager of Liverpool from 1985 to 1991. King Kenny was a Liverpool legend as a player, but he then became an iconic manager who helped heal a community in the wake of the Hillsborough disaster and raised millions to fight cancer, for which he was honoured with the Lifetime Achievement Award at this year's Mirror Pride of Sport Awards in partnership with TSB.

He amassed 26 major honours, including 13 league titles and three European Cups with Liverpool, Blackburn Rovers and Celtic as player and then manager. Following 1989's Hillsborough disaster and the deaths of 96 fans, he organised hospital visits to the injured, spent time with bereaved families and made sure Liverpool were represented at every single funeral, attending many himself. In addition he raised millions of pounds for charity, and in 2004 he founded The Marina Dalglish Appeal after his wife successfully fought breast cancer.

The horrors of Hillsborough is something that will forever be etched into Dalglish's memory, and I should know how much it affected him as I was at the semi-final and witnessed it all; it was something that affected everyone but as Liverpool manager Kenny took it upon himself to suffer the most. For my part I campaigned vigorously as the Chief Football Writer of the *Daily Mirror* on behalf of the club's supporters who were vilified in certain sections of the media.

He might now be a Sir, but at Anfield Kenny is still King. He is universally recognised as one of the greatest players of his generation, he was offered the job of player-manager at the age of 34 just days after

Kenny took over as player-manager in 1985 and won the League and Cup double in his first season, the first of 8 honours across two spells as manager.

the terrible tragedy at Heysel stadium in Brussels. These were difficult times for English football but especially for Liverpool. Kenny had the experience of Bob Paisley to help him through such a tumultuous time with English clubs banned indefinitely from European competition. After the club was vilified for what happened in Brussels, Kenny helped rebuild Liverpool's reputation, then he helped other people to rebuild their lives when a similar tragedy struck Liverpool's own supporters.

Kenny coped with his new role as player-manager so well that Liverpool won the League and FA Cup Double in his first season in charge and it could have been a triple success because the club also reached the semi-final of the League Cup but were surprisingly beaten by Queens Park Rangers.

The team had made a good start to the league programme with just one defeat from their opening 10 matches but they were still nine points behind Manchester United, who had a perfect record from the same number of games. Liverpool gradually chipped away at United's lead but eventually their rivals for the title would be Merseryside rivals and reigning champions Everton. Dalglish was reluctant to pick himself and he wasn't in the team when a below-par Liverpool lost a crucial home fixture with Everton towards the end of February.

After that he played every minute of the final seven league games, all were won and he scored at Chelsea on the final day of the season to ensure Liverpool were champions for the 16th time. At Wembley a week later Everton were beaten 3-1 in the Cup Final. Ian Rush grabbed the headlines for his two goals, but Craig Johnston and Jan Molby were outstanding.

The following season Everton regained the championship as Liverpool finished without a trophy for the second time in three seasons after losing the League Cup final to Arsenal, the first time Liverpool had lost when Ian Rush scored. Kenny knew Rush would be going to Juventus in the summer but he was already planning ahead with boyhood Liverpool fan John Aldridge arriving from Oxford United before the end of the 1986-87 season. In the close-season the manager brought in the exciting talents of Peter Beardsley and John Barnes and shortly after the season started Ray Houghton. All were influential as Liverpool won the championship by nine points from Manchester United with some breathtaking displays, destroying Nottingham Forest 5-0 at Anfield four days after beating the same opponents to reach the FA Cup final. Liverpool were strong favourites to beat Wimbledon in the 1988 FA Cup final but Beardsley had a goal ruled out because referee Brian Hill failed to play an advantage and called play back for a free-kick to be taken in Liverpool's favour. Instead of being a goal up, a few minutes later they were a goal down following Laurie Sanchez's header. A penalty was awarded to Liverpool in the second half for a perfectly fair challenge but John Aldridge saw his spot-kick saved by Dave Beasant as another double slipped away.

Ian Rush returned from Italy after just a season. Aldridge was the main striker with 21 league goals during the 1988-89 season, although Rush was injured for much of the season and scored only seven league goals, his least productive year since becoming a first-team regular. When they lost at Old Trafford on New Year's Day it was their fifth league defeat and their chances of catching leaders Arsenal seemed slim but 48 points were taken from the next 54 and that meant Liverpool could afford to lose their final league game, at home to Arsenal, by one goal and still take the title. But Michael Thomas, who would later join Liverpool, scored an injury-time winner that took the championship trophy to Highbury.

It was hard to imagine the manager could lift his players as a month earlier in the FA Cup semi-final with Nottingham Forest was the biggest disaster in English football history.

My experience with the initial Inquiry into the Hillsborough Disaster summed up the miscarriage of justice that it took Liverpool supporters 30 years to overturn. I made a statement which never saw the light of day in the many court proceedings which followed, and I was never given an explanation as to why, in fact I never heard from the police again after giving this statement! This is what I told police investigators at the time…

"In addition to writing about the actual game of football I have observed crowd behaviour including riot situations both abroad and at home. I have also been a keen observer of police methods in relation to football games at home and abroad.

"Having arrived in Sheffield with the ground visible in front of us, we asked a Police Officer on duty where the official press car park was. This officer stated he did not know and there were other officers at this location who also did not know. I thought to myself that it was quite amusing that police officers on duty at the ground did not know the geography of the stadium. This is not an uncommon problem when visiting grounds.

"In retrospect I believe this is a key area in keeping things running smoothly and that the officers outside the ground should know the key areas to direct people to. This should be part of a nationwide co-ordinated strategy.

"On Saturday 15th April 1989, I attended Hillsborough football ground to cover the FA semi-final between Liverpool and Nottingham Forest, for the Daily Mirror newspaper. Having entered the ground we went as a group to the main entrance. I believe one of our group had to collect his press pass. I had mine, in fact I also had a press overflow ticket. In fact I was asked if I had a spare ticket by a group of youths near to the main entrance and I must admit I was tempted to give it away. I did not as it would have meant the fan sitting in the press area. We then all went to the press room.

"From the press room I went to the press box and took up my seat at about 2.45 pm. The atmosphere was as I expected, a massive turnout of both sets of fans, and in particular the Liverpool fans. I was aware that the West Stand was heaving with Liverpool fans who were swaying which is exactly what I expected to see and I thought nothing of this at that stage.

"The teams came out and kick off was to schedule. Then virtually after the kick off there was a surge by the Liverpool fans in the Leppings

Lane end behind the goal and at this point I became aware there was trouble at that end. Also within a minute it was clear that people at that end were in trouble and I noticed one guy was already over the fence and in distress.

"During the next couple of minutes it was crystal clear that people were in distress and escaping over the fence. Even at this early stage, it was clearly obvious to me that this was not a riot situation but a genuine case of fans being in peril on the terraces. I make this point because although it was obvious to me in the press box that this was the case, it was not obvious to the police on the touchline who were clearly treating this as a pitch invasion.

"I then made a note of an incident I found particularly disturbing when a police officer who had gone to that end tried to put a fan back over the fence. He was clearly unaware of what was happening and it was a clear indication that the police were not co-ordinated in their operations and sadly lacking in communication.

"As an experienced sports writer as previously described I have a number of observations regarding the tragedy which I hope will be of benefit to the enquiry. I would like to start with my comments regarding the football authorities but I must state that I am not holding anyone more responsible than any other, it is just a convenient starting point.

"The whole of football has abdicated its responsibility for the safety, the convenience, the facilities and the well being of its paying customers. There is a distinct lack of leadership in formulating any policy for the benefit of the ordinary fan. Instead a squabble over everything and anything that effects them and their football clubs such as the distribution of TV money, the voting structure, the allocation of cup final tickets to County FA's instead of the game of football. They should have minimum criteria for major football stadiums in respect of safety and well being of the spectator and that minimum criteria should go far beyond the present Government safety legislation.

"The Football Authorities have abdicated their responsibility in the policing of major soccer matches. It is the police not the clubs who decide on strength of numbers, strategies, treatment of fans, etc, paid for by the football club. It should be the club's responsibility and therefore the League and FA's responsibility rather than any suspicion that the number of policemen inside grounds should be dictated by cost rather than necessity.

"A whole series of errors were made by the police in respect of this match. I suspect that officers outside the ground did not have detailed knowledge of the geography of the stadium and delays may have occurred if the police were unable to give the fans direction as to where to park for example.

"There was a failure to advance filter fans without tickets, and a clear breakdown in communications from the events I witnessed, not only in relation inside the ground and outside the ground but also to ensure there were officers to direct fans when the door was opened for instance blocking off the tunnel.

"There appears to be an unwritten policing policy that if there is trouble outside then let the fans in. This seems an easy option to take and clearly had disastrous consequences on this occasion. It also encourages fans to turn up without tickets. "Ticket touting is an abhorrent practice, more significantly it encourages fans to turn up without tickets hoping to get in. There should be Court legislation to ban this practice within a five mile radius of any football ground. It is also the FA's responsibility to clamp down on the sources of such tickets.

"The points that I have made are both criticisms of the events at Hillsborough and items that need to be addressed to prevent such a tragedy again. Lastly, a point I would like to add is the significant lack of medical facilities at such a major match which should be the responsibility of the FA.

The points I made in his statement were seemingly ignored – and the same may well have applied to the version of events of others. Perhaps the eventual verdict could have been reached sooner.

Liverpool won the replayed game and it was perhaps appropriate that it was again their neighbours Everton who would oppose them in one of the most emotional cup finals ever staged. Liverpool won 3-2 but the city and football was still in shock at what had happened in Sheffield. The 15th April, 1989 changed a lot of people's lives for ever. It changed Kenny Dalglish too. He may have been loved by Liverpool supporters but he was perceived as a dour man by the media. The manager and some of his senior players attended many funerals and made themselves constantly available to counsel bereaved families. Just by being there and showing that they cared, they gave support, comfort and strength to people whose lives had been torn apart in the face of such a massive tragedy.

Although his playing days were now over, apart from a brief cameo in the final league match after the championship had been won, Kenny led Liverpool to their third title in five seasons the following year. They achieved their biggest-ever league win with a 9-0 destruction of Crystal Palace. Ten of the players who started that rout against Palace also started the F.A. cup semi-final against the same opponents nearly seven months later and Liverpool lost 4-3 after extra-time! For the first time since he took over as manager, Dalglish was the victim of some criticism from a section of the fans who were unhappy with team-selections for away games that they saw as unnecessarily negative and also for a couple of purchases of decidedly average players.

The following season the Merseyside clubs were paired together in the FA Cup 5th round. The match at Anfield was drawn and three days later the clubs met again at Goodison Park. On an extraordinary night, Liverpool took the lead four times but on each occasion parity was restored by Everton. Dalglish was exhausted physically, mentally and emotionally. At the press conference at Anfield the next day Dalglish reached the end of the line and knew that for once in his life he had to put himself and his family before his job. Kenny looked a broken man and it was impossible not to feel for him and wonder how much of a part Hillsborough and its aftermath had played in his decision to quit.

A refreshed Kenny returned with Blackburn Rovers. Jack Walker's millions helped but it was some achievement in eventually taking an unfashionable club to the League championship. I am not sure Kenny was too happy with me when, again with the Daily Mirror, I broke the story of his imminent sacking at St. James's Park. Kenny was driving to the training ground when he heard the 'news' on his car radio, stopped the car, called chairman Freddie Shepherd, who requested he turned round and meet him at the ground rather than continue to the training ground. As the day unfolded, Kenny was dismissed by Newcastle and replaced by Ruud Gullit just as the Mirror headline had forecast that morning.

GRAEME SOUNESS

1991-94 - Honours: FA Cup 1992

AFTER TWO YEARS WITH SAMPDORIA, GRAEME Souness returned to become player-manager of Glasgow Rangers in 1986 where he enjoyed a stellar start to his managerial career accruing 3 Scottish League titles and 4 Scottish League Cups before, almost inevitably as one of Liverpools' greatest-ever players and captains, returning to Anfield as the clubs' manager shortly before the end of the 1990-1991 season.

He was introduced to the crowd before the home game with Norwich City on the 20th April. Five league matches remained but Liverpool's chances of catching Arsenal were slim and successive away defeats to Chelsea and Nottingham Forest early in May ended the faint hope of retaining the title.

During the summer Mark Wright and Dean Saunders were signed from relegated Derby County and Mark Walters arrived from the manager's former club Rangers. The team won four of the opening half dozen matches but there was only one victory from the next nine league games, scoring just six. After scoring in successive home matches at the end of August, the goals dried up from Saunders and even though Steve McManaman was emerging, neither he nor Walters were ever seen as prolific. Ian Rush missed the early weeks of the season and Souness bought Rob Jones from Crewe early in October and the full-back made an impressive debut against Manchester United at Old Trafford.

Stoke City and Port Vale held Liverpool to draws at Anfield before being defeated in cup replays, but Liverpool suffered an embarrassing 4th round defeat at Peterborough United.

Liverpool were allowed to enter European club competitions for the first time in six years since the 1985 European cup final in Brussels (other English clubs had been re-admitted in 1990) but there were still restrictions on the number of foreigners that could play.

Souness had to pick his team carefully for the opening round against Finnish club Kuusysi Lahti who were finished off with a late flourish at Anfield but won their meaningless home encounter a fortnight later.

Souness failed to maintain the success of the Boot Room and an interview with the reviled Sun newspaper proved to be a step too far for supporters.

Another away defeat followed in the 2nd round at Auxerre but there was a thrilling fight-back in the home leg when Liverpool overturned a 0-2 deficit with goals from Molby, Marsh and Walters.

Souness had a reputation of being an aggressive player and some of that abrasiveness stayed with him as a manager. After finishing first and second in the previous two seasons, the Liverpool team was no longer good enough to challenge for the championship. With only three of 21 league fixtures won away from home, the title was out of reach but it was the FA Cup that saved Liverpool's season but even that came at a price, certainly where the manager was concerned. Michael Thomas was bought from Arsenal shortly before Christmas and it was his goal against Aston Villa that saw Liverpool through to the semi-final where they would meet outsiders Portsmouth. After the drawn match with the south coast club at Highbury on the 5th April, Souness announced to the media that he would be going into hospital immediately to undergo a triple by-pass heart operation. There had been no warning, so it was a big shock.

But sympathy turned to outrage from supporters when on the anniversary of the Hillsborough disaster the manager's picture and story were splashed on the front page of the Sun newspaper. An apology later came but although Souness defended the timing of the article and might not have had any say in the actual date it would be printed, many supporters saw his decision to sell his story to that newspaper as unforgivable. However Souness was able to attend the cup final against Sunderland with a doctor in close attendance but the die was cast with supporters following the Sun article.

That summer Paul Stewart arrived for more than £2m but he wasn't they only one the manager bought in who failed to make much impact. Winning just three league games away, Chesterfield came to Anfield in a cup tie and led 3-0 before the home team somehow scraped a 4-4 draw. Only 12,500 bothered to attend and probably a quarter of those were in the visitors end. When Liverpool went to Middlesbrough in the middle of March, the Teesiders occupied one of the relegation places but could have joined Liverpool on the same number of points if they had won. Thanks to a late winner from Rush and a flurry of goals from the Welshman as the season reached its conclusion, the club climbed into a more respectable sixth. But when Liverpool played Spurs at Anfield on the final day of the season, the manager was absent with rumours that he had resigned or been dismissed. He survived any attempt from the club to remove him but possibly only because of his close friendship with chairman David Moores.

Nigel Clough and Neil Ruddock arrived during the summer of 1993, making an immediate impact as Liverpool won their opening three matches in style and went top of the table. However all four league games lost in September without a single goal, and a public disagreement during the defeat at Goodison where Grobbelaar and McManaman came to blows.

Souness gave Robbie Fowler his first-team debut in the League Cup at Fulham and the youngster scored at Craven Cottage and then all five goals when Liverpool won the return leg. Robbie was an immediate success but not Julian Dicks signed from West Ham in September with Mike Marsh and David Burrows going the other way.

Shortly after New Year, Manchester United came to Anfield and swept into a 3-0 lead with the visiting supporters taunting the home crowd and its manager with a sarcastic chant of "Souness must stay". On one of the final occasions in front of a standing Kop, Clough (2) and Ruddock brought the score back to 3-3. The team survived a tricky FA Cup tie with Bristol City at Ashton Gate and brought the West Country club back to Merseyside for a replay. But for the second season in a row Liverpool were dumped out of the competition in front of their own supporters. This was a far worse defeat than to Bolton in 1993. There was deserved applause from the home fans towards the victors at the end but also boos aimed at the Liverpool team and its manager, Souness's time was up.

Souness has since brought other teams to Anfield but resentment persists. At the time of his appointment in 1991 there probably weren't too many who disagreed with the choice. "I should have resigned there and then," he writes in his 2017 autobiography about the Sun article. "It ultimately soured my relationship with the Liverpool supporters forever and it's something I deeply regret. If I could turn one thing round in my football career, it would be that." Souness's explanation at the time was that he had been managing in Scotland at the time of Hillsborough and, not being on Merseyside, misjudged the depth of outrage that led to Liverpool supporters boycotting the Sun. Regardless, his goose was cooked with the fans from that day on and the form of his team didn't help. More recently he said: "It was an obvious mistake I made in agreeing to do that. Liverpool will always be the place I look back in terms of the place where I enjoyed playing, it was just unique. The dressing room - if you are winning every week it's very easy to have a great dressing room - but we went through hiccups and had a real bond. Liverpool will always be a very special place to me. There are things that happened there when I was manager which I deeply regret but I can't turn back the clock, how I wish I could, but I can't, and that hurts me badly, that I am perceived by some people to be something I'm not."

Souness won five league titles and three European Cups as a player with Liverpool, but despite winning the FA Cup in 1992 as their manager, Liverpool's dominance of English football ended with him. He admits he tried to change the culture of the club too fast. "That was a job that I was always going to be offered and I took it at the wrong time. There is no doubt about it. I got the Liverpool job when I was 38. I had five years at Rangers that had gone really well, I had tremendous support from David Holmes and then David Murray, and I was running the show there and it went very well. I was offered the Liverpool job twice and said no twice, and then ultimately said yes. I thought I would go in there and change it. The one thing I learnt going to Italy was there's no real change in how the game should be played, but how players look after themselves. I was one of the chaps when it came to enjoying myself, and I tried to change that, and it was very easy when I went to Rangers to change that because that was a team that hadn't won the league in nine years. I was saying 'this is what we are going to do and this is what we will do after the game'. At Rangers they bought into it because they were young boys, so then when I go to Liverpool and say I don't want to see fish and chips after the game and I don't want to see lager under the seats on the bus for the way back, the response you would get would be 'we have always done that'. It was very hard for me to argue that because I had been part of that culture. I made many mistakes and my biggest crime was trying to make the changes too quickly

"One of the biggest mistakes I made was, Peter Robinson, who ran the show at Liverpool and was the chief executive and made all the decisions, said to me 'do you want to do the contracts'? I had done the contracts at Rangers so I said 'yeah, I'll do those'. I felt that was a monster mistake. I remember one incident where we signed Dean Saunders and Mark Wright and they had gone on to earn slightly more than Rushy and Ronnie Whelan. I remember Rushy knocking on the door and saying 'you're going to have to give me more money' and I said 'I understand why you are saying that, but the money is sneaking up and sneaking up, they have come on big transfer fees and that's why they are getting paid more than you'. But he said 'everything I done for this club…' That might have been a Wednesday or Thursday and I was saying to Rushy 'sorry I can't, that's the way it is' and then on Saturday at 2.45pm I have to put my arm around him and say 'make sure you give me everything now'.

ROY EVANS

1994-98 - Honours: League Cup 1994-95

ROY EVANS TOOK OVER THE ANFIELD OFFICE after Graeme Souness was forced out by the club due to a run of back results. Evans had been an integral part of the Boot Room dynasty begun by the legendary Bill Shankly. Having supported the club as a boy, he signed for them as a teenager, played for the first team and then served as an assistant coach, manager and co-manager. Evans had been selected for just nine league games in as many years prompting the Shankly quip "the lad's pace can be deceptive – he's much slower than you think"! It may have been a cruel jibe but a succinct Shanks appraisal of Evans limited playing career. When Paisley succeeded Shankly in 1974, Evans entered the Boot Room and enjoyed great success as reserve team manager. The club won the Central League seven times in nine years and Evans was responsible for bringing through Liverpool greats such as Ian Rush, Ronnie Whelan and Sammy Lee.

Evans belief was that they had to be all-rounders. "We didn't really have people who were qualified," Evans says. "For example, we had a doctor who would make the key decisions but we would do most of the medical work. We all took a first-aid course. I went to Lilleshall [the FA's former school of excellence] for a course just to make sure we could get an injured player off the pitch safely."

Their approach to injuries would not stand up to modern standards. "Early on Bob Paisley acted as the physio even though he hadn't been trained," writes Peter Hooton in The Boor Room Boys. "Tommy Smith used to say that Paisley didn't know how the equipment worked, so he was understandably a bit reticent when getting any sort of electric shock treatment." This is a million miles away from today's environment, where the current team doctor Andy Massey has 24 trained medical staff working for him across Melwood and the academy, including several fitness and conditioning coaches, two masseurs and a nutritionist.

"We would also take all the coaching sessions for all the different levels at different times," says Evans. "Joe Fagan, Ronnie Moran and myself would even have to take the kit home to get it washed. But none of us had a coaching badge. Whether it be Shankly, Paisley, Fagan or Ronnie Moran, not one of them held a coaching qualification." Evans recalls when Ian St. John told Shankly that he was going to do a coaching course at Lilleshall, Shankly responded: "'Tell them nothing, son'. But it wasn't quite as polite as that and had a few more swear words!"

Although Evans acknowledges the need for specialists in the modern game, he says the simplicity of the boot room served them well. "There were four or five of us doing all these different jobs that are now carried out by 15-20 people," Evans says. "The upside is as the manager you only had to listen to a handful of opinions. Sometimes the more people you've got, the more difficult decision-making becomes."

Evans benefited from the autonomy while in charge of the reserves. "They let me get on with it, so I had the pick of all the players who were not in the first team. If you were 16 and good enough you were in and playing against men," Evans says. "That made them better players who were not overawed if they then made the step-up to the first team." Today's academy players rarely play outside their specific age group, so do not get opportunities to mix with more experienced players.

As an example of the way the Boot Room worked, Bob Paisley once asked Evans, then reserve team coach, which of the young midfielders Sammy Lee or Kevin Kewley to put on the Liverpool bench for the home game against Middlesbrough on 2 January, 1978. Evans suggested Kewley. 'Are you sure?' asked Paisley, who was clearly unconvinced. However he took Evans opinion on board and it was Kewley, brought off the bench the following night, for what turned out to be the only game for Liverpool. Lee went on to appear for the club nearly 300 times! "I'm a 25-year-old guy and he is asking my opinion," Evans recalls. "He is saying, 'You might not get it right but you might get one little thing we don't.' They gave you your voice, your confidence, and that's the only way you could learn, really. It showed he wanted the people below him to have a voice and to speak."

Evans was brought in as manager just after the midway point of the 1993/94 season. Liverpool had sacked Souness after poor performances and "£9m of transfer debt". The club looked to Evans to save the club's season with sixteen league games to turn it around. He got off to a reasonable start with a two-all draw at Norwich. A Merseyside derby win was the highlight of that debut half season but a defeat by bottom of the table Sheffield United at Anfield left doubts about Evans as the clubu finished the season losing 1-0 to Norwich at Anfield adrift in

Roy Evans represented the last of the Boot Room Boys. His reign saw some great attacking football and the rise of local stars such as Robbie Fowler and Steve McManaman but only one trophy.

eighth place.

With England failing to qualify for the 1994 USA World Cup, Evans saw a chance to build but the only signing was young Danish keeper Michael Stengaard. Out went Bruce Grobelaar and Denmark's Torben Piechnik. Supporters questioned Evans as bookmakers set the worst odds for some considerable time of Liverpool winning the title at 20-1. It was not a good start to his first full season with player unrest and Julian Dicks and Don Hutchison sold off to West Ham and Mark Wright was relegated to the reserves. Yet in an early game Liverpool put six past Crystal Palace before teenage striker Robbie Fowler caused a shock by destroying Arsenal with a hat-trick in under five minutes, setting a Premiership record for the quickest hat-trick at the time. With John Barnes and Steve McManaman enjoying Evans' new tactics, Liverpool continued their run of form but a draw with West Ham and a defeat to Manchester United at Old Trafford started a run of bad league form. Liverpool finished a respectable fourth but Evans took Liverpool to Wembley and won his one and only piece of silver wear beating Bolton Wanderers 2-1 in the League Cup final.

Before the 1995/96 season Evans splashed £8m on Nottingham Forest's Stan Collymore and for a time it seemed possible that Liverpool could nip in between Manchester United and Newcastle to nick the title, especially after a thrilling 4-3 win over the Geordies during the title run-in. Yet inconsistency proved to be their undoing, although Evans took them back to Wembley again, this time losing the final of the FA Cup 1-0 to Manchester United who secured the league and cup double.

The following season Evans brought in Euro 96 star Patrik Berger from Dortmund and promoted two bright stars through the youth team; Michael Owen scored on his debut at Selhurst Park, going down 2-1 to Wimbledon during the 1996/97 season that would see Liverpool come within a few games of winning their coveted 19th title.

Michael Owen finished top Premiership scorer for the 1997/98 season but the team had faded badly by this point and Collymore was sold to Aston Villa for £7m. During the summer of 1998 Evans brought in Frenchman Gerard Houllier to join him in a managerial partnership. The partnership was not a success. Despite a good pre-season and start to the Premiership campaign, a bad run of results included elimination from the League Cup 3-1 to Spurs at Anfield.

In November 1998, Evans left after forty years in the club's service as a player, coach and finally manager, leaving Houllier in sole charge. Evans' departure effectively signalled the end of the Boot Room era. Although Jürgen Klopp will not be converting any broom cupboards in the near future, he knows football management is a team game. "I feel very blessed to be supported by both Pep Lijnders [first-team coach] and Peter Krawietz [assistant coach], as well as John Achterberg [goalkeeping coach], Andreas Kornmayer [head of fitness and conditioning] and the countless others at Melwood who are vital to us." The Boot Room principle remains the same, but the working conditions, salaries, and sheer volume of staff are vastly different.

GERARD HOULLIER

1998-2004 - Honours: FA Cup: 2000–01, Football League Cup: 2000–01, 2002–03; FA Charity Shield: 2001; UEFA Cup: 2000–01; UEFA Super Cup: 2001

GERARD HOULLIER CONSIDERED HIMSELF one of the most avid admirers of the Liverpool Way, and was a students of the Anfield club. He attended Reds matches while working at Alsop Comprehensive School, three decades before he took charge of the team! It was therefore a thrill and an honour when he became manager, and in a throw back to the Boot Room philosophy he brought influential former captain Phil Thompson back to the club as his assistant, a hugely popular appointment.

For the first time the board decided to let two managers run team affairs. If the appointment of Kenny Dalglish as the club's first player-manager in the middle of the 1980's was a surprise, this was an even bigger shock. Houllier's appointment was regarded as a demotion for Roy Evans. Long after he left Anfield, Evans wrote about the odd job situation in his book 'Ghost on the Wall'.

Initially the relationship seemed fine but it didn't take long for rumblings of discontent. A good start had been made to the league programme with three wins and a draw from the opening four fixtures, then an away match with West Ham and an apparently disagreement over whether Karl-Heinz Riedle should start the game or not. One wanted to save him for the European match in midweek; the other thought he should play from the start at Upton Park. In the end Riedle didn't start. He came on as a substitute and scored but the game was lost.

Two defeats and a draw in next three away matches in the league with no goals had the fans fearful, although attendances at Anfield for league games remained high but only 22,000 turned up to watch Fulham in the League Cup towards the end of October and less than 21,000 for the visit of Spurs in the next round. Spurs won 3-1 and this defeat came only three days after Derby County had also won a match at Anfield in the league. Evans had had enough. By the time Leeds United came to Anfield the following weekend, Houllier was in sole charge of team affairs.

Houllier's reign 'proper' started with a home defeat to Leeds United, their third loss at Anfield in a week, followed by an early exit from Europe as Celta Vigo won both legs of their European tie, although at the time there were still restrictions on the number of foreign players that could participate, it all added to the general feeling that club needed to halt the slide.

Steven Gerrard was introduced as a late substitute against Blackburn at Anfield at the end of November but results remained inconsistent and a seventh place finishing failed to generate European football. Defeat at Old Trafford in the FA Cup 4th round was hard to take as Liverpool held on to Michael Owen's early goal only to concede two goals in injury-time. United went on to win the Treble.

Sami Hyypia and Stephane Henchoz arrived in the summer to bolster a fragile defence and19 fewer goals were conceded in the league programme than during the previous season. Striker Titi Camara and Vladimir Smicer also arrived. Four league defeats before the end of September did not suggest the awaited turnaround. However a solid second half of the season included a run of one defeat in 18 league matches. Chances of a lucrative place in the Champions' League, ended with no wins and no goals in the final five games. Defeat on the final day at Bradford City consigned Liverpool to the UEFA Cup.

Several more signings arrived, the experience of Markus Babbel and Gary McAllister were vital but the Liverpool careers of Nicky Barmby, Christian Ziege and Jari Litmanen would be brief. Nevertheless the team was difficult to beat and although nine league defeats was the same as the previous season, three of those, all away, came during a poor spell in November. The final league position was improved by one place to third. Again a win was required in the final match again to qualify for the Champions' League, this time it was achieved at the Valley, with a comfortable 4-0 victory.

The following season the trophies flowed at last as Liverpool took their place in the history books with an unprecedented triple success. It took penalties to beat Birmingham City in the League Cup and luck was on their side in the FA Cup final win over Arsenal, Owen's two late strikes provided revenge for three previous final defeats by the Gunners, but Liverpool were not the better side on that day.

The UEFA cup proved a tough ask as they were paired with Roma, Porto and Barcelona. Winning in Rome's Olympic Stadium was a

Gerard Houliier brought 6 trophies to Anfield during his 6 year reign but the coveted league title proved to be beyond him.

massive achievement, the second leg ended in controversy after the Spanish referee appeared to give the Italians a chance of equalising the aggregate score only to change his mind and give a corner-kick after seeming to originally point to the spot following a handball in the area by Babbel. Gary McAllister's confident penalty was the only goal of the semi-final with Barcelona and he repeated that feat in Dortmund when Liverpool prevailed over Alaves with a 'golden goal' own-goal in the closing minutes of extra-time!

Liverpool finished runners-up the following season and 80 points might have won the title in other seasons but it wasn't enough to beat a rampant Arsenal side who went on to win the double. Sander Westerveld was axed after a late error at Bolton with Jerzy Dudek and Chris Kirkland immediately arriving to replace him. Houllier also sold Paul Ince and his decisions showed a ruthless streak.

During the home match with Leeds in October 2001, the manager failed to emerge for the second half and it was later announced that he had been rushed to hospital for immediate and life-saving heart surgery. Phil Thompson deputised and did an admirable job until Houllier returned to take his place back on the bench before an emotional match with

Roma in the middle of March. The team navigated the two group stages of the Champions' League and had real hopes of further progress when they drew Leverkusen. But a narrow home victory was not enough. Houllier controversially substituted Hamann for Smicer after an hour and the tie was eventually lost 3-4 on aggregate.

Liverpool made a blistering start to the league programme in 2002-03 with nine wins and three draws from the opening dozen matches but during the next game at Middlesbrough, Houllier was criticised for a cautious approach that resulted in a 1-0 defeat. Liverpool hit a shocking run that hadn't been seen since the relegation season of 1953-54. Despite splashing big on Diouf, Cheyrou and Diao, none proved to be value for money. Houllier failed to negotiate the opening group stage of the Champions' League and Liverpool were knocked out of the UEFA cup by Celtic despite a 1-1 draw in the away leg in Glasgow, although the Frenchman earned a reprieve following another success in the League Cup against bitter rivals Manchester United.

Harry Kewell arrived from Leeds and two French starlets Antony le Tallec and Florent Sinama Pongolle were acquired pre-season. Houllier reached his target of finishing fourth to qualify for the Champions League as Newcastle faltered toward the end to the season but it wasn't enough to pacify the Liverpool board and during the following week a press conference was called to announce that the manager would be leaving with one year of his contract still to run. The Reds trailed Premiership champions Arsenal by 30 points and were 15 points behind third-placed Manchester United, as the board lost patience.

While some of his expensive signings failed, he changed a lot of the culture regarding diet and lifestyle. Four trophies in five seasons gave the supporters some unforgettable memories, and he believed he was the man to take Liverpool that one step further.

The then Liverpool chief executive Rick Parry said at the time: "After considerable thought and discussion the board have decided to part company with the manager and Gerard has accepted this with typical good grace. We have always said we would review our position at the end of the season and that is what we have now done. Although we have reached the Champions League, that is a minimum standard and not a goal. For a variety of reasons the board decided that change was necessary if we were to realistically challenge for the title next season.

"But this is not a day for anger, recrimination or speculation. It is a day for dignity and respect and I want to publicly thank Gerard for his considerable achievements during his time in charge. We all have very fond memories of the historic treble and the other trophies won but there were many other special occasions and I will personally never forget the reception given to Gerard after he returned from illness for the Champions League game against Roma. We had many good times together."

When Houllier left Anfield, the Frenchman insisted: "I may have left Liverpool, but Liverpool will not leave me."

His farewell statement read, "I arrived here six years ago as a Liverpool supporter and I leave as an even bigger supporter. I may have left Liverpool, but Liverpool will not leave me. I will return to watch the team as a fan. I have four special memories that I take away with me. Michael Owen scoring the winner against Arsenal with his left foot [in the FA Cup final], Gary McAllister being handed the man of the match award against Alaves [in the UEFA Cup], the mosaic when I was recovering from heart surgery and Steven Gerrard taking his daughter around the pitch on the last day of the season."

A year after leaving Liverpool, Houllier signed a two-year contract with Lyon, the French club which had just won four consecutive Ligue 1 championships. He increased that run to six but was unable to convert Lyon's dominance of their domestic game on to the European stage. Towards the end of May 2007 he left Lyon. He returned to the English game in September 2010, taking over from Martin O'Neill at Aston Villa, appointing Gary McAllister his assistant, knowing him well from his Liverpool days.

On the 20th April, Houllier was taken to hospital to undergo tests after falling ill in the night. This was clearly a concern because of his previous illness in 2001 while he was Liverpool's manager. Early reports from Birmingham indicated that his condition was stable but he was not immediately discharged and therefore was unable to attend training so Gary McAllister took over that responsibility. Gérard was expected to be discharged from coronary care by the end of April after intensive tests showed that his heart was "working properly". It wasn't a major surprise when Aston Villa announced early in June 2011 that Houllier would be leaving less than a year after taking over. Villa officials were concerned that a return to the dugout could cause the Frenchman further health issues.

RAFAEL BENITEZ

2004-10 - Honours: European Cup 2004-05; FA Cup 2005-06

BENÍTEZ KNEW LITTLE OF BILL SHANKLY WHEN he became Liverpool manager in June 2004 but he soon learned of the man who revolutionised the club, and while still in charge of the team the Spaniard discussed the spirit of Shankly as the 50th anniversary of the great man's departure from the club approached.

Benitez suggested at that time that the appointment of Sammy Lee as assistant manager was partly designed to rediscover the spirit of the club's modern founding father. "Everything has changed in football and everything is different in society nowadays. Everyone has iPods or Wiis and in a hurry to do things. But still we try to have the same ideas as Shankly," said Benítez. "When people talk about the 'Liverpool Way', it was always to win. We try to do this and that is our priority if possible. We try to do things properly, like Shankly did.

"When we decided to bring in Sammy we had someone who knew the philosophy and the ideals of the club. One of the things we did after Sammy came was to change a little bit of decoration at Melwood. We now have a lot of photographs of former players, the legends and the managers and quotes from different people. We have been trying to bring this spirit. It is much better now. When people come to training now, they can look around and it is an inspiration to them. It would have been an honour to have met him [Shankly]. I didn't really know much about him before I came but I started reading books about him and made sure that I spoke with a lot of people. I kept reading all those little phrases and sentences. But I also listened to an old radio interview he did, over and over again when I was at home or when I was in my car. I struggled at first with the accent but once it all became clear, I was really impressed with his ideas. He was so ahead of his time. He was talking about training sessions and if it had been raining and the players were wet, he would tell them to careful and he would look after them, make sure they recovered properly and ate the right food."

Rafa continued the work Gerard Houllier had done in lifting Liverpool from mid table to the top of the table. The highlight of his reign

Rafa Benitez with the coveted European Cup after a remarkable final in Istanbul. Benitez never quite realised his ambition of winning the league title at Anfield, coming closest in 2009.

was undoubtedly winning the Champions League in his first season in Istanbul with a side which very few regarded as top class. However Rafa had the great fortune to find a gem in Steven Gerrard and it was the local lad who would be go on to make his name in the final, hauling Liverpool back from the brink and overturning a 3 goal half time deficit. Yes, luck played its part with opponents AC Milan spurning chance after chance but there only seemed to be one winner once the final went to penalties. The much maligned Jerzy Dudek proved to be the hero and Liverpool paraded the trophy the following day to delirious crowds on Merseyside.

Benitez struggled to live up to that in the seasons that followed but an FA Cup followed in 2006, inspired again by Stevie G, as well as another Champions League final appearance against the same opposition, this time in Athens, in 2007 - although Milan took their revenge with a 2-1 win. Arguably the high point of the Benitez reign came in 2009 when a combination of a superb run of league form and a wobble by front-runners Manchester United seemed to open the way for that long-awaited Premier League title. In the event, United kept finding late goals from the most unlikely sources and Liverpool dropped points at home to Arsenal in a chaotic 4-4 draw, ultimately costing them the title. However with Steven Gerrard and scoring sensation Fernando Torres in sync, the end to the long wait for a league crown seemed to be at hand.

Unfortunately the wheels came off the following season as Xabi Alonso was sold and a few dubious signings led to disquiet among supporters. Rafa left Anfield at the end of the season as the team ended the season in 7th place. That title seemed as far away as ever...

ROY HODGSON

2010-11

IN A MANAGERIAL CAREER SPANNING 43 YEARS, Roy Hodgson has had some high profile jobs which saw him manage Italian giants Inter Milan, yet his credibility remains questioned due to ill-fated spells with Liverpool and England that left a stain on an otherwise impressive and wide-ranging CV. Hodgson's stock had never been higher after he guided Fulham to seventh in the Premier League and the Europa League final – overcoming Juventus and Shakhtar Donetsk along the way – in the 2009/10 season. It got him the job at Anfield. But it ranks as arguably his worst spell as manager, the fans never took to him and his brand of football was openly criticised as dull and uninspiring. Unsurprisingly, Hodgson is the shortest-serving manager in the club's entire history, sacked after just 31 games in charge between 2010 and 2011. He won only seven of his 20 Premier League games in charge before being given his marching orders with the Reds languishing in 11tth with Kenny Dalglish returning as caretaker boss.

In the summer of 2010 Hodgson signed a three-year deal to become manager after the six-year tenure of the revered Rafa, and told the assembled press, "This is the biggest job in club football and I'm honoured to be taking on Britain's most successful football club," The then 62-year-old joined from Fulham, where he took charge in December 2007 and had guided the homely London club to a Europa Cup final. Club captain Steven Gerrard believed Hodgson's extensive experience in Europe made him the "right man for Liverpool". "I think it's been worth the wait and I'm sure he's just keen now to get on with it and start to quickly put in place his plans for the new season," said the then 30-year-old Gerrard.

Kenny Dalglish, who was then an ambassador at the club and was linked with the manager's job, insisted he welcomed Hodgson's appointment. "I look very favourably on it," he told the Daily Mail. "I have known Roy a long time and have a great respect for him. We've not had detailed conversations yet but my interests are in Liverpool."

Hodgson was a somewhat unexpected appointment, but the club

Roy Hodgson was the wrong man at the wrong time for controversial Liverpool owners Gillet and Hicks.

were gripped by the poisonous reign of their new American owners, and the affable Hodgson was seen as someone thought to be non contentious. Liverpool chairman at that time Martin Broughton assured Hodgson, and the fans, the new manager would not have to offload players to service the club's huge debts of about £350m.

Liverpool supporters knew Hodgson was dropped into a difficult job in trying circumstances due to detested owners Tom Hicks and George Gillett. With a civil war in the boardroom during the final months of the ownership under Hicks and Gillett, the manager was in an intolerable situation without funds, coupled with key injuries. Poor Roy was labelled a man out of his depth, repeatedly alienating supporters with PR gaffes.

Asked after a rare home win whether there was anywhere quite like Anfield for an atmosphere, Hodgson replied "the San Siro and Old Trafford are excellent". True. But not what the die hard fans want to hear. Overcoming Trabzonspor in the Europa League play-off round was hailed as "a famous European night". Really? No, not really! Asked to respond to Alex Ferguson's claims that Fernando Torres had been playacting to try to get John O'Shea sent off, he said: "Maybe Sir Alex had a better view of it than me". Oh dear! Liverpool's derby display was described as "our best performance of the season". No, it was worse than that.

Hodgson is the last Liverpool manager to have been beaten in a Merseyside derby, losing 2-0 at Goodison Park. A defeat to Blackpool left the Reds in the bottom three for the first time in nearly half a century and Hodgson confessed he felt in a relegation battle. Unable to lift even the likes of Steven Gerrard and Fernando Torres, it was the manager who would go. Torres decided he could no longer play for Hodgson. The Kop chanted 'Hodgson for England' in a universal desire for their manager to go. Hodgson's complaint that "the famous Anfield support has not been there ever since I came here" was yet another PR own goal.

He lasted just over six months, a 3-1 defeat at Blackburn with Steven Gerrard missing a penalty, proved to be the last straw in January 2011. Hodgson's final team included David N'Gog out wide and Sotirios Kyrgiakos at centre-back. Yet he said after that defeat: "I still see a lot of things positively and my glass is absolutely half-full rather than half-empty at the moment," When the Blackburn supporters chanted "You're getting sacked in the morning", those that had travelled from Liverpool joined in. Two days later he was sacked and Kop legend Dalglish stepped in as caretaker manager.

Hodgson's wife was from Liverpool and born into a family of Evertonians. He should have known the expectations at Anfield. But he failed miserably to lock into the fans psyche and instead he became known for his Royisms, a succession of saying the wrong things at the wrong time, and not getting his message across.

"The protest does not help," Roy advised supporters as they continued to campaign against the American owners who were leading Liverpool towards potential administration having taken over the club with a lot of talk and not so much money. Liverpool were not the cash cow that Manchester United had been for the Glazer family but the club's eventual sale paved the way for the New England Sports Ventures takeover.

Ray Lewington, Hodgson's long standing right hand man, observed: "It was the wrong time to go to Liverpool when everything was on a downer; the money side wasn't great. People on the outside will see that probably as one of the bad things that happened for him. But people within the game, we always know the circumstances. You hear the whispers."

SIR KENNY DALGLISH

2011-12 - Honours: *League Cup: 2011–12;*

KOP LEGEND KENNY DALGLISH TOOK OVER the reigns from Roy Hodgson and steadied the ship. At last here was a man who knew Liverpool inside and out and someone guaranteed to say the right things, although his second coming as Anfield boss wasn't all plain sailing.

Having returned to Anfield as a club ambassador in 2009, fans had been calling for Dalglish to replace Hodgson for months before the latter's dismissal. Kenny's appointment helped Liverpool pull towards the top of the table and he was confirmed as permanent boss for a second time in May 2011.

The sale of Fernando Torres and purchase of Andy Carroll for an eye-watering £35m raised eyebrows, as did his attempts to defend hot-shot striker Luis Suarez following allegations of racism against Manchester United's Patrice Evra during a heated exchange during a game at Anfield. The players warmed up wearing T-shirts protesting Suarez's innocence after the FA imposed an eight match ban on the Uruguayan.

Nevertheless, under Dalglish Liverpool lifted their first trophy for 6 years by beating Cardiff City on penalties in the League Cup but lost the FA Cup final 2-1 to Chelsea. A disappointing eighth place meant that Dalglish was dismissed at the end of the season but returned to the club as a non-executive director in October 2013.

BRENDAN RODGERS

2012-15

BRENDAN RODGERS WAS THE LEFT-FIELD choice to succeed Dalglish in 2012. The Swansea manager had earned a glowing reputation for playing expansive football and gained the Welsh club promotion to the Premier League and then kept them in the top flight taking the scalps of several big clubs along the way. Yet he faced a daunting task in taking over at Anfield where expectations remained sky high and supporters waited impatiently for that first ever Premier League title.

Upon his take over in June 2012 Rodgers said, "I am better when I have control. I am not a power freak" which stood out as one of the first of many 'Brendanisms' that littered an entertaining spell as Liverpool boss. Rodgers would also produce such gems as "My biggest mentor is myself because I've had to study and that's been my biggest influence"; "It's not just about training players, it's about educating players. You train dogs"; "I use a quote with the players, 'Per aspera ad astra', which is Latin for 'through adversity to the stars'"; "I think there's three players who will let us down this year — the cause, the fight, everything – and I have written them down already in these three envelopes. Make sure you are not in one of the envelopes"; "I believe a young player will run through a barbed wire fence for you. An older player looks for a hole in the fence." These faux pas undermined the Ulsterman at times and was a distraction from the man who at one point looked like ending that quarter of a century wait for the league title.

Rodgers took Liverpool to within touching distance of the title in April 2014. They had taken the league by storm; embarking on an 16 match unbeaten run including 11 straight wins which saw them overhaul Manchester City at the top of the table and the title looked theirs to lose after a 3-2 win over their title rivals at Anfield. Another 3-2 win over Norwich in the following game was greeted with lusty choruses of "We're going to win the league" by the away end at Carrow Road and for once even the most pessimistic Liverpool fan had to admit that it was within their grasp. All they needed were two wins from the last three games – Chelsea at Anfield, Crystal Palace at Selhurst Park and then Newcastle back at Anfield. Not only that but Chelsea were weakened by injuries and preparing for a Champions League semi-final second leg against Atletico Madrid with Chelsea boss Jose Mourinho claiming he would pick a weakened team. In the event Liverpool froze on the day as Chelsea sat deep. An untimely slip from Steven Gerrard let in Demba Ba on the stroke of half time; it was a sickening moment for the home crowd, compounded by Willian's second in injury time and Mourinho's ludicrous celebration at the final whistle. A week later Liverpool surged into a three goal lead and went in search of more goals to pull back the goal difference on City when they conceded three in 11 minutes to draw the game. The final games were academic and City won the league by 2 points, thanks largely to Liverpool's sudden loss of nerve and form.

That proved to be the zenith for Rodgers as his deflated squad never recovered. They had been carried towards the title on a wave of euphoria but the reality of being so close left them bereft the following season. The sale of Luis Suarez to Barcelona didn't help as Liverpool slumped to sixth but they reached the semi-finals of both domestic cups, losing to Chelsea in the League Cup and Aston Villa at Wembley in the FA Cup and didn't progress beyond the round of 32 in the Europa League.

Brendan's reign lasted just 8 league games into the following season. He became the first Liverpool manager since the 1950s not to win a trophy in his first three seasons. Rodgers was dismissed after a 1-1 draw at Everton which left the Reds tenth in the Premier League, but the decision was made before the game. After the draw with Everton, Rodgers spoke of a "constant rebuilding" job and highlighted the impact of losing "four real catalysts" of his side; Rodgers was referring to the likes of Jamie Carragher, Luis Suarez, Raheem Sterling and Steven Gerrard who had all left the club since that title charge of spring 2014.

As he left his final media questioning as Liverpool manager walking out of the door at Goodison Park, within an hour he was out of the door at Anfield! Liverpool had won just four of their 11 games in all competitions that season, including a victory on penalties against League Two Carlisle at home in the Capital One Cup. Owners Fenway Sports Group issued a joint statement from principal owner John W Henry, chairman Tom Werner and president Mike Gordon: "We would like to place on record our sincere thanks to Brendan Rodgers for the significant contribution he has made to the club and express our gratitude for his hard work and commitment. All of us have experienced some wonderful

Brendan Rodgers got Liverpool to within 3 games of winning the league, the closest they had come until the arrival of Jürgen Klopp.

moments with Brendan as manager and we are confident he will enjoy a long career in the game. Ambition and winning are at the heart of what we want to bring to Liverpool and we believe this change gives us the best opportunity to deliver it."

Liverpool had spent £80m in the summer signing Christian Benteke, Danny Ings, Roberto Firmino, Nathaniel Clyne and Joe Gomez. Ex-Borussia Dortmund boss Jürgen Klopp was the first choice to succeed him, although former Chelsea and Real Madrid manager Carlo Ancelotti and Ajax boss Frank de Boer had also been linked with the Liverpool job in recent weeks. "The search for a new manager is under way and we hope to make an appointment in a decisive and timely manner," added the statement.

Alan Shearer said at the time: "No-one wants to see a manager get sacked but the bar was set when the owners sacked Kenny Dalglish for finishing eighth, getting into two cup finals and winning one of them. From there to now I don't really see much progression. Looking from the outside now, I don't seen an identity, I don't see who their best players are, what the plan is or what the best system is. So from that point of view I was pretty confused. From the beginning of this season, with his two coaches going I thought Brendan was a dead man walking. As soon as he was going to have a bad run I felt the inevitable would happen."

Ian Wright commented, "I am shocked. He was meant to be the new kid on the block but he had run out of time. It is unfortunate for him but I don't think Liverpool owed him that time. They gave him a lot of money to spend. The club are nowhere near where they want to be. A club of Liverpool's size do not need to answer to anyone."

Former Liverpool centre-back Jamie Carragher said, "Rodgers can't argue in some ways. He's been there three years, he hasn't won a trophy and they've played Champions League football once. That's not good enough for Liverpool. Liverpool are becoming Tottenham. They think they are a big club but the real big clubs aren't concerned about what they do. What are these owners going to do to get the club back to where it needs to be?"

Garry Monk, who played under Rodgers at Swansea, commented, "I don't understand it. It is a very harsh decision and he did not deserve that at all. He is a top manager. You do not know what happens behind closed doors. I am not sure who would do a better job at Liverpool. He will bounce back. He was so supportive to me, giving me advice when I got the job [at Swansea]. He is a top man and a top manager."

Arsene Wenger believed Rodgers was very unlucky not to have won the Premier League. "I'm always sad when that happens as I think he is a quality manager. Unfortunately the pressure is always bigger on the managers. He was very unlucky to not win the Premier League. He was closest certainly to winning the Premier League of all the managers that have been working for the club, but that is the way it goes now and I wish him good luck. I'm sure he will find a job again."

Rodgers went on to win 7 trophies in less than three seasons at Celtic before taking over at Leicester City in February 2019, meanwhile Liverpool resumed the search for the man who would end their title agony.

THE HEIR APPARENT

FOLLOWING FOUR YEARS OF PREPARATION, IT all came together for Jürgen Klopp and Liverpool in 2019 and they appear to stand on the brink of world domination yet again. Not only that but the German mastermind has signed a new deal which will keep him at Anfield until 2024; given the current rate of improvement, who knows how many trophies he will have won by then. But what of the future beyond Klopp? Is it possible that a new Boot Room philosophy will emerge or will the Anfield club sink back into relative obscurity once the German's tenure ends?

As a new decade began, Jürgen Klopp clearly believed Steven Gerrard was the perfect man to replace him when he eventually left Anfield. On the very day Klopp signed a long-term deal with, the fans were convinced Gerard was earmarked to succeed him because a few hundred miles north Gerrard also agreed a new contract to manage Rangers, that would keep him at Ibrox until… 2024! Many are convinced the deals go hand-in-hand, with Gerrard eventually replacing Klopp at Anfield having served his apprenticeship north of the border.

Klopp was fleshing out his vision to create a new Anfield dynasty and his desire to oversee it leaving Liverpool in the best possible shape. "The club was asking for a while already if we could talk about an extension and I thought it makes sense before things are getting a bit intense – not now, I was completely calm – but maybe in the summer we would have started again," said Klopp, whose old deal ran until June 2022. "With new players when you want to bring them in they ask 'How long is the manager going to be here?' We all wanted to avoid that so it's done and I am really happy about that. We agreed a contract on a really bad weather day but I'm used to it. It's a really happy family. I feel the club is in a good place and we have the chance to develop. There are a lot of exciting things coming up with the new academy and maybe a new stand. But there will be cloudy days as well and you have to be there and make decisions and I feel very responsible for all the things here. I wanted to sort this thing and we did that. Great!"

Klopp could be at Anfield for nine years, the longest managerial reign at Anfield since Bob Paisley, longer than the seven years he spent at Mainz and Borussia Dortmund. "The one reason for this contract extension is that we don't speak about it anymore," said Klopp. "For the next three-and-a-half years at least no-one has to talk about it. We will see what happens. The plan is to make it the best time of our life. It was not too bad till now but we don't feel that it could not be better so let's try to make the best time of our lives. Enjoy the ride, enjoy the journey."

It also emerged at Steven Gerrard regularly asks Klopp for managerial advice. "We exchange messages quite a lot. I have said it before and I will say it again, he has been fantastic for me, even going back to when I had the first chat with him at the Academy. I thought about 'Am I doing the right thing? What would you do in my situation?' I asked him all these types of things and he has always been there to give me sound advice. We were messaging each other just a few days ago and obviously we've both had big weeks and weekends, so yes, he has been fantastic and I can't thank him enough really."

Steven Gerrard said he took something from every one of the managers he played under during his brilliant playing career with the club. "I have tapped into them all, Rafa, Brendan, Gerard Houllier, Roy Hodgson, all of them. Probably unknown to them but I have tried to tap into all of them and use it myself, and having that around what I do. But, if we talk about the Porto fixture, there are certain things we tried to do as a team that we would have done as a team when I played. What Rafa would have said to us in that situation? What would Brendan have said in and out of possession? So you try and take things from them all."

After a year back at Liverpool before embarking on his own management career with Rangers, Gerrard thanked Klopp for his on-going help and support. Klopp first let him return to Anfield to train during the MLS close-season just months after arriving at Liverpool, before welcoming the 38-year-old back to the club as part of the coaching staff. "I was like a sponge, watching and learning" Gerrard said. "I watch him on TV and see how he handles situations. I could never be Jürgen with his charisma and energy. But if I can take a few things from him it will be such a help. And if I text, call or see him, Jürgen's always got time for me. Jürgen's really good at switching off. When the game is on he's very emotional but once it's over he can park the emotion. That's why he's so good at handling the pressure. After cup finals and a big set-back he'll be the one to start the party. Tomorrow is a different day and that's a big lesson I have to learn. I have to live my life outside football while still being a manager. It is difficult but I'm trying. I love Jürgen Klopp and I

The success of Steven Gerrard at Ibrox has led to speculation that he will one day succeed Jürgen Klopp

believe he can help Liverpool win the Premier League. I know what it will mean to the fans because they suffered so much in 2014. So we're in a great place – and I say 'we' because I'm a fan and al- ways will be. But I've got two teams in my heart now. Rangers and Liverpool."

Earlier Klopp had told FourFourTwo that Kenny Dalglish might step forward to replace him, although probably more in an emergency, but long term Gerrard was the man. Klopp emphasised that both Dalglish and Gerrard gave him "big support" from the moment he came to the club.

Klopp said: "If you ask who should follow me, I'd say Stevie. I help him whenever I can. If someone gets your job, it's not about them, it's about you not being good enough. I'm old enough to know that I give this job everything. I'm not a genius, I'm not perfect, but I give the club 100 per cent. If that's enough, great. If it's not, then it's just the problem of the situation. I'm not jealous, I'm not sceptical. I'm completely open. If you want my help, you'll get it. My family often thinks that I'm too quick to open up, but I think being any other way is a waste of time. I love life, I love my job, I like most people – that's how it is."

Klopp's future looks likely to be back in Germany, probably as the national coach, possibly in charge of Bayern. Hans-Joachim Watzke had asked Klopp to return to Dortmund in 2018, even though the German club's CEO always knew it was a non-starter. Lucien Favre took charge but before prising him away from Nice, Watzke attempted to persuade Klopp to make a grand return - three years after his exit from the club he twice led to the league title. In his new book 'Real Love - A life with Borussia Dortmund', serialised by Bild, Watzke revealed that he contacted Klopp in the summer of 2018. "I knew Jürgen would fulfil his contract until the end. Jürgen has always fulfilled his contracts. That's how he is. But if you want to go in new ways, and I wanted a new path at BVB at this point, then I at least had to ask Jürgen to consider."

Klopp was mid-flight when he took the call from Watzke, with whom he had previously worked for seven years during his time at Dortmund. "My phone rang while I was on the plane Aki was on it: 'Jürgen, you have to come back'" reveals Klopp. "I thought he was kidding. 'Are you stupid, have you been drinking, how did you get the idea, I've got a few more years in Liverpool.'"

Klopp did not know how serious he was, Watzke admits: "I would not have forgiven myself for not asking him at that moment." Klopp would also consider helping his old club if they were in dire straights and in need of him.

Bayern Munich president Uli Hoeness approached Klopp when he was at Mainz in 2008. Klopp was also angry with Bayern for announcing they had exercised an escape clause to take Gotze before Dortmund's semi-final with Real, the player wanting to work with Guardiola who was due to arrive at Bayern the following season. "This is not a bit personal or whatever," said Klopp, "the story Uli Hoeness brought up, or whoever brought up, that in 2008 we had one, no two phone calls. I have known that since 2008, but never told anyone. Now they say it. I can say 'Yes, that's how it was' so no problem. I never expected that they would go for me. I was a second division manager in Germany, and who would expect that Bayern calls you? It was more of a shock in the first moment. Then a couple of days later they called and said they went for the other Jürgen. Making kind of these personal battles out of it I don't understand. It is two big clubs facing each other and I am really happy to be part of this game."

After Liverpool beat Bayern Munich on the way to winning their 6th European Cup, former club president Beckenbauer felt Klopp, who won two titles with rivals Dortmund, would be an ideal fit for the club. "Jürgen Klopp at Bayern. That would be the highlight. Jürgen was the one who taught the Germans how to play football quickly," the German legend commented. Klopp reacted, "Someone told me what Franz said that after the game. It doesn't put pressure on me. I am blessed that I have known him for 14 years. Knowing him is something quite special. We are friends, even if we don't talk a lot, but I am not surprised that he said positive things about me. When he always speaks about me, he speaks positively. It is just like the king knighting a man 'Sir'. There is no bigger football legend in Germany than Franz Beckenbauer. It is great. It is a compliment to Liverpool, but Bayern have done most things right in the last 10 or 15 years without making many mistakes. Hopefully in 50 or 60 years, I will be remembered without referring to managing many different clubs. I am happy with the clubs I've had now.

"Liverpool is a really good fit for me. I love it. There are a lot of opportunities to develop an already really good football team. So let's work and try to make the most of it. I have enough confidence to say I am the right manager for this club at the moment, but we will see how it is in the future. We are at the right place, but we all constantly have to prove ourselves. So far, it has worked out, and hopefully it will last a lot longer. That would be cool. We are very happy about the situation and very positive about the future. We are fine with what we've done so far, but now we have to finish the season the best way possible. It is a big opportunity. We have improved a lot, but people judge it only on winning titles. We know that, but we can change it in the future."

ABOUT THE AUTHOR

Multi-Award winning author Harry Harris with Alan Kennedy, Nigel Spackman and Jimmy Carter with his best selling book last year "Liverpool: Diary of the Season" a an event to promote the book at Berystede Hotel in Ascot.

Harry Harris best seller "Liverpool: Diary of the Season" continued his long association with the club having written the autobiography of Steve McMahon and who campaigned immediately on behalf of the supporters in the aftermath of Hillsborough when chief football writer of the Daily Mirror.

He is a double winner of the British Sports Journalist of the Year award and the British Variety Club of Great Britain Silver Heart for 'Contribution to Sports Journalism'.

Double winner of the Sports Story of the Year award, the only journalist ever to win the Sports Story of the year accolade twice. Total of 24 industry awards.

Regular football analyst on TV news and sports programmes; Richard & Judy, Newsnight, BBC News and ITV News at Ten, Sky, Setanta. Radio 5 Live, Radio 4, and TalkSport. Interviewed on Football Focus, formed original Hold The Back Page and Jimmy Hill Sunday Supplement on Sky.

Arguably the most prolific writer of best selling football books of his generation. Among 80 plus books are the highly acclaimed best seller in the UK and the States "Pele - His Life and Times", 'Gullit: The Chelsea Diary', 'All The Way Jose', Chelsea Century, Chelski, 'Wayne Rooney -The Story of Footballs Wonder Kid'. Autobiographies: Ruud Gullit, Paul Merson, Glenn Hoddle, Gary Mabbutt, Terry Neill, Bill Nicholson:'Glory, Glory - My Life With Spurs.' Biographies: Roman Abramovich, Jürgen Klinsmann, Sir Alex Ferguson, Jose Mourinho, Terry Venables, Franco Zola, Luca Vialli. George Best's last book and best seller, 'Hard Tackles and Dirty Baths'.

One of the most influential football columnists for three decades, one of the most acclaimed investigative journalists of his generation. Worked for Daily Mail, Daily Mirror, Daily Express, Daily Star, Sunday Express and Star on Sunday, ESPNsoccernet Football Correspondent,

BT Sport. More recently in the Daily & Sunday Telegraph as part of an Investigative Team. Directed documentaries: Ossie Ardiles, Kenny Sansom, Kerry Dixon, Ron 'Chopper' Harris.

Ray Clemence and Jimmy Carter at the book launch of "Liverpool:Diary of the Season" at Planet Hollywood in central London.

Printed in Great Britain
by Amazon

66989496R00144